Strategic Maintenance Planning

Strategic Maintenance Planning

Anthony Kelly

AMSTERDAM • BOSTON • HEIDELBERG • LONDON • OXFORD •
NEW YORK • PARIS • SAN DIEGO • SAN FRANCISCO • SINGAPORE •
SYDNEY • TOKYO

Butterworth-Heinemann is an imprint of Elsevier
Linacre House, Jordan Hill, Oxford OX2 8DP, UK
30 Corporate Drive, Suite 400, Burlington, MA 01803, USA

First Edition 2006
Reprinted 2007

British Library Cataloguing in Publication Data
A catalogue record for this book is available from the British Library

Library of Congress Control Number: 2006921204

ISBN: 978-0-7506-6992-4

Plant Maintenance Management (set of three volumes)
ISBN: 978-0-7506-6995-5

For information on all Butterworth-Heinemann publications
visit our website at books.elsevier.com

Printed and bound in *Great Britain*

07 08 09 10 10 9 8 7 6 5 4 3 2

Contents

Preface

Strategic Maintenance Planning is the first of three companion books covering material which has been developed (and updated) from my 1997 publications *Maintenance Strategy* and *Maintenance Organization and Systems,* which were subsequently expanded and converted into distance-learning units which comprised the first half of a 2-year Masters program offered by an Australian and a UK university.

The main approach adopted throughout all three books, and which determines the direction and content of all the material, is that of business-centered maintenance (BCM) the starting point of which is the identification of the business aims. These are then translated into the maintenance objectives which, in their turn, are used to underpin the formulation firstly of strategy (the subject of this book, *viz.* the *planning* aspects of maintenance management), secondly of the design of the appropriate organization (the subject of Book 2, *Managing Maintenance Resources, viz.* the *doing* aspects of maintenance management) and finally the creation of the necessary systems (the subject of Book 3, *Maintenance Systems and Documentation, viz.* the *controlling* aspects).

Because the material has come from a distance-learning program all three books contain numerous review questions (with answers), exercises and case studies – these last having been selected to ensure coverage of the care of physical assets across a wide range of industries (process, mining, food, power generation and transmission, etc). In addition, every chapter has its own clearly specified objectives and learning outcomes – as well as a route map which enables the reader to see where the chapter is in relation to the rest of the topics covered.

Although the BCM approach integrates all three books into a unified maintenance management methodology, I have tried to ensure that each one can stand alone, i.e. be studied and understood in isolation from its companion works. It is therefore inevitable that there is some overlap, *viz.*:

- To explain the principles and concepts of BCM, the same case study (of a food processing plant) is used at the beginning of each book.
- To illustrate the linkage between maintenance planning, organization and systems, a full audit of a chemical plant is presented at the end of each book.

The overall aim of each book is to provide managers of physical assets with a better understanding of the operation of the maintenance function, an understanding which will enable them to identify problems within their own organization and prescribe effective solutions. As asserted by Henry Mintzberg (Managers Not MBAs, *Financial Times*, Prentice Hall, 2004):

> What managers really need from a course of a book is insight – theories or models that enable them to make sense of practice, learn from experience and reach better judgements.

The provision of such insight is the overriding purpose of these three books.

Strategic Maintenance Planning, Book 1 of the series, aims to impart an understanding of the concepts, principles and techniques of preventive maintenance, and shows how the complexity of maintenance strategic planning can be resolved by a systematic *top-down bottom-up* approach (TDBUA). It explains that strategic maintenance planning is concerned with:

- Establishing objectives, for the physical assets and the maintenance resources.
- Formulating an appropriate life plan for each unit of plant, a comprehensive program of maintenance tasks (e.g. lubrication, inspection, repair, replacement) spanning the life of each unit.
- Formulating, from the work identified in the life plans, a preventive maintenance schedule for the plant as a whole.
- Designing a maintenance organization and establishing a budget to ensure that the maintenance work can be resourced.

Chapter 1 reviews the role of maintenance within the context of an industrial organization. Chapter 2 then discusses the importance of plant acquisition policy to maintenance life-cycle costs. Chapter 3 – the key chapter – explains the BCM approach to understanding and establishing a maintenance strategy, and outlines the overall structure of the three-book series. Chapter 4 shows how systems of physical assets can be modeled, and Chapter 5 defines and discusses the maintenance objectives.

Chapters 6–8 focus on the principles and concepts of preventive maintenance decision-making, and relates these to decision processes that can be used to establish life plans for plant units. Chapter 9 shows a procedure for establishing a preventive schedule for a complete plant. Chapter 10 looks at models of plant reliability control, showing how this may be achieved, in part, by reviewing existing life plans.

Chapter 11 gives the reader the opportunity to attempt two exercises in maintenance strategy. The final chapter then presents ten case studies from a wide variety of industries, these being used both as a vehicle for review questions and also to illustrate the similarities of – and differences between – the maintenance of process plant and the maintenance of physical assets in other technologic sectors.

Anthony Kelly
a.kelly99@ntlworld.com

Acknowledgments

Firstly, I wish to acknowledge a special gratitude to John Harris who has edited the complete text, and also contributed Reading 8.1 and Appendix 3. I also acknowledge Ian Bendall for contributing the example of Chapter 8 and Dr. H.S. Riddell who contributed a number of figures in Chapter 2.

I thank the people in industry, most recently – Bill Sugden, Ian Peterson, Gudmunder Bjornason, Leonard Bouwman, Kevin Hardman, Nigel Beard and many others – who provided access to their plants and without whose help this book could not have been written.

Finally, I wish to thank Vicky Taylor for typing the text and Denise Jackson for producing the artwork.

Author's biography

Dr. Anthony Kelly served a trade apprenticeship before obtaining a first degree in mechanical engineering from the University of Wales and a Masters Degree (in corrosion engineering) from the University of London. He then held several industrial positions, in which he was responsible for the management of maintenance resources, before joining, in 1969, the University of Manchester, UK, where he specialized in maintenance management, its teaching and research, and obtained his doctorate for a thesis on maintenance organizational design. Dr. Kelly has published numerous technical papers and seven textbooks which have been translated into several languages.

Over the last 15 years Dr. Kelly has run his own consultancy partnership, operating worldwide and carrying out more than 60 major investigations and audits of a wide variety of industrial activities: mining, power generation and distribution, chemical processing, manufacturing, building services, etc. Over the last 15 years he has also held visiting/industrial professorships at Central Queensland University (Australia), University of Stellenbosch (South Africa) and Hogskolen i Stavanger (Norway).

Author's Biography

PART 1

Introductory chapters

1 Maintenance and the industrial organization

*'Management means the substitution of thought for muscle,
of knowledge for folklore, and of cooperation for force.'*

Peter Drucker

Chapter aims and outcomes

To explain and define the maintenance management function within the industrial organization.

On completion of this chapter you should be able to:

- visualize an industrial organization as a complex open system;
- understand the role of management and the different management philosophies that can be used for the management of industrial organizations;
- appreciate that the maintenance department is not 'an island unto itself' – it influences, and is influenced by, many other industrial subsystems.

Chapter route map

Book divisions

- Introductory chapters
- Maintenance objectives and task selection
- The top-down bottom-up approach
- Controlling plant reliability
- Exercises
- Case studies

This chapter in the division

- Chapter 1 Maintenance and the industrial organization
- Chapter 2 Plant acquisition policy and maintenance life-cycle costs
- Chapter 3 Formulating maintenance strategy: a business-centered approach

Chapter topics

- 1.1 Introduction
- 1.2 A systems view of maintenance management

1.1 Introduction

Etzioni defined organizations as groupings of human beings (of individuals and sub-groups of individuals) constructed and reconstructed to seek specific goals [1]. Various material resources will also be needed, he said. A better understanding of organizations may be obtained through the so-called *systems* approach. In this, organizations can be viewed as *open systems* taking inputs from their environments and transforming them – by a series of activities and with some objective in view – into outputs (see Figure 1.1).

> *Open system: An open system is in continual interaction with its environment and achieves a steady state while still retaining the capacity for work (transformation). The system is open in the sense it can react not only to the direct 'inputs and outputs' but also changes in the environment surrounding it.*

Organizations can be categorized, on the basis of their objectives, into public and private enterprises. An industrial company exemplifies the latter and Riddell has pointed out that

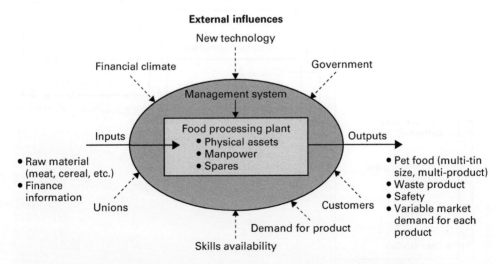

Figure 1.1 An organization producing pet food, viewed as an open system

if it is to achieve its primary objective of maximizing its long-term profitability – while also providing an in-demand service – it will need to carry out two prime functions [2]:

1. The internal mechanisms of the industrial enterprise itself must be made to operate well. The right product must be made at the right time, by the right plant, using the right raw materials and employing the appropriate workforce. *The physical assets must be carefully selected and properly maintained.* Effective long-term research and development plans must be implemented and new capital investment generated. In short, the internal efficiency must be high.
2. The interaction with the outside world, with external influences and constraints, must be made to be co-operative and beneficial, rather than antagonistic and damaging, i.e. the overall, externally measured, efficiency must also be high.

Riddell sees the *role of management* as being concerned with carrying out these functions in order to ensure the ongoing success (profit) of the organization. He sees management as the designer, constructor, director and controller of the organization so that it can achieve its objective.

Several helpful approaches to carrying out this role have evolved (see Table 1.1). These, in particular the *administrative* and the *human relations* approaches, will be used in this book to develop a framework (or methodology) of maintenance management principles and procedures (see Chapter 3).

Table 1.1 Summary of management theories

Mechanistic management: Monitors and controls the way the job is performed at shop-floor level; includes method, timing and direction.

Administrative management: Applies universal management functions and structural principles to the design of an organization and to its operation.

Human relations management: Studies characteristics and relationships of individuals and groups within an organization, and takes account of these factors when designing and administrating the organization.

Decision management: Applies procedural and quantitative models to the solution of management problems. A theory for communications and decision-making in organizations.

Systems management: Studies organizations as dynamic systems reacting with their environment. Analyses a system into its subsystems and takes account of behavioral, mechanistic, technologic and managerial aspects.

Contingency management*: Takes the view that the characteristics of an organization must be matched to its internal and external environment. Since these environments can change it is important to view the organizational structure as dynamic.

*Contingency (dictionary definition) is a thing contingent on an uncertain event. Contingency management is related to systems' theory. It emphasizes the complexity of organizations (see Figure 1.2) and attempts to understand how organizations operate under varying conditions and specific circumstances. The contingency theory of management is directed toward proposing organizational designs and management actions most appropriate for specific situations.

Review Question

R1.1   Read through Case study 1 (Chapter 12) and identify where at least one of the management theories listed in Table 1.1 has been used to describe/discuss/model the maintenance management procedures of Fertec Ltd.

1.2 A systems view of maintenance management

Several writers have modeled the industrial organization as a socio-technical system comprising various subsystems. For example, Kast and Rosenzweig saw it as an open, socio-technical system (see Figure 1.2) with the following five subsystems, each with its own input–conversion–output process related to, and interacting with, the other subsystems [3]:

  (i) A *goal-oriented arrangement*: people with a purpose.
 (ii) A *technical subsystem*: people using knowledge, techniques, equipment and facilities.
(iii) A *structural subsystem*: people working together on integrated activities.
(iv) A *psychosocial subsystem*: people in social relationships, co-ordinated by a managerial subsystem.
 (v) A *managerial subsystem*: planning and controlling the overall endeavor, i.e. ensuring that the activities of the organization as a whole are directed toward the accomplishment of its objectives.

The author prefers to view the industrial organization as an open system, converting raw material or information into finished products of a higher value. It can be considered to be made up of many interacting subsystems (e.g. maintenance, production,

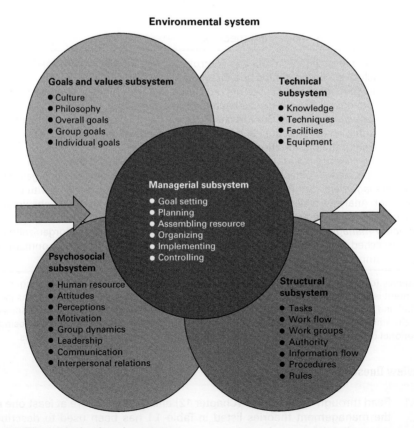

Figure 1.2 The organizational system

stores, capital asset acquisition, safety, design, finance, corporate finance), each carrying out distinct organizational functions:

- The function of *corporate management* (the master subsystem) is to set the organizational goal and strategy and direct, co-ordinate and control the other subsystems to achieve the set goal.
- The function of *capital asset acquisition* is to select, buy, install and commission physical assets, a function which is carried out through the combined efforts of a number of other subsystems (e.g. design, finance, projects).
- The function of *maintenance* is to sustain the integrity of physical assets by repairing, modifying or replacing them as necessary.

Each such subsystem requires inputs of information and resources from one or more of the other subsystems and/or the external environment in order to perform its function. The output from one subsystem can be an input to another or an output to the external environment (see Figure 1.3), e.g. maintenance management uses information from production management on the way the physical assets are going to be operated (the operating pattern: 15 shifts week) and the availability they require to meet the output. Similarly, production management needs information from the marketing/sales management on the demand for the product(s) which allows them to determine the production schedule.

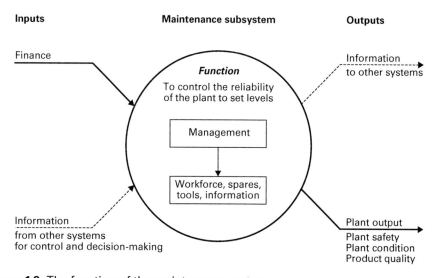

Figure 1.3 The function of the maintenance system

Review Questions

R1.2   How does the maintenance system influence the production system?
R1.3   Identify the essential information the maintenance system requires from the production system if it is going to operate well?

This systems' view of an organization shows that the maintenance subsystem influences, and is influenced by, many of the other subsystems. Two aspects of this are of particular importance:

(i) Because the asset acquisition function, which influences reliability and maintainability, has a considerable effect on the maintenance function, a necessary preliminary to developing the main arguments of this book to clarify the nature of the relationship between them (see Chapter 2).

(ii) The relationships between maintenance and the other organizational subsystems, e.g. production, must also be clarified, and must form part of any description of the operation of the maintenance subsystem or of any of its parts (see Chapter 3).

Review Question

R1.4   Outline the main ways in which plant procurement (asset acquisition) can adversely affect the operation of the maintenance department.

References

1. Etzioni, A., *Modern Organisations*, Prentice Hall, Englewood Cliffs, NJ, USA, 1964.
2. Riddell, H.S., *Lecture notes on engineering management*, University of Manchester, School of Engineering, Manchester, 1994.
3. Kast, F.E. and Rosenzweig, J.E., *Organisations and Management* (3rd Ed), McGraw Hill, Singapore, 1974.

Review Questions Guidelines

R1.1   Decision management: see point (iii) on page 229 of Case study 1 of Chapter 12 regarding the operating period of the ammonia plant.

R1.2   The main outputs from the maintenance system are plant availability, plant performance, plant condition for longevity and safety. All of these factors are essential for the effective operation of the production department.

R1.3   The long- and short-term production plan for the manufacturing equipment. This is influenced by many factors to include the market demand for the product, production maintenance (e.g. catalyst changes), plant-production rate, inter-stage storage and plant structure (redundant plant units). This information is essential for long- and short-term maintenance planning.

R1.4   The plant acquisition procedure should ensure that the selected equipment can carry out the required production specified performance over the required life cycle at minimum maintenance cost. The selection of the wrong equipment can result in poor performance, low availability and high maintenance costs.

2 Plant acquisition policy and maintenance life-cycle costs

'Maintenance Engineers solve the problems that Project Engineers miss.'
With apologies to Albert Einstein

Chapter aims and outcomes

To define the phases of the life cycle of industrial equipment. To show how a proper consideration of the factors that affect maintenance [direct costs (wages, spares, etc.) and indirect costs (loss due to unavailability, quality, etc.)]. in decisions taken at the pre-usage stages (design, commissioning, etc.) of equipment is essential if the aim is to optimize the balance of life-cycle costs and incomes.

On completion of this chapter you should be able to:

- describe and model an industrial equipment life cycle;
- understand that maintenance costs (direct and indirect) can be a significant proportion of the total costs of ownership over the life cycle of industrial plant;
- understand the 'capital asset management' approach that can be used to ensure that maintenance costs are given proper consideration in decisions that are taken in the pre-usage phase of industrial equipment.

Chapter route map

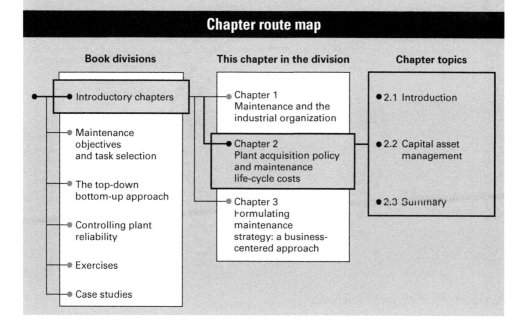

2.1 Introduction

One way of considering the profitability of plant is on the basis of its complete *life cycle*. Figure 2.1 models the principal phases of this, and Table 2.1 lists the main cost-influencing factors. The importance of these various phases and factors will vary with the technology concerned, e.g. in power generation fuel costs may be the overriding factor, in petroleum refining the plant availability, in the provision of buildings their anticipated useful life.

Investment in the plant occurs from its conception to its commissioning, and perhaps into its early years of operation. If all goes well, the return on this investment begins

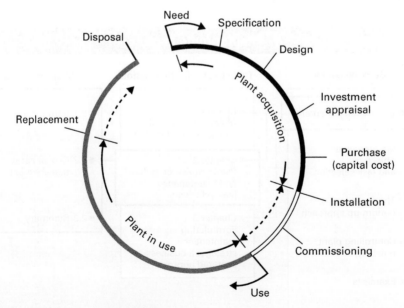

Figure 2.1 Plant life cycle and costs

Table 2.1 Factors influencing life-cycle profitability

Acquisition costs
  Capital cost
  Installation cost and time
  Commissioning cost and time
	Running costs
	  Production cost
	  Maintenance cost
	  Fuel cost

Output parameters
  Useful life
  Plant performance
  Product quality
  Plant availability
	Outside management control
	  Product demand
	  Product price
	  Obsolescence

soon after the plant comes into use and continues until the plant is disposed of. An example of a life-cycle cost profile is shown in Figure 2.2. The data of this example have been used to plot Figure 2.3, which demonstrates that in some cases the total maintenance cost can be considerably greater than the capital cost.

A company might have as its objective the maximization of its plant's life-cycle profitability within the constraints imposed by the need for safe operation. Achievement of this would necessitate, among other things, an investment appraisal which sought an economic compromise between such factors as capital cost, running cost, performance, availability and useful life.

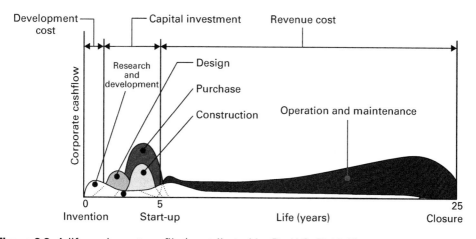

Figure 2.2 A life-cycle cost profile (contributed by Dr. H.S. Riddell)

2.2 Capital asset management

Almost invariably, the application of life-cycle cost analysis is rendered difficult by:

(i)   the lack of definition of the capital asset acquisition subsystem;
(ii) the complex relationships between the many factors involved in the economic compromise;

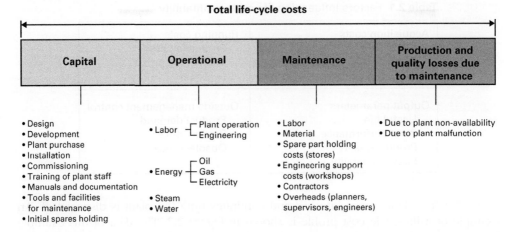

Figure 2.3 Factor in the build-up of total life cost (contributed by Dr. H.S. Riddell)

(iii)   the uncertainty of much of the life-cycle information, i.e. concerning such matters as the projected need for the product, whether and when the plant would become obsolescent, the estimated plant reliability and availability, anticipated costs, and so on.

Because of these and other difficulties the equipment acquisition appraisal is usually dominated by considerations of plant performance and capital cost. Little or no thought is given to reliability and maintainability, the inevitable consequence being that installation and commissioning times and costs will be extended and that plant operation will be dogged by low equipment availability (i.e. high maintenance costs, both indirect and direct).

The question therefore arises as to how this situation can be improved or corrected. Is it via the so-called *terotechnologic* approach? This evolved in the UK in the early 1970s.

It was defined, at first, as follows [1]:

> *A combination of management, financial, engineering and other practices applied to physical assets in pursuit of economic life cycle costs.*

A little later, the following was added:

> *...its practice is concerned with the specification and design for reliability and maintainability of plant, machinery, equipment, buildings and structures, with their installation and replacement, and with the feedback of information on design, performance and costs.*

In short, the idea quite rapidly enlarged from being an approach in which maintenance and unavailability costs were of central importance to one which was much more general, and therefore less tangible. Because of this the concept never took root in British industry.

Capital asset management, outlined in Table 2.2, is a more recent approach – preferred by the author – to this area [2]. It is based on the idea of 'optimizing total maintenance costs over the equipment life cycle'. This is best achieved through an understanding of the effects that decisions taken in the plant's *pre-operational* phases can have on the direct and indirect maintenance costs of the *operational* phase [3] (see Figure 2.4).

Table 2.2 Capital asset management

Definition	Practice	Implementation
A co-ordinated management of the design, procurement, use and maintenance of a firm's fixed assets, in order to maximize the contributions to the firm's profit over the life cycle of those assets.	Is concerned with: • the specification and design for reliability and maintainability of plant, equipment, buildings and services; • their installation, commissioning, maintenance, modification and replacement; • feedback of information on design, performance and costs.	• Correctly specify, design and acquire the asset. • Use the resources efficiently. • Determine and provide the appropriate level of care through effective maintenance. • Determine the optimum replacement periods.

Source: Contributed by H.S. Riddell.

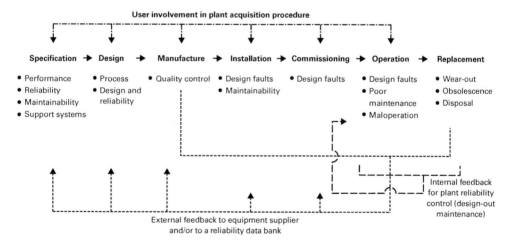

Figure 2.4 Factors influencing maintenance costs over the life cycle

The *specification* for new plant must include requirements for reliability and maintainability (i.e. availability) as well as for performance, capital cost and safety. As far as possible, the expected or useful life of the plant should also be specified. In support of this the equipment manuals, drawings, spares lists, spares security-of-supply and training needs should all be specified and, where necessary, this should be included in the contract.

At the *design* stage, reliability, maintainability and useful life are of paramount importance, and should be considered alongside performance. The method of production is particularly important. For example, if a continuous rather than a batch process is adopted careful consideration should be given to the much higher maintenance costs that inevitably occur.

In addition, it must be understood that design stage considerations of reliability and maintainability can also affect the duration and cost of commissioning. It is self-evident that quality control during the *plant manufacturing* stage will strongly affect the subsequent level of maintenance.

At the *installation* stage, maintainability will continue to be an important consideration because it is only then that the multidimensional nature of many of the maintenance problems becomes clear.

The *commissioning stage* will not only be a period of technical performance testing but also one of learning – where primary design faults, that might reduce availability, might be located and how they could be designed out. Failure to do this will mean serious maintenance problems and high unavailability early in the operational life. Operating equipment past its *useful life* stage will result in low availability and high maintenance costs.

> The model is looking at the acquisition procedure from the equipment purchaser/owners' viewpoint with the emphasis placed on maintenance costs. The model shows that it is essential for the equipment purchases/owner to:
>
> - get involved in all stages of the acquisition procedure (indicated by the dashed & dotted line);
> - feedback information from all stages of the equipment life cycle to the equipment supplier (indicated by the dotted line);
> - set up a plant reliability control system to identify low reliability/high maintenance cost hot spots and design them out (indicated by the dashed line).

Clearly, the best time to influence maintenance and unavailability costs is before the plant comes into use (see Figure 2.5).

- The opportunity for maintenance cost reduction is high at the design stage but drops rapidly (via several key, gateway, decisions) to a relatively low level after commissioning.
- It is important that the often conflicting requirements of non-maintenance departments (represented, in Figure 2.5, by the downward-pointing arrows) are balanced against the maintenance requirements (represented by the upward-pointing arrows).

Review Questions

R2.1   Identify some of the important decisions taken in the pre-usage phases of an industrial equipment life cycle that can have a major impact on the direct and indirect maintenance costs at the usage phase of the equipment.

R2.2   What is the importance of the maintenance history record in the plant acquisition procedure?

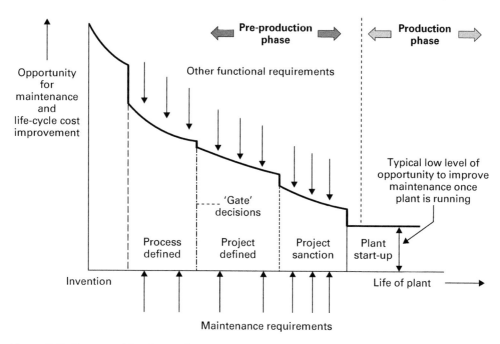

Figure 2.5 Opportunities for maintenance and life-cycle cost improvement (contributed by Dr. H.S. Riddell).

The above arguments suggest the following rules for the effective application of the capital asset management, life-cycle approach to maintenance management:

(i) Decisions to buy a new or replacement plant should be based on a present-value life-cycle analysis of costs which should consider both maintenance and unavailability costs, these being estimated, wherever possible, from documented experience.

(ii) The owner–operator of the plant should co-operate with the designer–manufacturer–installer in a full analysis of its reliability, maintainability and safety characteristics. Such an exercise should include assessment of spare part provisioning, of maintenance personnel training and of supplier support systems. The higher the potential costs of maintenance and unavailability, the more vital is this exercise.

(iii) The owner–operator should set up a system to record and analyze plant failures, and identify areas of high maintenance cost. Such a system should operate from the commissioning (with the supplier's assistance) to plant replacement. It should identify causes and prescribe solutions with the aim of minimizing the total of direct and indirect maintenance costs. Because plant design is a continuing process, information thus gathered should, ideally, be fed back to the equipment supplier or manufacturer. In certain circumstances it could be fed further to a data bank shared on an inter-company, national or international basis. (The difficulty of implementing such information feedback continues to pose a major obstacle to the successful implementation of capital asset management; communication systems are expensive and different organizations, with their different objectives, are involved during the equipment life cycle.) A model of such a system is shown in Figure 2.6.

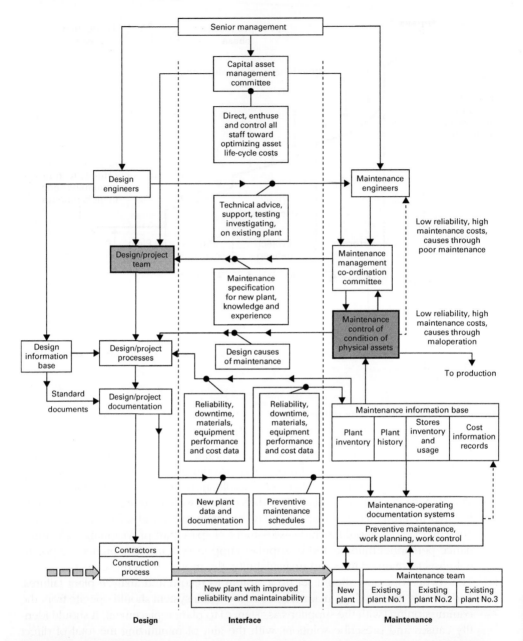

Figure 2.6 Capital asset management control system (contributed by Dr. H.S. Riddell)

Figure 2.6 shows the interrelationships between the maintenance and design departments in a large industrial organization. The two main systems highlighted (see also Figure 2.4) are continuous improvement (see the right side of the model) and the feed-forward of equipment maintenance history to assist the acquisition procedure (see the left side of the model).

(iv) Within the organization concerned, a capital asset management system (CAMS) should be defined and established. This should transcend traditional functional boundaries for decision-making and will require considerable commitment from the most senior management for its effective operation.

> The CAMS is charged with the function acquiring new or replacement equipment. A number of other departments, at senior management level, are involved in CAMS or in providing information to it (*viz.* engineering, production, finance, corporate management and maintenance). This results in decision-making procedures that are complex and open to considerable influence from 'human factors', e.g. polarization between design engineers and maintenance engineers resulting in poor communication, and lack of maintenance input to equipment specification.

Review Question

R2.3   You are the Maintenance Manager of Fertec Ltd. and involved in a project team concerned with purchasing a new syn-gas compressor (see Case study 1 of Chapter 12) to replace the existing compressor. The team have already agreed on performance, availability/reliability issues and have asked you to identify the information you would expect from the syn-gas compressor manufacturer to enable you to carry out effective maintenance. Identify the information in order of importance.

2.3 Summary

The application of the terotechnologic/capital asset approach involves much higher expenditure than the traditional lowest-bid, lowest-cost, shortest-time approach. The difficulties of its implementation are many – e.g. cash constraints, time constraints, the uncertainty of forecasting demand and product life – so in some situations it has to be accepted that the extra effort and cost might not be worth the return. However, with the present trend toward automated, large, expensive plant, the adoption of this approach will usually bring considerable benefits. It requires the commitment and foresight of the most senior management. It is therefore no accident that the successful industrial examples of its application appear to have one common factor, at least, an engineering director who is convinced of the long-term advantages of keeping maintenance firmly in mind when designing, installing and commissioning.

The maintenance manager's basic task is twofold: the determination of strategy and the organization of resources (i.e. labor, material and tools). These are difficult and important tasks in their own right, but failure of the organization to appreciate the fundamental ideas of capital asset management will probably mean that the maintenance manager will be wasting his time on unnecessary tasks when the plant comes into operation.

References

1. Committee for Terotechnology, *Terotechnology, An Introduction to the Management of Physical Resources*, Department of Industry, HMSO, 1975.
2. Riddell, H.S., Life cycle costing in the chemical industry, *Terotechnica* 2(1), Elsevier, 1980.
3. Kelly, A., *Maintenance Planning and Control*, Butterworths, Oxford, 1984.

Exercises

E2.1   Outline the plant acquisition procedures of your own company to consider the extent to which maintenance issues are incorporated into these procedures. Identify any 'human factors problems' that hinder this linkage.

E2.2   Carry out a brief Internet search to see if you can find information on more recent capital asset management case studies than that outlined in Reading 2.1.

Review Questions Guidelines

R2.1   At the design stage, the method of production, i.e. batch processes involve lower maintenance costs than continuous processes. At the specification stage it is necessary to emphasize to the supplier/manufacturer the need for properly thought out life plans, spares requirements, etc.

R2.2   Considerable information about the failure history and maintenance costs will have been built up in the history record, say for pumps. This information is invaluable when deciding on a new pump specification and selection.

R2.3   The life plan for each unit of equipment with recommended spares list; the name of original manufacturer of spare parts; logic fault-finding information; maintenance specification for standard jobs with safety information. Perhaps all of this incorporated into a manufacturers' equipment manual.

Reading 2.1   Application of capital asset management to a steel mill

Some of the advantages of the terotechnologic approach are illustrated in Harvey and Eastburn's plant procurement (Harvey and Eastburn, 1979), see Case Study 4. The project described was part of a steel bar mill rationalization. It involved an investment of £34 million in a 400,000 ton/year plant occupying a 265-acre site.

Preliminary work was started in mid-1970 by the development engineering department who set up a Preliminary Project Steering Committee chaired by a Works Manager and having representatives from engineering, quality control, sales, accounts, market research, strategy studies, and research and development. The basic parameters such as product range, size, output rate, packaging and process requirements were established by this Committee.

When approval for the project was given, in 1972, a project management organization was formed. At an early stage, consideration was given to the problem or organizational communication. To ensure adequate control, several committees covering production control, quality control, production and commissioning, engineering co-ordination, recruitment and training, and project management were established.

In addition, Joint Consultative Working Groups were established, involving management and labor. These groups discussed plant designs, working procedures, safety, and so on. Regular design, manufacture, installation and other co-ordination meetings were held with contractors. A computerized network analysis of the project was used for planning and control of all phases of work. The Factory Inspectorate was involved from a very early stage to advise on, and approve, safety features and procedures.

Specifications were drawn up for all items of plant covering performance, reliability and maintainability. This was not easy and plant personnel were closely involved with suppliers in explaining, training and assisting with the preparation of logic fault-finding systems. Maintenance manuals, including preventive maintenance schedules, overhaul schedules, lubrication programs, spares listings, fault diagnosis information and training programs were also specified. The need for modular construction, ease of access for maintenance and ergonomic considerations were also included. A percentage of the purchase cost was withheld until delivery of all maintenance manuals and initial spares was completed.

Initial **design** work included the collection of historic information on plant performance, listing of maintenance characteristics, layout and flow studies. Maintenance records for previous plant were examined in detail in order to estimate maintenance manpower and frequencies for preventive maintenance schedules. Plant availability estimates were based on recorded mechanical and electrical breakdown.

The productivity services department carried out simulation studies of the plant's likely performance. The 'lowest-bid' temptation was avoided on many occasions, notably so when selecting automatic bundling equipment and FSD. An ergonomist was employed in the design of control panels, control cabins, crane cabs, etc.

Other notable design features were the quick-stand-change facilities, the stand-by lubrication system, the considerable rationalization of pumps, drives and motors, rigorous application of modifications to standard equipment in order to improve reliability and maintainability, the design for maximum accessibility for maintenance, the use of modular construction concepts, the functional grouping of equipment in order to facilitate FSD, plant-mounted sensors for vibration detection and fault location, the use of an 'alarms computer' for detecting and reporting faults and process variations.

All equipment drawings were examined for **spares** requirements, one of the aims of the rationalization program being the reduction of the variety of spares. For example, all pipework was designed in seven basic sizes and only three types of hydraulic pump were used. Extensive rationalization was also achieved in the required electrical spares.

In order to carry out much of the above it was essential that an experienced maintenance engineer was recruited as a senior member of the management team. He was involved in all stages of the project, including the design. A notable consequence of this was that the building exhibited some unique features that were designed specifically to facilitate maintenance organization. For example, the mill bay had two floor levels, an elevated rolling level and a lower services and maintenance level. The advantages of this underground services floor were considerable and included routing of distribution and services pipework which was an improvement from the point of view of both installation and maintenance. It gave ease of preventive maintenance (with underground test points), lubrication points and readily accessible drive equipment, without disrupting production flow on the upper level. In addition, scrap collection was facilitated by a 'drive-in' arrangement and road vehicles. Maintenance of rolls was facilitated by passing the roll assemblies through the floor of the production bay directly into the roll and guide shop. After preparation the new roll assemblies were simply craned up to the production floor and refitted.

Installation was supervised by a team of installation engineers who formed part of the project management team. Normal recording of plant installation problems was carried out.

Commissioning procedures (plant performance testing, training programs, a commissioning check-card system) were rigorously formalized for both the static and running phases. The installation engineers compiled lists of checks required for each plant, this work demanding considerable study of drawings and design information prior to installation, and ensured that they gained considerable familiarity with the plant design. Control of the issue of the commissioning check cards was related to a computerized installation network program and cards were issued to appropriate staff when predetermined stages were achieved in the program. A computer terminal was available for regular updating of the network, and for reviewing checks required, on a day-to-day basis while maintaining an overall picture of the installation and commissioning phase.

The company's own experience, supplemented by visits to similar plants in other countries, suggested that lengthy plant commissioning times had been due to insufficient attention to **training**. It was therefore decided that all management, operatives, artisans, engineers and supporting personnel should be adequately trained in the theory and practice needed to meet both the desired reduction in commissioning time and the required operational performance of the new mill. A recruitment and training committee was established, consisting of the project manager, production engineer, personnel officer, production manager, maintenance engineer and training officer. Initial instruction and training was given in 2 to 4 weeks of formal lectures and discussion groups. Multi-skill training was given where considered desirable. Simulated control panels and layouts were built and used extensively.

Each artisan's dossier of experience was matched against a skill and knowledge of matrix based on a job description, and was then used to compile a training program designed to suit the individual's needs. Electricians and fitters were recruited 3 months before mill startup and were given formal lectures, site work and project work. Regular tests were given and the training programs were also reviewed in the light of the participants' comments on their effectiveness. Pipe fitters were recruited 2 months before mill startup and welders, boilersmiths and auxiliaries 1 month before start-up.

Maintenance engineering staff selection was given some thought at an early stage. For example, the recruitment of the installation engineers took account of their potential for subsequent transfer to maintenance department when the mill became operational. As a result, nine installation engineers were transferred to permanent maintenance engineering positions. Team training was also applied and the management team were involved in a series of courses designed to improve personal and team effectiveness. Weekend sessions, for fostering teamwork, were undertaken by the management, production operatives, artisans and engineers of each shift.

As a result of the considerable prior effort described, the **operational** and **maintenance** practice that will now be outlined was made much easier.

The plant was to be operated on a continuous 15 shift systems for 5 days a week. During initial commissioning a one shift system was run, this being subsequently increased to two and eventually three shifts.

Performance standards were derived, for output, yield, defectives, accidents, fuel consumption, labor, maintenance, etc., for each product group. These were supported by a formal system of reporting production problems, delays, utilization, scrap, lost time and many other factors, such reporting being completed on a shift basis. Daily meetings were held between production and maintenance at top management level, and formal reports issued on a weekly and monthly basis. Preventive maintenance routines and tasks were designed to be carried out, wherever possible, while the plant was running, the remainder being done at weekends or when the plant was standing for product changes, etc.

As equipment was installed, plant history cards were opened, maintenance routines analyzed, preventive maintenance frequencies determined and a computer-controlled preventive maintenance system adopted. A readily assessed and continually updated inventory of routines and repetitive jobs was established in the computer data bank, which also contained more detailed information for the execution of specific jobs. Work planning was based on computerized job cards and used 'work measured' job times for repetitive work. Information on failure cause could also be recorded on the job cards for subsequent analysis alongside the maintenance reports compiled for each shift by the shift engineer. Any delays that could be clearly attributed to design faults were charged to the design department and booked separately on the shift report for further investigation.

Downtime plots were kept up-to-date and displayed in the maintenance engineer's office and the planning officer. Availability figures were recorded and graphed for major items of plant, and a maintenance engineering report issued monthly. Standards for maintainability and plant availability were established. Network analysis was used on major maintenance jobs.

As a continuing, long-term operation, **feedback** of the experience gained would be directed both to the company's maintenance data bank and to the equipment suppliers.

In achieving its worked-up tonnage level in 1 year, the plant outstripped the performance of any other recent and major bar mills, worldwide. A planned second commissioning year was not needed.

A 5.4% target for engineering delays was seen as unrealistic and in 1977 management agreed to set the standard at 6.6%. As it turned out the level attained in 78/79 was 5.6% which compared favorably with the 8% figure of the other major mills.

Summary

The application of the approach that has been outlined involves a much higher capital expenditure than the traditional lowest-bid, lowest-cost, shortest-time approach. The difficulties of implementing such an approach are many, e.g. cash constraints, time constraints, the uncertainty of forecasting demand and product life; therefore, in some situations it has to be accepted that the additional effort and cost might not be worth the return. However, with the present trend toward automated, large, expensive plant, the adoption of this approach can, in the majority of cases, benefit a company to a considerable extent. It requires the commitment and foresight of the most senior management. It is therefore no accident that the successful industrial examples of the application of terotechnology appear to have at least one common factor – an Engineering Director who is convinced of the long-term advantages of keeping maintenance firmly in mind when designing, installing and commissioning.

Reference

Harvey, G. and Eastburn, K., Terotechnology: a case study in the application of the concept, *Terotechnica* 1(1), 1979.

3

Formulating maintenance strategy:
A business-centered approach

'Strategy without tactics is the slowest route to victory,
Tactics without strategy is the noise before defeat.'
Sun Tzu, 490 BC Chinese Military Strategist

Chapter aims and outcomes

To explain the business-centered maintenance (BCM) procedure and show how it can be used to develop or modify the maintenance strategy for a complex industrial plant.

On completion of this chapter you should be able to:

- understand the methodology of BCM and why it is so called;
- understand that maintenance strategy is concerned with deciding how to maintain the plant, with setting up an appropriate maintenance organization and with establishing and using systems for directing the maintenance effort;
- understand how the BCM methodology can be used to map and model the maintenance department of an industrial plant in order to improve the maintenance strategy — the strategic thought process.

Chapter route map

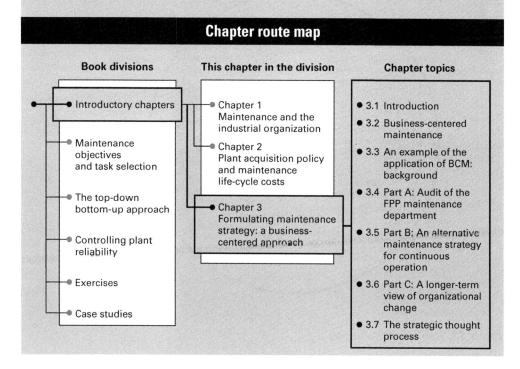

Book divisions	This chapter in the division	Chapter topics
Introductory chapters	Chapter 1 Maintenance and the industrial organization	• 3.1 Introduction
Maintenance objectives and task selection	Chapter 2 Plant acquisition policy and maintenance life-cycle costs	• 3.2 Business-centered maintenance
The top-down bottom-up approach	Chapter 3 Formulating maintenance strategy: a business-centered approach	• 3.3 An example of the application of BCM: background
Controlling plant reliability		• 3.4 Part A: Audit of the FPP maintenance department
Exercises		• 3.5 Part B: An alternative maintenance strategy for continuous operation
Case studies		• 3.6 Part C: A longer-term view of organizational change
		• 3.7 The strategic thought process

Key words

- Business-centered maintenance
- Maintenance strategy
- Maintenance auditing
- Strategic thought process
- Business objectives

3.1 Introduction

Devising optimal strategy for maintaining industrial plant can be a difficult task of quite daunting complexity. The purpose of this chapter is to provide the maintenance manager with an overview of a comprehensive and systematic approach for tackling this problem, i.e. a methodology – or framework of guidelines – for deciding maintenance objectives, formulating equipment life plans and plant maintenance schedules, designing the maintenance organization and setting up appropriate systems of documentation and control.

I have called this approach business-centered maintenance (BCM), because it springs from, and is driven by, the identification of business objectives, which are then translated into maintenance objectives and underpin the maintenance strategy formulation (see Figure 3.1).

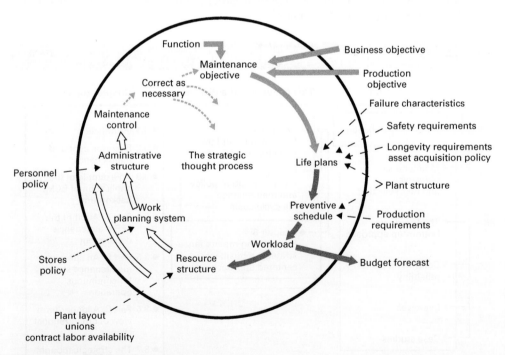

Figure 3.1 A BCM methodology

It is this approach, i.e. BCM, which therefore informs at every stage the treatment of the maintenance management problem presented in this series of three companion books:

- This, the first volume in the series, is concerned with the strategic side of mainte- nance – identified in Figures 3.1 and 3.2 as function, objective and plan (*in simple terms, the planning aspect of maintenance management*).
- '*Managing the Maintenance Resources*', the second book in the series, is concerned with the organization of the maintenance resource to carry out the maintenance work – iden- tified in Figure 3.1 as workload, resource structure, work planning and administrative structure (*in simple terms, the doing aspect of maintenance management*).
- '*Maintenance Documentation and Systems*', the third book, is concerned with the documentation and control systems that are needed – identified in Figure 3.1 as con- trol (*the controlling aspect of maintenance management*).

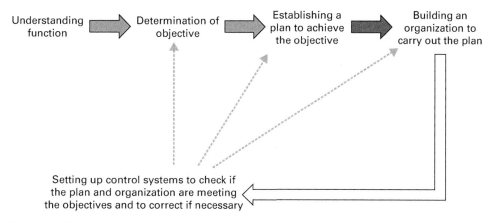

Figure 3.2 Basic steps of the management process

This chapter is key to this present book because it covers (in outline via a case study) the concepts, procedures and models of all three books, i.e. those concerned not only with the planning of maintenance but also with its organization and control.

3.2 Business-centered maintenance

The structure of a methodology for developing a maintenance strategy, which I call the BCM approach, is outlined in Figure 3.1. It is based on well-established administrative management principles (see Figure 3.2) and provides a framework for identifying, map- ping and then auditing the elements of any maintenance management system [1].

In order to better understand the purpose of Figure 3.1, it is useful to put yourself in the position of a maintenance manager thinking through how he is going to set up a maintenance department for a new plant. Obviously he needs to understand the way the plant operates, its relationship with its market and the function of maintenance within this context. The large circle is his strategic thought process starting with the plant maintenance objective (which is subordinate to the business objectives) and proceeding via life plans and organization through to control (this procedure is essentially the same as the basic management procedure of Figure 3.2). From outside of the large circle come the numerous factors (from other departments or from the environment, e.g. industrial relations) that can affect the strategic thought process.

One way of describing the *function* of maintenance was defined in the previous chapter, *viz.*:

to sustain the integrity of the physical assets by repairing, modifying or replacing them as necessary.

This can also be expressed as:

to provide and control the reliability of the plant.

The ways in which the maintenance function might be affected by its dynamic relationship with the production function need to be clearly understood. Once this has been achieved the *maintenance objective* can be established. This can only be carried out in conjunction with the production department because the maintenance and production objectives are inseparable and both need to be compatible with the corporate objectives – associated with '*maximization of profitability in the long term*' (which recognizes company survival as an objective in itself). It is for this reason I call the approach *business centered*, the maintenance decision-making process stemming from the business objectives.

This assumes the production and maintenance departments are separate, i.e. have separate managers and budgets. Even where production and maintenance are fused into a single department the maintenance function and objective remains distinct from the production function and objective. In this later case, it is much easier to ensure that the production and maintenance objectives are compatible.

Any decision on 'how best to maintain a plant equipment' or 'how best to organize the maintenance resources' must be based on how that decision affects the company's bottom line. A generic expression for the maintenance objective for a plant might therefore be:

to achieve the agreed plant operating pattern, availability and product quality within the accepted plant condition (for longevity[1]) and safety standards, and at minimum resource cost.

By setting maintenance objectives at plant level (a power station) and then bringing these down to unit level (a boiler), we are in a better position to establish each maintenance *life plan* (the way it is proposed to maintain the unit throughout its expected life) at this level.

---

[1] Longevity: dictionary definition, long duration of existence. In this case, the term is associated with the designed life of the plant.

The *preventive maintenance schedule* for the plant as a whole is made up from the jobs identified in the life plans for each unit. This schedule is influenced by many factors, including the plant-operating pattern, statutory safety requirements, equipment redundancy, etc.

The preventive schedule defines the *maintenance workload* (see Figure 3.1).

> For example, consider a power station using three 500 MW turbo-generators. Traditionally each one has a life plan based on 3-yearly major overhauls, each lasting for about 8 weeks and requiring up to 1000 men. The maintenance schedule would involve one of the three units coming out in the summer each year. This would generate a major peak of work for 8 weeks, the workload then dropping back for the remainder of the year to a level appropriate to the base staffing of about 100 men.

The maintenance workload in turn has the largest single influence on *organizational design*.

> At the station the management would be forced to consider contract labor to handle the work peaks. In addition they may have to consider shift working to handle the high-priority work occurring on a 24-hour basis.

Finally, *control systems* are required (see Figure 3.1), to ensure that the maintenance effort is achieving the objectives and, if not, to correct the life plans or organizations as necessary.

Review Question

R3.1   You have been asked by your Managing Director to explain in a concise way what exactly is BCM. Write down an explanation – keep it as short as possible.

3.3 An example of the application of BCM: background

A more detailed and comprehensive explanation of BCM may be gained by referring to an industrial application, in this case its use in auditing the maintenance department of a food processing plant (FPP).

The plant layout was shown in Figure 3.3, and an outline process flow diagram being shown in Figure 3.4. At the time of the audit the production pattern was three shifts per day, 5 days per week and 50 weeks per year. There was also considerable spare capacity. For example, only three lines out of four (see Figure 3.4) were needed to achieve full capacity. However, each line had its own product mix to satisfy the market demand. Thus, the availability of any given line for maintenance depended on the market demand and the level of finished product stored. Offline maintenance could be carried out in the weekend windows of opportunity or, by exploring spare capacity, during the week. In general, the maintenance manager found it easier to carry out most of the offline work during the weekend.

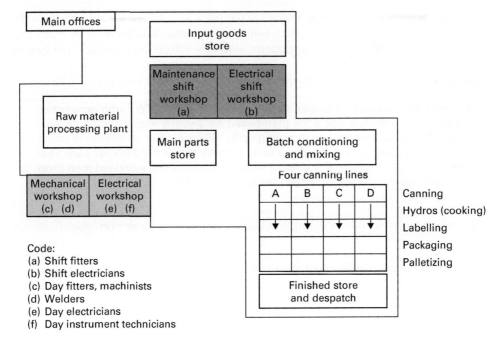

Figure 3.3 Layout of FPP

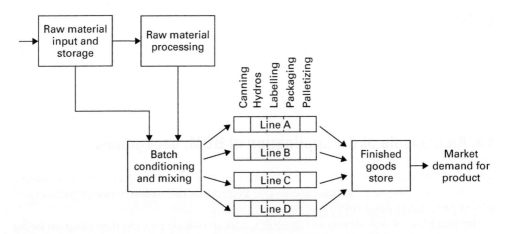

Pattern of operation 50 weeks x 5 days x 3 shifts, Monday/Friday

Figure 3.4 Process flow for FPP

The relationship between the plant and the market demand for its product (and/or raw material supply) has a considerable influence on maintenance strategy. It governs the way production will use the plant — the plant-operating pattern. This in turn determines the frequency, duration and cost of scheduling the plant for offline maintenance — maintenance windows. The market demand is different across different industries. For example, base-load power stations (stations that provide the cheapest electricity) are required to operate for as long as possible because of a constant and continuous demand. The FPP of this example is a multi-product company where the demand for each product may well vary with time, often seasonally.

The problem the company faced was that they wanted to increase their output by using the weekends for production and by operating each line for as long as possible. Experience had led to the feeling that each line could operate continuously for about 4 weeks before coming out, for two shifts, for maintenance. The company wanted to know how this was going to affect their maintenance strategy and the following tasks were requested:

A To audit their existing maintenance department in order to compare it to international best practice.
B To propose an alternative maintenance strategy that would facilitate the new mode of continuous operation.
C To provide an organizational vision (via models) of where the company should be heading in the next 5 years.

The audit of the FPP (task A above) will be used to provide a detailed and comprehensive explanation of BCM. This will include descriptions of each of the main elements of BCM, e.g. objectives, and will also introduce a number of generic models that can be used to map and understand the operation of these elements. You may find it necessary during your progress through the audit to refer back to the master diagram of Figure 3.1. It is important as you progress through the audit that you consider how you would modify the organization to comply with tasks B and C above — the answer to these tasks will be incorporated into this chapter as exercises.

3.4 Part A: Audit of the FPP maintenance department

The audit procedure follows the main elements of the methodology model shown in Figure 3.1.

3.4.1 Maintenance objectives

At plant level this could be stated as being:

to achieve the 15-shift operating pattern, product mix and output (cans/week) within the accepted plant condition for longevity and safety requirements, and at minimum resource cost.

It is the responsibility of the production, safety and engineering departments to specify the plant requirements, and the maintenance department to develop the strategy to achieve these requirements at minimum cost.

If the maintenance department were to develop the 'best way of maintaining the plant' the maintenance objectives needed to be interpreted in a form that is meaningful at a lower level of equipment, the plant unit – a hydro, say, or the cooker (see Figure 3.5). This allowed the maintenance *life plans* for the various units of plant to be established.

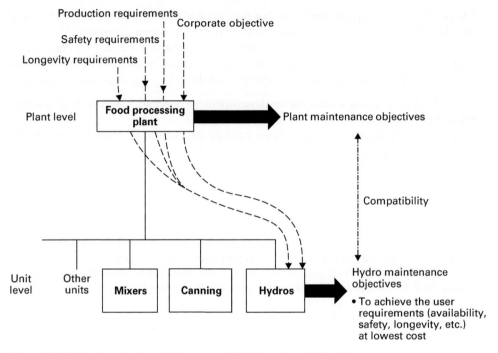

Figure 3.5 Bringing plant maintenance objectives to unit level

The audit established that the FPP were using a management-by-objectives (MBO) procedure. Business objectives were set, and translated into maintenance objectives by the chief engineer. These in turn were translated into key result areas (KRAs) which, rather than being objectives, were a series of future actions to achieve the maintenance objectives. The auditors considered the procedure to be excellent but the KRAs were not well enough directed toward maintenance objectives and were not sufficiently numerical.

3.4.2 Life plans and preventive schedule

A generic model of a life plan for a unit of plant (a hydro, say) is shown in Figure 3.6. Such a plan can be considered as a program of maintenance jobs (lubrication, inspection, repair, replace and carried out at set frequencies) spanning the expected life of the unit.

The main decision regarding the life plan is the determination of the preventive policy (replace or repair at fixed-time or fixed-operating periods, or via some form of inspection), which, in its turn, determines the resulting level of corrective work. The life plans should be established, using the well-documented principles of preventive maintenance [1] and should be reviewed periodically to ensure their effectiveness.

These principles and concepts of preventive maintenance will be discussed in depth in Chapter 6.

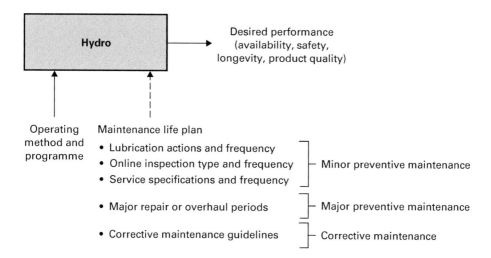

Figure 3.6 Outline of a life plan for a unit of plant

The preventive maintenance schedule for the FPP was assembled from the preventive jobs identified in the life plans (see Figure 3.7). Such a schedule is only one part of the maintenance workload and has to be carried out in conjunction with the corrective work which has a shorter scheduling horizon, and often higher priority. (Sometimes restricting the maintenance department's ability to carry out corrective work – an aspect that will be discussed in more detail when we come to work planning.)

The schedule is influenced by the production plan – which itself is a function of the market demand (multi-product fluctuating demand requiring a flexible production plan), operating pattern, plant redundancy, inter-stage and final-stage storage, etc. In the FPP case, the important factor was the operating pattern which gave six shift-weekend windows and a 2-week annual window that provided enough time to carry out the necessary preventive (and corrective) work without affecting the production plan.

In spite of the criticism of the objectives the unit life plans investigated were good (e.g. see Table 3.1) for the life plan for the hydro. The work content of the hydro overhauls (the major maintenance) was based on the monitoring and inspection of their condition. The frequency of overhauls, once every 8 years, was determined only by an experience-based, and approximate, judgment. Nevertheless, it did give an indication of the future major workload, and its resource scheduling and budgeting. The preventive schedule was based on the scheduling guidelines outlined in Table 3.2. This meant that most of the second-line work was carried out at weekends. Little attempt had been made to schedule this latter work into the weekend, by exploiting spare capacity.

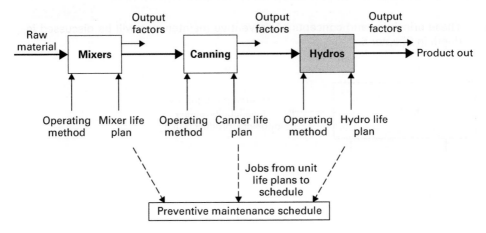

Figure 3.7 Build up of plant preventive schedule from unit life plans

Table 3.1 Outline the hydro life plan

Weekly	Cleaning, check operation of critical parts, lubrication.	4 hours	
2 weekly/monthly	Lubrication routine.	4 hours	
3 monthly	Inspection of main drive to include oil analysis.	8 hours	Minor Work
6 monthly	Inspection of all flights and conveyor drives. Clean hydro internally. Oil analysis of conveyor drives.	3 shifts	
12 monthly	Fixed-time replacement of sprocket bearings. Overhaul drive unit and rewind motors.	1 week	
2 yearly	Replace with speed drive belts.	1 week	
8 yearly	Major rebuild. Exact frequency on condition.	3 weeks	Major work

Workload

The maintenance schedule generates the maintenance workload (see Figure 3.1). The mechanical workload for the FPP is mapped in Figure 3.8 by its scheduling characteristics (the electrical workload can be mapped in the same way). *First-line work* is made up from emergency jobs (which can be defined as work needing to be carried out in the shift of its occurrence) and jobs (corrective or preventive) that are small and do not require detailed planning – they can be 'fitted in'.

It can be seen that this work is carried out during the shifts over Monday to Friday. Management had manned up the shift resource to ensure all the emergency work received attention during the shift of its occurrence.

Table 3.2 Scheduling guidelines for the FPP

	Maintenance philosophy	*Work type*
Monday to Friday	'Keep the plant going' and 'Keep an eye on its condition'	Reactive maintenance Operator monitoring routines Trade-force line-patrolling routines Condition-based routines
Weekends	'Inspect the plant carefully and repair as necessary in order to keep it going until next weekend'	Schedule corrective jobs by priority Inspect and repair schedule Fixed-time minor job schedule (services, etc.)
Summer shutdown	'Schedule out the major jobs to see us through another year'	Schedule corrective jobs Fixed-time major jobs schedule

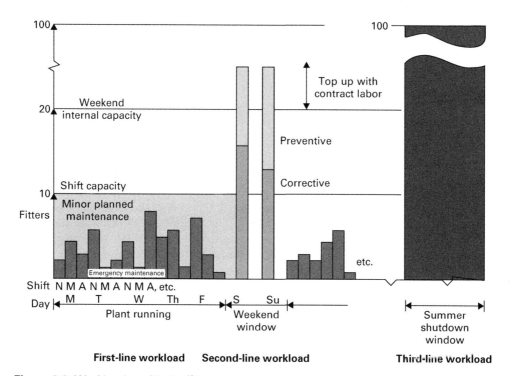

Figure 3.8 Workload profile for fitters

Second-line work involves the larger preventive jobs (services, small overhauls, etc.) and corrective jobs that require planning and, via a priority system can be scheduled to be carried out at weekend (or in some other available window).

> When the weekend workload exceeded the internal weekend resource (two
> of the four shift-groups – 20 fitters) contract labor was used to cover the excess.

Third-line work involves major plant (or parts of the plant) overhauls. It requires the plant to be offline for considerable periods and is carried out at medium- or long-term intervals – in the FPP case in the annual 2-week windows. The planning lead time for such work can be many months.

A more detailed categorization of a maintenance workload is shown in Table 3.3.

> The audit revealed a 50% over-manning on the mid-week shifts, caused by lack
> of clear definition of emergency work – much of which could have been carried
> out at the weekends as planned second-line work.

3.4.3 Maintenance organization

The workload is the biggest single influence in the size and shape of the maintenance organization. At the FPP the first-line emergency work required shift cover and the yearly shutdown peak required contract labor. Designing the organization requires many interrelated decisions to be made (where to locate manpower, how to extend inter-trade flexibility, who should be responsible for spare parts, how to decide the responsibilities for plant operation and maintenance), each influenced by various conflicting factors. Thinking in terms of the methodology of Figure 3.1 reduces the complexity of this problem, by categorizing the decisions according to the main elements of the organization, *viz.* its resource structure, its administrative structure, its systems, and then considering each one in the order indicated – the procedure is iterative.

Resource structure
The resource structure is the geographic location of workforce, spares, tools and information, their function, composition, size and logistics. For example, Figure 3.9 shows the Monday-to-Friday structure that had evolved at the FPP, to best suit the characteristics of a 24-hour first-line emergency workload. The emphasis is on rapid response, plant knowledge via specialization, shift working and team working with production. In theory, the shift-groups had been sized to match the reactive workload with the lower-priority jobs being used to smooth the workload. The weekday centralized group carried out second-line work to include weekend preparation, reconditioning and also acted as a first-line work overspill for the shift-groups.

Figure 3.10 shows the structure that matched the second-line weekend workload. The shift roster was arranged to ensure that two of the four shift-groups are available for 12 hours on Saturdays and Sundays (to include some overtime). Contract labor was used to top-up, as necessary the internal labor force. A similar approach was used for the annual shutdown, but in that case the contracted workforce exceeded the internally available labor. The spare parts store and tool store was an integral part of the resource structure and in this case both were centralized, serving the whole site.

> The resource structure (e.g. see Figure 3.9) can be regarded as a simple matrix
> of plant specialization against work category (first line, second line, etc.). To

Table 3.3 Detailed categorization of maintenance workload by organizational characteristics

Main category	Subcategory	Category number	Comments
First line	Corrective emergency	1	Occurs with random incidence and little warning and the job times also vary greatly. A typical emergency workload is shown in Figure 3.8. This is a workload generated by operating plant, the pattern following the production-operating pattern (e.g. 5 days, three shifts per day, etc.). Requires urgent attention due to economic or safety imperatives. Planning limited to resource cover and some job instructions or decision guidelines. Can be offline or online (*in-situ* corrective techniques). In some industries (e.g. power generation) failures can generate major work, these are usually infrequent but cause large work peaks.
	Corrective deferred minor	2	Occurs in the same way as emergency corrective work but does not require urgent attention; it can be deferred until time and maintenance resources are available (it can be planned and scheduled). During plant operation some small jobs can be fitted into an emergency workload such as that of Figure 3.8 (smoothing).
	Preventive routines	3	Short-periodicity work, normally involving inspections and/or lubrication and/or minor replacements. Usually online and carried out by specialists or used to smooth an emergency workload such as that of Figure 3.8.
Second line	Corrective deferred major	4	Same characteristics as (2) but of longer duration and requiring major planning and scheduling.
	Preventive services	5	Involves minor offline work carried out at short- or medium-length intervals. Scheduled with time tolerances for slotting and work smoothing purposes. Some work can be carried out online although most is carried out online during weekend or other shutdown windows.
	Corrective reconditioning and fabrication	6	Similar to deferred work but is carried out away from the plant (second-line maintenance) and usually by a separate trade-force.
Third line	Preventive major work (overhauls, etc.)	7	Involves overhauls of plant, plant sections of major units. Work is offline and carried out at medium- or long-term intervals. Such a workload varies in the long term as shown in Figure 3.8. The shutdown schedule for large multi-plant companies can be designed to smooth the company shutdown workload.
	Modifications	8	Can be planned and scheduled some time ahead. The modification workload (often 'capital work') tends to rise to a peak at the end of the company financial year. This work can also be used to smooth the shutdown workload.

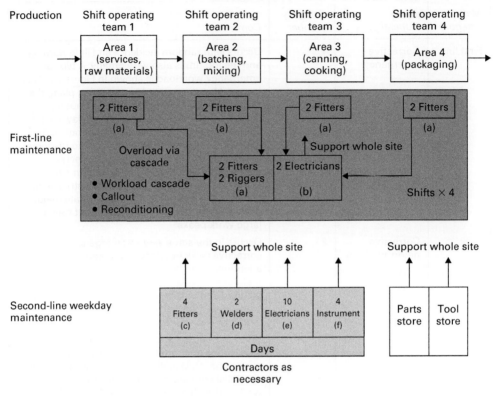

Figure 3.9 Weekday resource structure

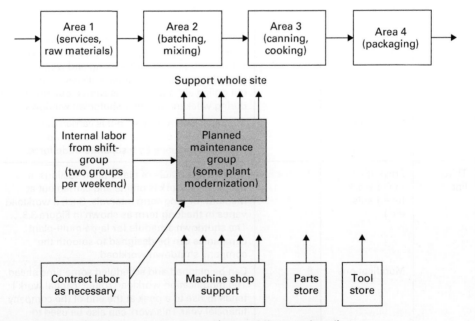

Figure 3.10 Weekend resource structure (second-line weekend)

enable the structure to be drawn it is necessary to construct the horizontal axis as the 'plant line' (i.e. the division of the plant into its main process areas) and the vertical axis as the 'work-type line' (i.e. operations above the plant line and maintenance work categories below the plant line). In this case, the complete structure (weekday and weekend) could have been drawn on the same diagram.

It would have then been necessary to explain on the diagram how the shift teams related into the weekend teams. Resource structures provide an outline of the way in which maintenance resources are used – they need to be supplemented by a description of trade flexibility, contract usage, shift rostering and human factors, etc.

The aim of any resource structure design (or modification) is to achieve the best resource utilization for a desired speed of response and quality of work. This, in part, involves the best match of the resources to the workload. Decisions in a number of other areas – e.g. in shift rostering, the use of contract labor, inter-plant flexibility, inter-trade flexibility and production-maintenance flexibility – can influence this matching process. Flexibility is clearly the key factor here. The structure is also influenced by the availability of trade-force skills and by various human factors.

The FPP audit revealed a number of deficiencies in the resource structure. The most important was the over-manning of the mid-week shifts (see the workload comments). The audit was carried out 13 years ago and it is not surprising that inter-trade flexibility, production-maintenance flexibility and contractor alliances were not being exploited. Human factors such as morale, motivation and a sense of equipment ownership were good.

Administrative structure

This can be considered as a hierarchy of work roles, ranked by their authority and responsibility for deciding what, when and how maintenance work should be carried out. The FPP structure is shown in Figure 3.11 (which uses the so-called organogram as the modeling vehicle). Many of the rules and guidelines of classical administrative theory [2] can be used in the design of such structures. The model shows the maintenance administration in the context of the full administration, simplified in this case. The key decisions in the design of the maintenance administration can be divided between its upper and lower structures. Regarding the former, the audit must identify how the responsibilities for plant ownership, operation and maintenance have been allocated. In the FPP case, production had responsibility for the operation of the plant, and in a sense its ownership, since they dictated how it was to be used and when it could be released for maintenance. Maintenance had responsibility for establishing and carrying out the maintenance strategy, and engineering for plant acquisition and plant condition standards. These responsibilities have to be clearly defined and overlapping areas identified.

Initially, the lower structure has to be considered separately from the upper because it is influenced – indeed, almost constrained – by the nature of the maintenance resource structure which, as explained, is in turn a function of the workload. Lower structure decisions are concerned with establishing the duties, responsibilities and work roles of the shop-floor personnel and of the first level of supervision.

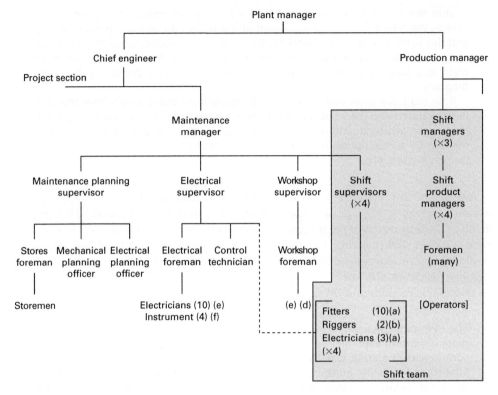

Figure 3.11 Administrative structure

The FPP was using the traditional supervisor – planner – trade-force structure. This needs to be compared with the more recent structures of self-empowered operator–maintainer shift teams and self-empowered second-line maintenance teams.

(Maintenance organization is covered in depth in the second book in this series – *Managing Maintenance Resources*, ISBN 07506 69934.)

3.4.4 Maintenance work planning

Figure 3.12 outlines a maintenance work planning system for the FPP resource and administrative structure previously shown. The design of this should aim to get the right balance between the cost of planning the resources and the savings in direct and indirect maintenance costs that result from use of such resources.

It can be seen that the planning system is designed around the resource structure – it has a shift planning system (first line), a weekend planning system (second line) and an annual shutdown planning system (third line, not shown in detail). The audit must

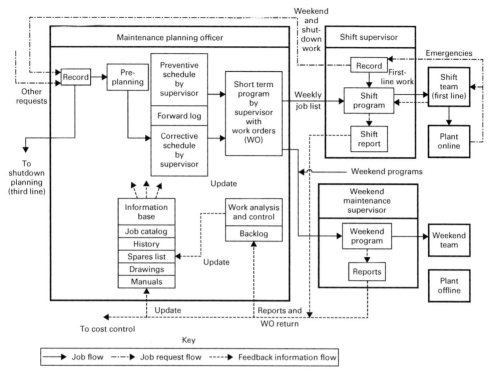

Figure 3.12 Work planning system

identify how well each level of planning is being carried out. At each level there are key procedures to verify, e.g. at FPP's second level:

- How good is the information base in terms of standard job procedures, spare part list, history?
- Who identifies the job method for monitoring jobs?
- Are job times estimated before they are put into the forward log?
- How are multi-trade jobs handled?
- How good is the return of information in terms of quantity and quality?

To understand the operation of the 'weekday planning system' refer to Figures 3.9 and 3.12. Work originates from the plant areas and goes to the maintenance shift supervisor (MSS) via the operators and production supervisors. The MSS carries out priority 1 work (emergencies, etc.) and passes back lower-priority work to the planning officer (PO) for planning and scheduling. The MSS smooths the ongoing emergency workload by feeding low-priority first-line work (from the weekly planned job list) to the trade-force (see also Figure 3.8).

To understand the operation of the weekend planning system, refer to Figures 3.10 and 3.12. Corrective jobs come into this system from the MSS and from other personnel – this work is priority 2 and above (plannable and schedulable).

Work that can only be carried out in a major shutdown (priority 5) is passed onto the shutdown planning system. The jobs are pre-planned (spares, method, esti-mated time) and slotted by priority into the corrective schedule. The planning of the jobs is aided by the 'information base'. A weekly meeting (Thursday) estab-lishes the 'weekend program' which is passed on to the weekend supervisor (one of the four MSS on a monthly rota) for detailed planning. The PO helps in co-ordinating the multi-trade jobs. Feedback to update the information base and for cost control comes back via completed work orders. In general such systems are now carried out electronically.

Figure 3.13 shows the work control system, which is complementary to the work plan-ning system, its main function being to control the flow of work (preventive and correc-tive) via a job priority procedure and via the feed-forward of information about future resource availability. At the FPP a number of performance indices were being used to assist this process, *viz.*:

- Total man-days in the forward log.
- Man-days in the forward log by priority.
- Man-days in the backlog.

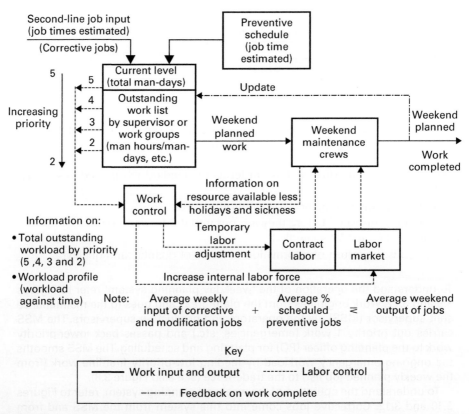

Figure 3.13 Principles of work control

- Percent planned work completed per period.
- Percent of preventive work completed per period.

> The audit revealed that the FPP's work planning system was satisfactory for what was essentially a weekly planning system, the work is planned during the week for the weekend. It was my opinion that the work planning system (and the associated software) would have to be up-rated if major jobs were to be planned at short notice during the week (see Section B of this case study).

3.4.5 Maintenance control system

This is needed to ensure that the maintenance organization is achieving its objectives (see Figure 3.1) and to initiate corrective action (e.g. change the life plan, if it is not). My own opinion is that the best practical mechanism for controlling the *overall maintenance effort* would be a properly designed maintenance costing system. This (see Figure 3.14) could be designed to provide a variety of outputs, including 'Top Tens', or Pareto plots indicating areas of low reliability, high maintenance cost, poor output performance, etc.

> The FPP audit identified that the plant had a costing system similar to that outlined in Figure 3.14 but used cost centers that were accountancy oriented rather than equipment oriented. In addition, the maintenance expenditure was not linked in any way to the output parameters.

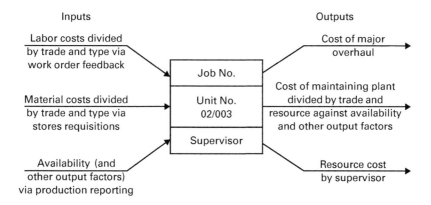

Job No.	Plant code		Trade and supervisor		Work type
	Plant	Unit	Electrician	Night shift	Preventive
521	02	003	2	NS	2

Figure 3.14 Outline of maintenance costing system

Even if properly designed, a maintenance costing system has to be a high-level, longer-term system, providing a means of controlling the overall maintenance effort. This needs to be complemented by control systems operating at a lower level and on a shorter time scale.

3.4.6 Maintenance documentation

Figure 3.1 indicated that some form of formal documentation system – for the collection, storage, interrogation, analysis and reporting of information (schedules, manuals, drawings or computer files) – is needed to facilitate the operation of all the elements of maintenance management. Figure 3.15, a general functional model of such a system (whether manual or computerized), indicates that it can be seen as comprising seven principal interrelated modules (performing different documentation functions). Considerable clerical and engineering effort is needed to establish and maintain certain of

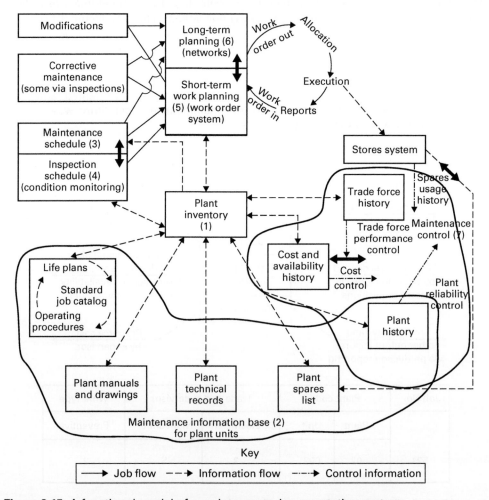

Figure 3.15 A functional model of a maintenance documentation system

these functions (e.g. the plant maintenance information base). The control module, in particular, relies on an effective data collection system. Almost all of the companies that I now audit have computerized maintenance documentation systems.

> The best way of understanding the generic functional documentation model of Figure 3.15 is to start with the plant inventory (Module 1). This is a coded list of the equipment that has to be maintained (e.g. a mixer; see Figure 3.4). The essential maintenance information needed to maintain the mixer (and the other units listed in the inventory) is held in the information base (Module 2) (e.g. life plans, history, spares lists, etc.). The preventive work listed in the life plans of various equipment is carried out via the preventive and inspection schedules (Modules 3 and 4). This work and the corrective and modification work are fed into the 'short-term work planning system' (Module 5) and where there are major shutdowns into the 'long-term work planning system' (Module 6). The feedback of information from the work planning system provides maintenance control (Module 7) and also updates the information base.

The large double arrows in Figure 3.15 indicate the possible linkages between the maintenance documentation system and other company information systems, *viz.*:

- Maintenance costing to financial management.
- Spare parts list to stores management.
- Work planning to shutdown scheduling (e.g. Primavera).
- Work planning to condition monitoring.

The majority of the systems I have audited have these functions connected, i.e. electronically – in fact, the most recent audit involved an integrated package – all the functions are on the same database. An audit needs to investigate each of the main modules of Figure 3.15, and also the sub-functions within each module, e.g. the spare parts list. In addition, it needs to identify the level and degree of integration with the other company functions.

> The maintenance package at the FPP was a stand-alone computerized system. The audit revealed that this was satisfactory for the weekend planning system that was then being used (i.e. 13 years ago). For its time the plant information base was good and was being kept up to date (history excepted).

(Maintenance documentation and the other systems outlined in this case study are covered in depth in the third book of this series – *Maintenance Systems and Documentation*, ISBN 07506 69942.)

3.4.7 Audit summary

A business-centered methodology, in conjunction with models and procedures that describes in more detail each of its elements, has been used as a framework to audit the maintenance department.

The audit revealed a number of problems, in particular shift over-manning caused by lack of clear definition and measurement of the shift emergency maintenance work. In addition, the organization needed modification – improved inter-trade flexibility, the creation of operator–maintainer self-empowered teams, closer production-maintenance integration – to bring it up to international benchmark levels.

Review Questions

R3.2   Define maintenance strategy.

R3.3   Consider how the 'market demand for the product/service' and/or the 'supply of raw materials' can affect the maintenance strategy for the following physical asset systems:

   (a) A sugar refinery.
   (b) A petroleum refinery (see Case study 3 of Chapter 12).
   (c) A local passenger bus fleet (see Case study 6 of Chapter 12).

3.5 Part B: An alternative maintenance strategy for continuous operation (see Table 3.4)

The existing maintenance strategy at the FPP was based on carrying out offline maintenance during the weekend windows of opportunity and during the once-per-year holiday window.

Little attempt had been made to exploit the excess capacity of the plant, or spare plant to schedule offline work while the plant was operating. The new, continuous, operating pattern meant that offline maintenance would have to be carried out in this way. Indeed, the life plans and schedule would have to move in the direction indicated in Table 3.4. This, in turn, would change the workload pattern – also indicated in Table 3.4.

Table 3.4 Changes in maintenance strategy to accommodate continuous operation

- The first-line work would extend to 21 shifts per week. However, investigation of the mechanical emergency workload had revealed considerable over-manning. When the first-line work was defined as '*the work that must be carried out during the shift of its occurrence*' and subsequently activity sampled, it was shown that it could be carried out by five fitters.
- The second-line work (line shutdowns, unit shutdown, preparation for shutdown, services, inspection) was more difficult to forecast in terms of pattern and size. The main peaks would come during line shutdowns at a frequency of about once per week for two shifts. The size of the workload was unlikely to decrease (even with better preventive maintenance) because the plant was going to be more heavily utilized.
- The third-line major work could still be carried out during the holiday window.
- A movement toward shutdowns of complete sections of plant based on the longest running time of critical units (e.g. the hydros — about 4 weeks). The frequency of these shutdowns will, as far as possible be based on running hours or cumulative output. However, for critical items, inspection and condition monitoring routines may be used to indicate the need for shutdowns, which will provide more flexibility about shutdown dates.
- All plant designated as non-critical, e.g. as a result of spare capacity, will continue to be scheduled at unit level (e.g. the smaller mixers).
- A much greater dependence on formalized inspections and condition monitoring routines, for reasons given in (a) and also to detect faults while they are still minor and before they become critical.
- A concerted effort either to design-out critical items (short life or poor reliability) or to extend their effective running time.

Exercises

E3.1 From the above comments it will be realized that immediate organizational changes are needed to match the new mode of operation (continuous operation for up to 4 weeks before a 3 shift shutdown of one line for essential maintenance).

Outline a revised resource structure to match the new plant-operating pattern and workload (the existing resource structure is shown in Figures 3.9 and 3.10). Modify the administrative structure to cope with any changes made to the resource structure (at this stage limit the changes to only those necessary to cope with the changed operating pattern).

E3.2 How would the new mode of operation affect the work planning system? Advise management on any changes required.

3.6 Part C: A longer-term view of organizational change

(This section uses the guideline solutions to Exercise E3.1, therefore it is advisable to answer Exercise E3.1 before reading this section.)

The organization outlined in the guideline solution to Exercise E3.1 (see Figures 3.17 and 3.18) – or in your own solutions – incorporated the immediate changes necessary for continuous operation. Their purpose was to allow the company to increase the plant availability (and output) while holding the resource costs steady. It may well be that with the experience of operation the size of the day-group of artisans will be reduced. However, in the medium and long term, when this organization is benchmarked against the best of international standards within the food processing industry, further improvements can also be identified (see Exercise E3.3).

Exercise

E3.3 Provide the management of the FPP with a model of a maintenance organization (a resource structure and administrative structure) that will bring them up to international benchmark levels.

In order to answer this question you may need to carry out a literature search of FPP maintenance organizations (or use your own experience).

3.7 The strategic thought process

The case study has shown that the maintenance department requires managerial strategic analysis in the same way as any other department. The thought process that was involved is indicated in Figure 3.16. It starts with the sales   production reaction to market demand, the resulting change in the plant-operating pattern and the increased plant operation time. This, in turn, requires amended maintenance life plans and a modified maintenance schedule. Thus, the maintenance workload changes, which brings in the training the need to modify the maintenance organization and systems.

Understanding and applying this type of strategic through process is the cornerstone of effective and fruitful maintenance management analysis.

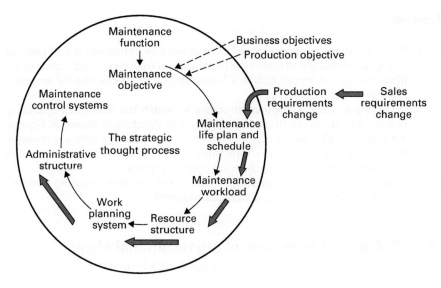

Figure 3.16 The influence of the market demand on maintenance strategy

Review Questions

R3.4   The sales department of the FPP wanted to increase output and the production department agreed to this. Can you explain the effect this had on the following:

- unit life plans,
- preventive maintenance schedule,
- maintenance workload,
- maintenance organization.

R3.5   From your answer to R3.4 and using Figure 3.16 explain the concept of the 'strategic maintenance management though process'.

References

1. Kelly, A., *Maintenance Strategy*, Butterworth-Heinemann, Oxford, 1997.
2. Kelly, A., *Maintenance Organisation and Systems*, Butterworth-Heinemann, Oxford, 1997.

Review Questions Guidelines

R3.1   Any decision involving the way maintenance is carried out should take into consideration its effect on the company's bottom line. For example, a reorganization might influence company profitability through changes in plant availability and maintenance resource costs.

R3.2   A maintenance strategy involves the complete maintenance management procedure, which includes setting maintenance objectives, determining the preventive maintenance schedule and setting up the maintenance organization.

R3.3 (a) The supply of raw cane sugar is seasonal lasting about 6 months over the Summer/Autumn period. Sugarcane has a short storage life and has to be processed shortly after cutting. The maintenance strategy of a sugar refinery is based on maintaining the plant over the 6-month sugarcane growing season to ensure high plant availability over the 6-month plant-refining period.

   (b) Petroleum refineries (see Case study 3 of Chapter 12) are mostly production limited, and involve high capital cost plant. The maintenance strategy is concerned with maintaining the plant during agreed shutdowns to achieve the longest possible production-operating period.

   (c) A local passenger bus fleet provides a service rather than a product. A typical demand for the service (number of buses in operation) is shown in Case study 6 of Chapter 12. Major maintenance is carried out using the 'spare buses in the fleet'. Minor maintenance is carried out in the low bus demand periods (the maintenance windows).

R3.4 This is explained clearly in the notes in Section 3.7.

R3.5 See Section 3.7 and Figure 3.16.

Exercise Guideline Solutions

E3.1 and E3.2 To match the new workload pattern the maintenance organization would also have to change. The most likely resource structure (see Figure 3.17)

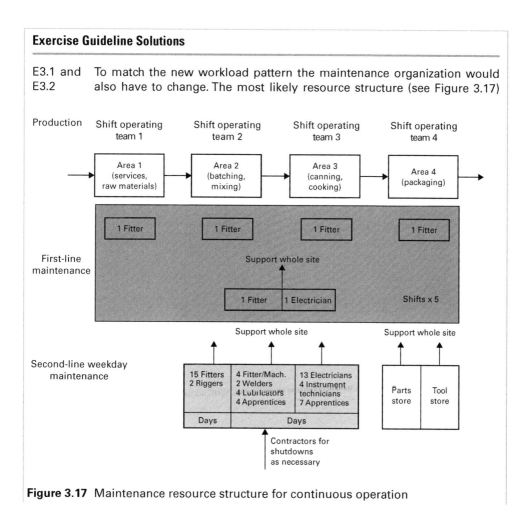

Figure 3.17 Maintenance resource structure for continuous operation

would be based on a first-line, 21 shift-group (the mechanical manning per shift being reduced to five fitters) and a second-line day-group of 15 fitters operating 5 days per week. This, in turn, would require a change the administrative structure as shown in Figure 3.18.

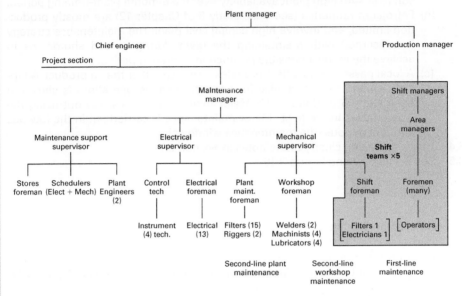

Figure 3.18 Maintenance administrative structure for continuous operation

Because of the changes in the way the work would be scheduled (the mid-week work peaks would occur at relatively short notice via the condition monitoring of the lines) it was also necessary to advise management that their work planning system would need to be improved, in order to be far more flexible and dynamic.

E3.3 A proposed improved maintenance organization is shown in Figure 3.19 (resource structure) and Figure 3.20 (administrative structure). The proposals incorporate the following actions:

- The introduction of self-empowered plant-oriented operator — maintainer teams.
- The introduction of self-empowered trade teams.
- Increase in the number of engineers, plant located for maintenance support.

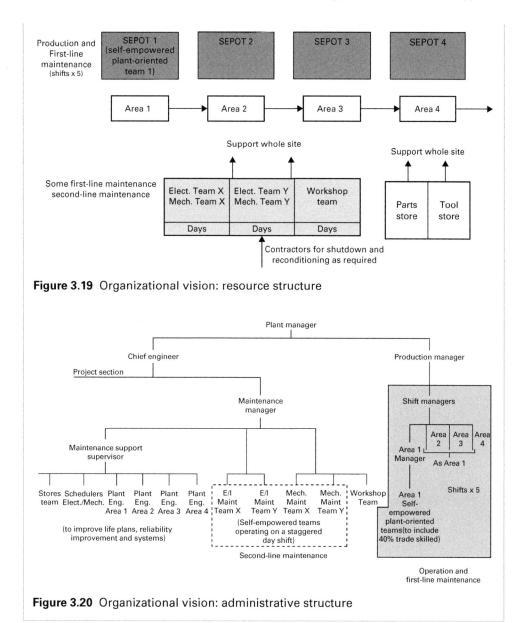

Figure 3.19 Organizational vision: resource structure

Figure 3.20 Organizational vision: administrative structure

PART 2

Maintenance objectives and task selection

4 The structure of industrial plant

'He presented me the parts of fifty locks, taken to pieces, and arranged in compartments. I put several together myself, taking pieces at hazard as they came to hand, and they fitted in the most perfect manner. The advantage of this when arms are out of repair are evident.'

Thomas Jefferson (1785)

Chapter aims and outcomes

To show how industrial plants can be modeled in order to understand their production and maintenance characteristics.

On completion of this chapter you should be able to:

- model an industrial plant using a process flow diagram;
- understand how to model the plant services (e.g. the control systems) and relate them to the process flow diagram;
- model an industrial plant as a hierarchy of parts down to component level;
- understand the basic reasons why maintenance is needed;
- understand the differences and relationships between maintenance strategy, capital replacement policy and production strategy.

Chapter route map

Book divisions	This chapter in the division	Chapter topics
Introductory chapters	Chapter 4 The structure of industrial plant	4.1 Introduction
Maintenance objectives and task selection	Chapter 5 Maintenance objectives	4.2 Physical asset systems
The top-down bottom-up approach	Chapter 6 Preventive maintenance decision-making Part 1: Principles, concepts and techniques	4.3 Modelling industrial plant
Controlling plant reliability	Chapter 7 Preventive maintenance decision-making Part 2: Maintenance task selection	4.4 The reason for maintenance
Exercises		4.5 Capital replacement policy
Case studies	Chapter 8 Maintenance task selection using reliability-centered maintenance	4.6 Maintenance strategy

Key words

- Physical assets
- Industrial plant modeling
- Assemblies
- Sub-assemblies
- Component parts
- Process flow diagrams
- Fleet 'status' models
- Capital replacement policy

Further reading

Reading 4.1 located at the end of this chapter.

4.1 Introduction

The main purpose of this book is to present and discuss methods for analyzing the complex problem of setting up maintenance strategies for industrial plant, that are both effective and efficient. In Chapter 3, the various necessary elements of a maintenance system were described – and illustrated by reference to the particular case of a food processing plant. This made it clear that the central problem is indeed the formulation of strategy. However, before enlarging on this we need to discuss:

- Methods of modeling and analyzing the operation of industrial plant, in ways that shed light on maintenance strategy.
- The reasons why such maintenance is needed.
- What exactly is meant by maintenance strategy.
- The relationship between maintenance strategy and capital replacement policy.

4.2 Physical asset systems

An industrial plant could be anything from a food processing plant, as described in Chapter 3, to an aluminum smelter (Case study 2 of Chapter 12), a car manufacturing plant or an agricultural chemical plant (Case study 1 of Chapter 12). While this course will concentrate on *industrial plant* it will also use case studies to discuss the maintenance management of other physical asset systems, *viz*. mining industry (Case study 4 of Chapter 12), transport fleets (Case study 6 of Chapter 12) and power utilities (Case studies 7–10 of Chapter 12).

4.3 Modeling industrial plant

An industrial plant will be required to carry out some overall production function, usually for some anticipated life. The effectiveness of the production function is usually measured in terms of its rate of output (e.g. tons of alumina per week).

In order to discuss an industrial plant in terms of its maintenance strategy it is useful to model the plant in two different but complimentary ways, *viz.* structural models and process flow models.

A *structural model* of an industrial plant can be envisaged as a hierarchy of parts, ranked according to their functional dependencies into units, assemblies, sub-assemblies and components (see Figure 4.1). A *unit* – e.g. a reaction vessel in a chemical plant (see Figure 4.2) or one of the mixers in the food processing plant – can be defined as:

> *collection of items interconnected mechanically and/or electrically to perform a specific production sub-function of the plant.*

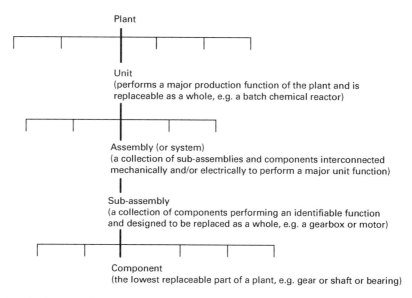

Figure 4.1 A plant modeled as a hierarchy of parts

A key part of this definition is the recognition that the unit performs a production function (e.g. mixes so many tons of pet food per hour). Each of the units can itself be informatively subdivided into a hierarchy of parts ranked largely according to their replaceability. For example, in Figure 4.3 the reaction vessel of Figure 4.2 is analyzed into assemblies (such as the agitator drive), sub-assemblies (such as the drive motor), and finally into components, the lowest level of replaceability (such as gears). This kind of analysis is particularly important when setting up the equipment inventory (usually based around the unit), and is especially useful when identifying the maintenance-causing assemblies, sub-assemblies and components of the unit. A similar analysis can be carried

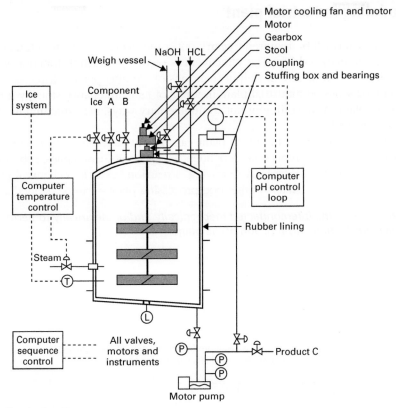

Reactor function:
To perform a defined stage of a production process,
i.e. chemical reaction under controlled pH and temperature

Figure 4.2 A batch chemical reactor

out of the plant control systems and other plant services such as air, water and electricity (see Figures 4.4–4.6).

> The model of Figure 4.1 could also be described using system theory, i.e. the unit is the subsystem of the plant and the unit can be further analyzed into its subsystems, etc. The author prefers to use the terms of Figure 4.1 because they are central to production maintenance communication, e.g. a plant unit performs a defined stage of a production process.

Exercise

E4.1 Identify examples of 'plant units' from your own plant. Select any one of these examples and draw the following:
(a) A schematic diagram of your selected unit (e.g. see Figure 6 in Case study 1 of Chapter 12).
(b) A hierarchical parts model of your selected unit (e.g. see Figure 4.3).

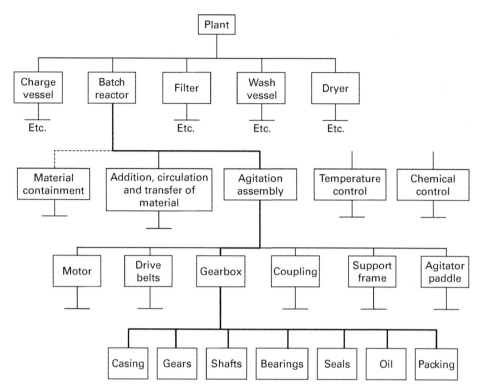

Figure 4.3 Hierarchical division of a batch chemical plant

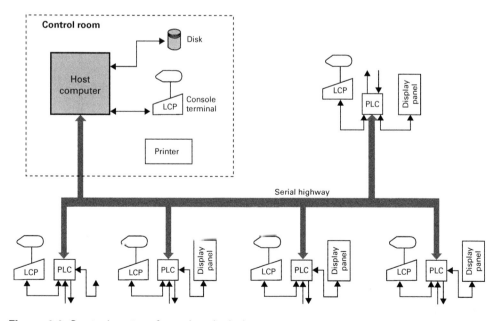

Figure 4.4 Control system for a chemical plant

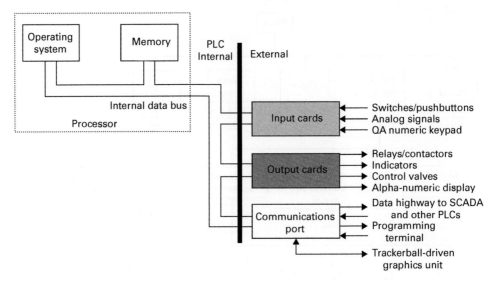

Figure 4.5 PLC internal/external block diagram

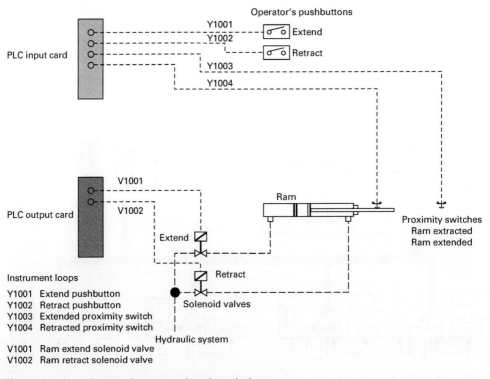

Instrument loops

Y1001   Extend pushbutton
Y1002   Retract pushbutton
Y1003   Extended proximity switch
Y1004   Retracted proximity switch

V1001   Ram extend solenoid valve
V1002   Ram retract solenoid valve

Figure 4.6 Local control system showing six loops

Most industrial plant can be informatively represented, or modeled, by a diagram show-ing the *process flow* between its various units. In this way Figure 4.7, e.g. charts the overall operation of a batch chemical plant and Figure 4.8 the detailed flows of one of its reaction streams. Models of this kind are an essential aid to understanding the production characteristics of plant and, hence the cost, safety and scheduling considerations which have to be taken into account when determining maintenance strategy.

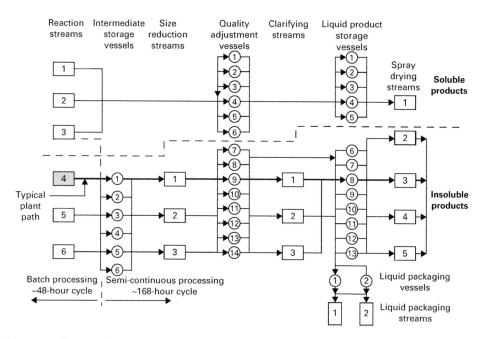

Figure 4.7 Process flow diagram: batch chemical plant

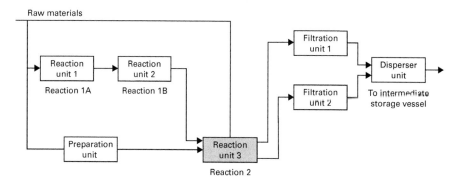

Figure 4.8 Process flow diagram: a reaction stream

In the other physical asset systems covered in this book, units can be identified, defined and modeled in a similar way to those in industrial plant. In the mining industry a conveyor or a coal shearer would be a unit (Case study 4 of Chapter 12). A bus would be a unit in a transport fleet (Case study 6 of Chapter 12) and a transformer in a power transmission system (Case study 10 of Chapter 12). However, different models are required to represent the overall operation of these physical asset systems.

Modified process flow diagrams are needed in the mining industry (see Figure 1 in Case study 4 and Figure 1 in Case study 5 of Chapter 12). In the case of transport fleets 'status diagrams' are used (see Figure 3 in Case study 6 of Chapter 12). In transmission and distribution of electricity simple transmission flow diagrams are used (see Figure 1 in Case study 9 of Chapter 12).

Although not covered in this book building maintenance could also be approached in a similar way. A building could be divided into its systems to include the building structure, air conditioning, heating and ventilation, electrical, etc. Within each of these systems units could be identified (e.g. a chiller unit).

The point that is being made here is that from the 'unit level of plant' downwards the principles and concepts of preventive maintenance can be applied universally across physical asset systems.

Review Questions

R4.1 Explain the essential differences between modeling industrial plant, e.g. an aluminum smelter, a petroleum refinery, a food processing plant and the following 'physical asset systems':
● an open cast coal mining operation,
● a bus fleet providing public transport,
● an electrical transmission/distribution utility.

R4.2 Define a 'unit of plant' and identify some examples from the Case studies 4, 6 and 9 of Chapter 12.

Exercise

E4.2 For your own company draw a process flow diagram of the type illustrated in Figures 4.7 and 4.8 (see also the way the physical asset systems have been modeled in Case studies 1–10).

4.4 The reason for maintenance

The need for maintenance originates at component level (e.g. at the bearings itemized in Figure 4.3). When a component is unable, according to some predetermined criterion, to perform its designated function it can be said to have failed, and this could be a *complete* or a *partial* loss of function. Such a loss could be contained at unit level (temporarily, at least) or have consequences at plant level, depending on the design of the plant, e.g. on the availability and capacity of inter-stage storage or redundancy (hence the importance of modeling plants in the way shown in Figures 4.7 and 4.8). The loss of function could also have safety or product quality consequences.

For technologic and economic reasons, many of the components of a plant will have been designed to have a useful life greater than the longest plant production cycle but less than that of the plant itself. In most cases such maintenance-causing parts, especially the short-life ones, will have been identified at the design stage and made easily replaceable at component level.

Other components will fail for reasons that are not easy to anticipate (such as poor design, poor maintenance or malpractice) and may be extremely expensive to replace, often requiring a substitution at a higher level of plant, i.e. of the complete assembly. In addition, as the plant ages, failure rates and maintenance replacement costs can be expected to increase as the long life, expensive, components – and eventually the assemblies and whole units – reach the limits of their useful lives.

> What can be asked at this point is why industrial plant cannot be made mainte- nance free, or at least designed for minimum maintenance. While this might increase capital cost it would reduce life-time maintenance costs. Perhaps work- ing against this is the fact that the equipment manufacturer knows that compa- nies purchasing equipment tend to use the 'lowest-bid approach' and do not think 'life-cycle costs' (see Chapter 2).
>
> In addition the equipment manufacturer makes much of his profit from the supply of parts and maintenance services.

Review Question

R4.3   Using your hierarchical parts model of Exercise E4.1(b) explain why main- tenance is necessary. Could a plant be designed to be (almost) mainte- nance free? Why is this not done?

4.5 Capital replacement policy

The delegation of the responsibility for taking replacement and repair decisions differs from one organization to another, but usually it is higher management that has to decide such matters for major units (or, indeed, for the complete plant) and maintenance man- agement for assemblies and below (see Figure 4.9). This division of responsibility is obligatory because the policy for major units and above is influenced by external, often longer term, factors such as obsolescence, sales trends or movements in the cost of cap- ital as well as internal, shorter-term, factors such as operating and maintenance costs.

Decisions involving the replacement of complete units or sections of plant should really be regarded as part of capital replacement policy.

Further reading on capital replacement policy is given in Reading 4.1 at the end of this chapter.

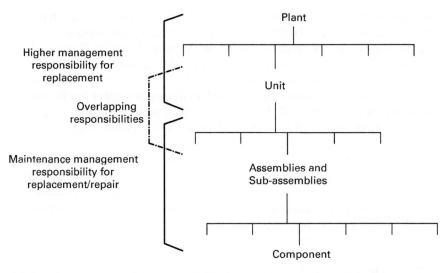

Figure 4.9 Levels of managerial responsibility for replacement/repair decision

Review Question

R4.4   Explain why, in general, maintenance managers do not on their own, make replacement decisions for large units of plant (capital replacement decisions).

4.6 Maintenance strategy

Maintenance can be considered as the replacement or repair of components and assemblies (before or after failure), so that the unit concerned can perform its designated function over its expected life.

A maintenance strategy involves the identification, resourcing and execution of many thousands of repair, replace and inspect decisions. It is concerned with:

- Formulating the *best life plan* (see Figure 4.10) for each unit. This is a comprehensive program of maintenance procedures – repair/replace/inspect at various frequencies – spanning the expected life of the unit.
- Formulating a *maintenance schedule* for the plant (see Figure 4.11). This should be assembled from the programs of work contained in the unit life plan(s) but should be dynamic, e.g. readily adjustable in the light of changes in the production schedule.
- Establishing the organization to enable the scheduled, and other, maintenance work to be resourced (see Figure 4.12, which also shows that maintenance strategy and capital replacement policy are interrelated, i.e. maintenance cost influences unit replacement decisions and vice versa).

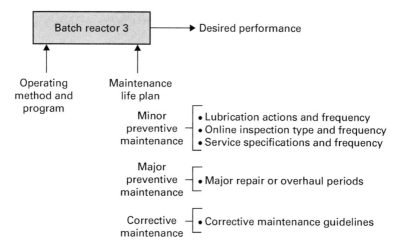

Figure 4.10 A typical unit and its maintenance life plan

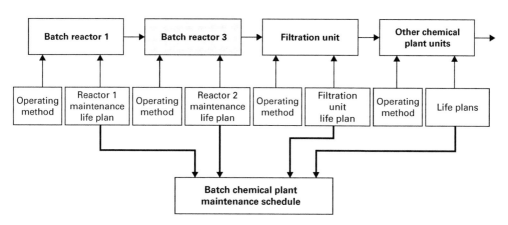

Figure 4.11 Assembling a maintenance schedule

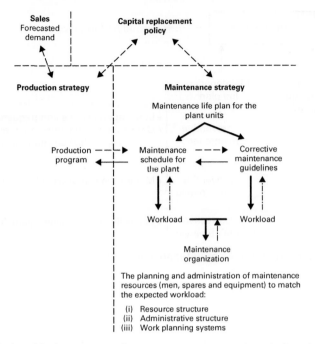

Figure 4.12 Relationship between maintenance strategy and capital replacement

---

Review Questions Guidelines

R4.1 With *industrial plant* the physical assets have a fixed location and are connected together via a batch or process arrangement to perform the overall plant function. The function is to provide a manufactured product to a market. The objective is to maximize long-term profitability. The best way of modeling such operations is by process flow diagrams down to the unit level of plant supplemented as necessary by systems diagrams for the services.

With an *open cast coal mining operation* the physical assets are spread over a wide geographic area and can be divided into mining assets, conveying/transport assets and coal preparation assets. The mining/transportation assets are mobile. The function of the operation is to provide mined coal to a market. The operation can be modeled using a combination of modified process flow diagrams (see Figure 1 in Case study 5 of Chapter 12) and status diagrams for the mobile plant (see Figure 2 in Case study 5 of Chapter 12).

With a *public transport bus fleet* the physical assets are mobile and operate over a wide geographic area. The function is to provide a public transport service. The best way of modeling fleets is via a status diagram (see Figure 1 in Case study 6 of Chapter 12).

The physical assets of a *transmission/distribution system* are spread over wide geographic area. The function is to provide electricity to consumers. With privatized utilities the objective is to maximize long-term profitability. With publically owned utilities the objective is to provide a defined level of service at best cost (these objectives are very different and have considerable influence on maintenance strategy). The operation is best modeled at the highest level as a complete generation/transmission/distribution system (see Figure 1 of the Power Utilities case studies introduction). Each part of the system, e.g. distribution can then be modeled in more detail – but in the context of the complete system (see Figure 1 in Case study 9 of Chapter 12).

R4.2   Definition of a unit: 'A collection assemblies, sub-assemblies and component parts interconnected mechanically and/or electrically to enable the whole to perform a specific production sub-function of the plant'.
  • A unit in an open cast coal mine would be a 'haulage truck'.
  • A unit in a bus fleet would be a 'bus'.
  • A unit in a distribution utility would be a 'transformer'.

R4.3   Many of the sub-assemblies and component parts of a unit have been designed with a useful life longer than the longest production run of the unit, but shorter than the expected life of the unit. Such parts have to be replaced/repaired during the life of the unit to ensure the unit remains reliable during production.
By selection of the best possible sub-assemblies and component parts a unit could be designed to be maintenance free over its designed life, say 25 years. This is not done mainly because it would be too expensive but also because in some cases such long-life parts would not be technologically possible.

R4.4   The replacement of large high-cost units of plant is influenced by many factors to include the availability of capital, taxation policy, production needs, maintenance costs and the availability record of the existing unit. The maintenance managers advice should be sought but in general he does not take the replacement decision.

Reading 4.1 Capital replacement policy

Capital replacement decisions have to take into account a multitude of considerations: production, maintenance and acquisition costs (and their variation), likely income from sale, plant reliability, fiscal considerations (tax incentives, import duty, etc.), cost of borrowing, obsolescence, alternative investment, etc. The greater the number of such considerations that a replacement calculation includes, the much greater is the complexity of the algebra. In general capital replacement models only take account of a few of the more important variables in any particular case and are, to that extent, always an approximation. The following simplified example is offered as an illustration. It is of deterministic nature in which averaged costs and trends are fairly predictable, as might be the case with a substantial unit of capital equipment.

A fixed-time replacement model for a unit of plant when new, the units-operating cost is 0 (£/year). Thus, rises linearly with time at a rate I (£/year/year) so that after n years the operating cost would be $0 + ni$ (£/year) and averaged over that time the mean-annual-operating cost would be $0 + (ni/2)$ (£/year).

If the equipment has cost £A to begin with, and were to be sold after n years for £S, the mean annual cost in this respect would be $(A - S)/n$ (£/year).

There will also be the cost of raising the above money which could have been done by borrowing £$(A - S)^{+}$ for n years (repaying this in annual installments over the period) and borrowing £S^{*} for n years (repaid at the time of sale). Assuming simple interest at rate r, and remembering that the amount borrowed decreases steadily, the mean cost of the first amount[+] borrowed would be $(A - S)r/2$ (£/year); the mean cost of the second amount* borrowed would be Sr (£/year). The total mean borrowing cost would therefore be the sum of these two, which is $(A + S)r/2$ (£/year).

So, the mean annual cost if the unit were to be replaced after n years would be:

$$C = 0 + \frac{ni}{2} + \frac{A - S}{n} + \frac{(A - S)r}{2}$$

The objective is to find the value of n which minimizes C. At this value:

$$\frac{dC}{dn} = \frac{i}{2} - \frac{A - S}{n^2} = 0$$

$$n = \left[\frac{2(A - S)}{i}\right]^{\frac{1}{2}}$$

If $A = £6000$, $S = £1000$ and $i = 400$ (£/year/year) then the optimum replacement age is:

$$n = \left[\frac{2(6000 - 1000)}{400}\right]^{\frac{1}{2}} = 5 \text{ years}$$

Models like this can be developed into as sophisticated a form as desired; the next step, for instance, might be to include discounted cash flow costing.

Extracted from Kelly, A. and Harris, M.J., *Management of Industrial Maintenance*, Butterworths, 1978.

5 Maintenance objectives

'First have a goal, an objective. Second, have the necessary means to achieve your ends; wisdom, money, materials, and methods. Third, adjust all your means to that end.'
Aristotle

Chapter aims and outcomes

To provide a general statement of a maintenance objective and to show how such an objective is used as the starting point of the maintenance strategic thought process.

On completion of this chapter you should be able to:

- identify the main factors that should be included in a statement of objectives;
- understand the relationship between maintenance resources and plant output factors (e.g. safety, longevity and availability);
- outline a generic statement of a maintenance objective and the procedure for establishing it;
- explain how maintenance objectives can be split into those concerning effectiveness and those concerning organizational efficiency;
- understand the relationship between maintenance objectives, maintenance performance indices and inter-firm comparison indices (benchmarks).

Chapter route map

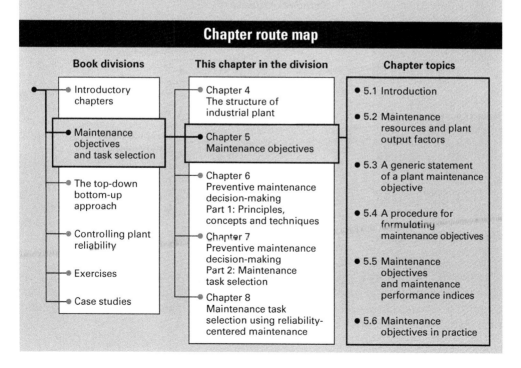

Book divisions	This chapter in the division	Chapter topics
Introductory chapters	Chapter 4 The structure of industrial plant	5.1 Introduction
Maintenance objectives and task selection	Chapter 5 Maintenance objectives	5.2 Maintenance resources and plant output factors
The top-down bottom-up approach	Chapter 6 Preventive maintenance decision-making Part 1: Principles, concepts and techniques	5.3 A generic statement of a plant maintenance objective
Controlling plant reliability	Chapter 7 Preventive maintenance decision-making Part 2: Maintenance task selection	5.4 A procedure for formulating maintenance objectives
Exercises		5.5 Maintenance objectives and maintenance performance indices
Case studies	Chapter 8 Maintenance task selection using reliability-centered maintenance	5.6 Maintenance objectives in practice

---

Key words

- Business objectives
- Maintenance objectives
- Management by objectives
- Safety objectives
- Key performance indices
- Inter-firm comparisons
- Benchmarks
- Overall equipment effectiveness
- Availability
- Organizational efficiency

5.1 Introduction

The previous chapters have stressed the importance of the *maintenance objective*, its starting-point role in the setting of a maintenance strategy, and hence the need for its clear formulation. Therefore, we need to establish what it should consist of, how it can be formulated and how it can then be used.

The main factors that should be taken into account in the formulation of a maintenance objective are shown in Figure 5.1. The maintenance resources are used to ensure that plant output (as specified under production policy), safety standards and plant design life are all achieved, and that energy use and raw material consumption are minimized.

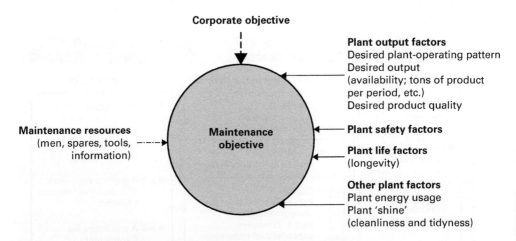

Figure 5.1 Factors influencing maintenance objective setting

In theory, the objective might be considered as being to achieve the optimum balance between the allocation of maintenance resources and the achievement of the plant outputs. In practice, however, the formulation of a maintenance objective is more complex than this.

It usually involves the users, owners and safety department specifying what they want from the plant in negotiation with the maintenance department. Only then can the last of these decide how best to maintain the plant (the maintenance strategy) in order to achieve the requirements at minimal maintenance resource cost. This process should provide the basis for maintenance budgeting and cost control.

5.2 Maintenance resources and plant output factors

Before considering the above process in more detail, it will be instructive to examine the relationships suggested in Figure 5.1, i.e. between maintenance resources and the various factors that are listed on the right-hand side of the diagram.

5.2.1 Maintenance resources (men, spares and tools)

Maintenance resources can be considered as inducing the *direct* cost of maintenance. This is relatively easy to measure, using a costing system, and is the maintenance cost the Financial Director is most aware of, it is what he sees maintenance budgeting as being all about. The maintenance manager can change the level of resources – very quickly in the case of contract arrangements, much more slowly if the resources are in-house.

5.2.2 Maintenance resources and plant longevity

A proportion of the maintenance resources is necessarily devoted to ensuring that major plant units – and, indeed, the whole plant itself – survive up to or beyond the design-operating life. Failure to ensure this will mean a corresponding loss of capital assets. The maintenance work involved is usually 'protective', e.g. preventing the corrosion of structures, but can also be major part replacement.

Although we all recognize that neglect can cause rapid deterioration, determining the relationship between the level of maintenance and the life of a plant is not easy. The best way of incorporating this into the objective is to establish the *standards of plant condition*, which will ensure that the plant will achieve its expected life, and in the light of which the actual plant condition can, periodically, be audited (taking into consideration such factors as obsolescence). Clearly, it is important to identify those parts of the plant that will have a major influence on its longevity. Although it is unlikely that – during the life of a plant – the standards of plant condition will change, the level of maintenance needed to ensure compliance with them will probably increase.

> One of the problems here is that maintenance that is aimed at prolonging plant life is likely not only to be expensive but also to be needed only very infrequently. Thus, because most costing systems operate on an annual accounting basis, the tendency is often to let such work go until it becomes 'someone else's problem'.

Review Question

R5.1   How would you incorporate 'longevity' into the maintenance objective and how would you check if longevity objectives were being achieved?

5.2.3 Maintenance resources and desired plant safety (equipment integrity)

Here again, there will usually be no clearly appropriate level or frequency of maintenance. The customary procedure is to set safety standards that take account of the estimated probability, consequences and costs of failure. For specific types of plant (e.g. pressure vessels), there are numerous maintenance requirements for ensuring safety – expressed in standards, Codes of Practice or legislation. For other items, safety standards will have to be set within the company, although again this will not be easy. Once again the sensible approach is to set safety standards by a process of engineering judgment based on experience and, wherever possible, analyses of plant failures. The extent to which such standards have been complied with should then be periodically audited.

Such a procedure should start with the most senior management. It is their responsibility to understand and comply with the ideas outlined in Figure 5.1, i.e. if there is pressure to cut back on maintenance resources at the same time as efforts are being made to increase output then plant safety standards must not be neglected. This is especially true in the case of ageing and hazardous plants. *Many major disasters have stemmed from companies' neglect of the relationship between maintenance resources and safety standards.*

Review Question

R5.2   How would you incorporate 'safety' into the maintenance objective and how would you check if safety objectives were being achieved?

5.2.4 Maintenance resources and product output

Product output can be expressed in various ways (see Table 5.1), the most useful of which is usually the output index because it combines several of the other parameters. In the case of the batch chemical plant (of Chapter 4), e.g. it is measured in tons of chemical – of a particular product mix, and of a defined quality – per period, all these factors determining the company's level of profit.

A possible relationship between output per period and the level of maintenance resources used is suggested in Figure 5.2. Here, it is assumed that the correct plant maintenance policy is being used, in this case one based on fixed-time maintenance, and that the resources are applied with maximum organizational efficiency. It should be noted that the relationship implies that the cost of achieving increased output rises as the output approaches its maximum.

Table 5.1 Measures of plant output

(i) Downtime due to maintenance (in hours, per production period, with causes)

(ii) Downtime index $= \dfrac{\text{Downtime per period}}{\text{Total planned production time per period}}$

(iii) Availability index $= \dfrac{\text{Uptime per period}}{\text{Total planned production time per period}}$

(iv) Output index $= \dfrac{\text{Planned output per period} - \text{Lost output per period}}{\text{Planned output per period}}$

Planned output per period $=$ Planned hours per period $\times$ Maximum rate per hour
Lost-output per period $=$ (Lost production hours per period $\times$ maximum
rate per hour) + (Average lost rate per period
$\times$ Hours + Wastage)

(v) Overall equipment effectiveness $=$ Availability $\times$ Performance rate $\times$ Quality rate

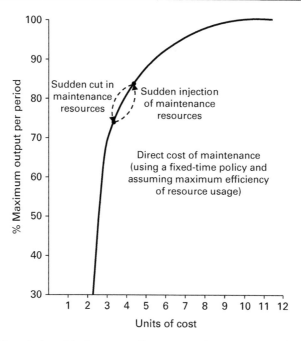

Figure 5.2 Possible relationship between direct cost of maintenance (fixed-time replacement) and output

It must be emphasized that the graphs shown in Figures 5.2–5.6 are illustrative only. It is unlikely that sufficient data will be available to construct such graphs.

In the case of the batch chemical plant the management wanted to increase overall plant availability from 92 to 95%. This would only be worthwhile if the income from the additional sales that would accrue from this increase would be greater than the direct maintenance cost involved in achieving it.

Note also the broken line in Figure 5.2; this indicates the result of imposing a sudden cut in maintenance expenditure. Little effect is felt for the first time period (6 months, say) but eventually the output will fall away and money will then have to be spent to bring the plant back to optimal level.

If the cost of lost production is known and is as shown in Figure 5.3 then, in theory and assuming a production-limited situation, the optimum-operating level can be established. Lost-output cost varies, of course, by orders of magnitude between different industries; in some cases, it can be substantially higher than maintenance resource costs. This pushes the optimum output toward the maximum (see Figure 5.4). In other words, the maintenance objective effectively becomes the maximization of output.

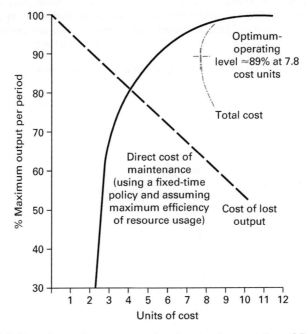

Figure 5.3 Establishing the optimum-operating level using a policy of fixed-time maintenance

The nature of this relationship can change with the plant's mode of operation, with its age and, in particular, with its maintenance policy. In the case of the batch chemical plant, e.g. the adoption of a condition-based policy might influence the relationship as indicated in Figure 5.5, *i.e. it is not just the level of resources that influences availability but also how they are used.*

Probably the main thing to emphasize here is that when considering the maintenance strategy for large complex plants the *principal focus should initially be not on the various relationships indicated in Figures 5.2–5.5 but on directing the use of maintenance resources toward the most critical production units.*

The relationships shown in Figures 5.2–5.5 have been based on the assumption that the maintenance resources have all been applied with maximum organizational efficiency.

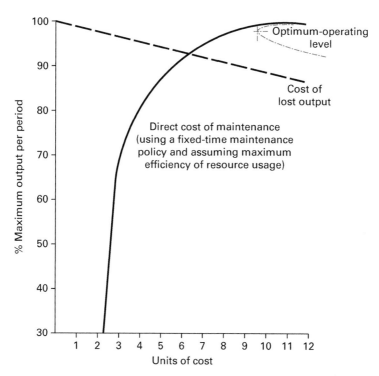

Figure 5.4 The effect of high lost-output cost on optimum-operating level

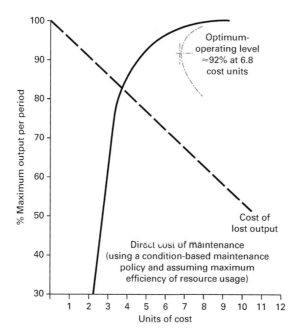

Figure 5.5 Establishing the optimum-operating level using a policy of condition-based maintenance

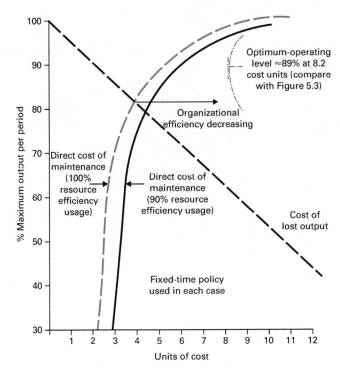

Figure 5.6 Effect of efficiency of resource usage on the location of the optimum-operating level

Figure 5.6 shows the effect of organizational efficiency on these relationships.

Decreasing organizational efficiency causes the curve to move horizontally to the right, i.e. the optimum-operating availability remains the same (see Figures 5.2 and 5.6) but at increased cost.

Review Question

R5.3   Draw a simple graph to illustrate a possible relationship between product output and direct maintenance costs.
        Think about how such a relationship might be affected by a change in maintenance policy (say from fixed-time maintenance to condition-based maintenance).
        Explain how the relationship might be affected by organizational efficiency.

5.3 A generic statement of a plant maintenance objective

Figure 5.1 and the subsequent discussion have identified the main factors, concerning maintenance resources and plant outputs, that need to be addressed when formulating a maintenance objective. Such considerations suggest the following general statement of the maintenance objective:

> *to achieve the agreed plant-operating pattern, product output and quality, within the accepted plant condition and safety standards, and at minimum resource costs.*

The relative importance of each of the factors included in this statement varies enormously from one technology to another and from one plant to another. With large, production limited, process plants the cost of lost output may be orders of magnitude greater than resource costs; with large buildings the longevity factor may be important, and so on.

Figure 5.7 shows that – while it is necessary to have such an overall maintenance objective – it may be desirable, in practice, to analyze this into sub-objectives concerning each of the output factors and resource areas. The main subdivision is into 'effectiveness' objectives – concerning selection of the best life plan (see Figures 5.2 and 5.5) – and into objectives concerning the efficient use of resources (see Figure 5.6).

> Figure 5.7 illustrates the two main tasks of the maintenance manager. Firstly, to determine the right maintenance strategy in order that the plant achieves the required output factors, i.e. availability, safety, etc. (maintenance effectiveness). Secondly, to ensure that the maintenance resources are used in the most efficient way (organizational efficiency).

Review Question

R5.4   List the main factors that should be included in a statement of a maintenance objective. Use these factors to write a generic statement of a maintenance objective.

5.4 A procedure for formulating maintenance objectives

A procedure is required for establishing maintenance objectives that will be acceptable to the maintenance department, and to all other departments – such as production – whose functions are affected by maintenance. To illustrate how this might be done let us look again at our example of the batch chemical plant.

> Clearly, the first thing is to get the various 'user departments' to specify what *they* want from each plant stream (see Figure 4.7). Negotiation to establish these plant objectives should take place at the companies' senior management level (see Figure 5.8). If it is to meet the market demand the production department will need to establish its operating pattern, its plant availability requirements, and the required product mix and quality. Plant longevity and safety requirements will also have to be identified (see Figure 5.9).
>
> This then enables the maintenance manager to establish the maintenance objective for the plant stream, *viz.*:
>
> > *To achieve continuous operation for 50 weeks per year at an average availability of 95%, with zero safety incidents and zero maintenance induced*

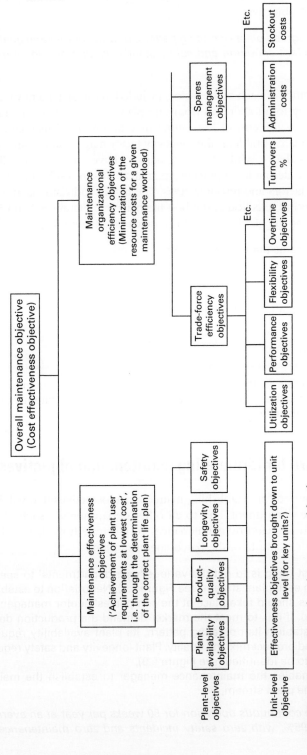

Figure 5.7 Hierarchy of maintenance objectives

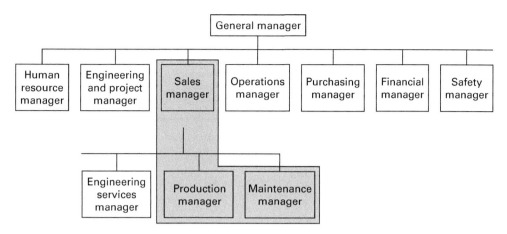

Figure 5.8 Senior management involvement in establishing maintenance objectives

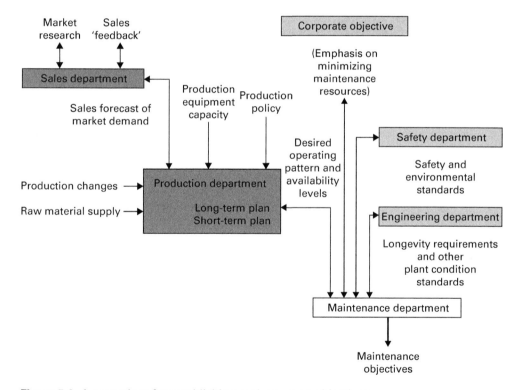

Figure 5.9 A procedure for establishing maintenance objectives

product-quality defects. In addition to maintain the plant in such a way so as to ensure a minimum of 30 years life.

To be meaningful, the above objectives need to be interpreted at plant unit level, e.g. a reaction unit (see Figures 4.8 and 5.10). This can only be accomplished

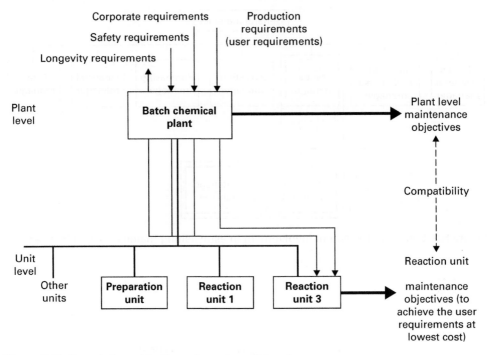

Figure 5.10 Translating objectives down to unit level

effectively if it is undertaken jointly by production and maintenance – with advice as necessary from those responsible for safety and longevity (where requirements tend to be more unchanging).

In the case of the batch chemical plant, it is the responsibility of the production manager with advice from the maintenance manager to establish the production requirements for the reaction stream and hence the individual units. For reaction unit 3 this might be stated as:

> 'to be available for continuous operation on a 48-batch cycle for 50 weeks per year to supply the planned product tonnage and mix at a specified quality'. The longevity and safety requirements might be for, say, 30-year life expectancy and zero safety incidents.

Taken together, these requirements form the basis of the user requirement for the reaction unit and effectively define the envelope with which it operates. The reaction units maintenance objective, which is compatible with the plant maintenance objective, can then be stated as being to achieve the user requirement for the reaction unit at least cost. Clear definition of this, and of the user requirement, are a necessary preliminary to establishing the maintenance life plan of the reaction unit (see Figure 4.10).

In addition to these *plant-oriented* objectives, *organizational* objectives of the type (illustrated in Figure 5.7) are necessary. These, if pursued, will improve organizational efficiency and therefore reduce, for a given workload, the direct cost of maintenance. The implication of Figure 5.7 is that a *single* organizational objective is insufficient. In practice, the establishment of objectives for each of the principal maintenance resources – labor and spares – is needed.

The trade-force objective might be:

to minimize, for the accomplishment of a given workload, the trade-force cost per period.

This could involve the setting of a target cost, or the setting of sub-objectives expressed in terms of performance targets, utilization levels, flexibility targets, etc. for the trade-force.

For spare parts the objective could be:

to minimize the sum of the stockout and holding costs,

which likewise could be used for setting cost targets or sub-objectives expressed via targets for stock turnover, stockout, etc.

Exercise

E5.1   Carry out a brief literature search on 'management by objectives'. Do you think this procedure could be used effectively in your own plant?

5.5 Maintenance objectives and maintenance performance indices

It is instructive at this early stage of this book to consider the relationship between maintenance objectives, maintenance performance indices (MPIs), maintenance control and benchmarks (inter-firm comparison indices).

MPIs* perform the same function as maintenance objectives, they are maintenance objectives. They can be derived from the objective hierarchy shown in Figure 5.7 (e.g. see Figure 5.11). As explained in Chapter 3 (Figure 3.1) objectives are the starting point of maintenance control. The monitoring of the MPIs should tell management if their maintenance effort is getting better or worse. The indices of Figure 5.11, perhaps in modified form, can also be used to compare (benchmark) the performance of maintenance departments in similar industries.

5.6 Maintenance objectives in practice

The setting of maintenance objectives is rarely done at all well. More often than not, a written statement of objectives will not exist. Where it does, it is not often based on

---

* Key performance indices (KPIs) are the set of most important indices (higher-level indices).

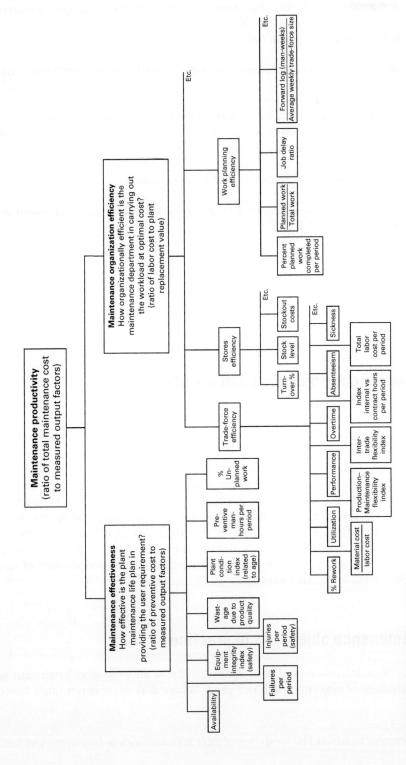

Figure 5.11 Hierarchy of MPIs

relationships of the type outlined in Figure 5.3; they are either not understood or ignored. Some of the reasons for this are as follows:

- It is unlikely that data will be available to produce plots such as Figures 5.3–5.6 (either at plant or unit level). At best there may unit-level data relating output to the level and type of maintenance resources. In the absence of such information production demand, to meet sales requirements, will dominate the setting of the maintenance objective. This is understandable because production generates the cash flow and has to be responsive to demand, and to variations in raw material availability, which are often unforeseeable.
- Financial managers often do not appreciate the relationship between maintenance resources and plant factors. They put pressure on the maintenance department to reduce costs without considering the consequences for plant performance and condition.
- Considerable pressure is put on the maintenance department to ensure that mandatory or Code of Practice safety standards are met and that safety-oriented maintenance work is carried out.

Under such pressures the maintenance objective more often than not places emphasis on the short as opposed to the long term. In practice, it is often stated along the lines:

> *to achieve the production-demanded output and operating pattern at minimum resource cost, subject to meeting mandatory safety standards.*

This might be acceptable in the short term but can eventually result in low availability (through neglecting preventive maintenance) and a shorter plant life.

> Sales, production and maintenance must co-operate if a credible maintenance objective is to be established. This will be effective only if the parties concerned appreciate the impact of the relationships modeled in Figures 5.2–5.6 and will be enhanced where such models (or even simple trends) are available to aid decision-making.

Reference

1. Kelly, A., *Maintenance Planning and Control*, Butterworths, 1984.

Exercises

E5.2   For your own plant examine the procedure for the setting of maintenance objectives.

- Is there a vision/mission statement for the company?
- Are there company and production objectives?
- Are there plant maintenance objectives and have they been put in numeric form?

- Have the maintenance objectives been linked with the production objectives?
- Have the plant maintenance objectives been brought down to unit level?
- Are there maintenance objectives associated with organizational efficiency?

E5.3   Outline the maintenance objectives and user requirements for the unit of plant identified in Exercise E4.1(b).

Review Questions Guidelines

R5.1   Identify those parts of the plant that when allowed to deteriorate too far will result in either reduced plant life or in a disproportionate maintenance expenditure. It is necessary to set standards of 'plant condition' for such parts to prevent them from deteriorating past the 'resource elbow' (see Figure 5.12). These parts and their condition levels should be subjected to periodic plant condition audits.

R5.2   Identify those parts/failure modes of the plant that if allowed to fail will cause an actual or potential safety hazard. Such parts/failure modes must either be designed out or a maintenance regime adopted to prevent their failure, e.g. the maintenance regime is developed to provide a level of plant safety, i.e. zero failures causing safety hazards.

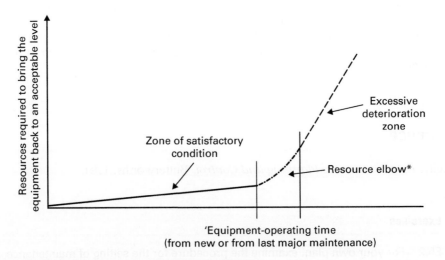

Figure 5.12 The concept of the 'resource elbow'.
*It has been observed that some parts (often mechanical structures in the process industry that are subject to wear/corrosion/erosion, etc.) have a deterioration curve as shown in Figure 5.12 – once the resource elbow has been passed (perhaps through neglect) deterioration proceeds rapidly

R5.3   Figure 5.3 illustrates the relationship between product output and direct maintenance costs.

Figures 5.3 and 5.5 illustrate the possible effect on availability and maintenance cost of moving from a policy of fixed-time maintenance to a policy of
condition-based maintenance.

Figure 5.6 illustrates how organizational efficiency effects the availability/
direct cost relationships.

R5.4   ● Maintenance resources (men, spares, tools, information)
● Output factors (availability, product quality, rate)
● Longevity (designed plant life)
● Safety (plant integrity, environmental factors)
● To achieve the agreed plant-operating pattern, product output and quality
within the accepted plant condition and safety standards, and at minimum
resource costs.

6

Preventive maintenance decision-making
Part 1: Principles, concepts and techniques

'A stitch in time saves nine.'

Anon.

Chapter aims and outcomes

To explain the principles, concepts and techniques of preventive and corrective maintenance.

On completion of this chapter you should be able to:

- understand the definition of a plant unit, a plant item and how the characteristics of a unit can be modeled by a maintainability diagram;
- define a maintenance task as being made up of a maintenance action (e.g. repair item) and the timing (the maintenance policy) of the action (e.g. on-condition maintenance);
- understand the repair vs replace decision and where *in-situ* repair techniques fit into maintenance decision-making;
- understand the principles of preventive maintenance policy decisions (i.e. regarding fixed-time maintenance, operate-to-failure and condition-based maintenance) and the techniques of condition-based maintenance.

Chapter route map

Book divisions	This chapter in the division	Chapter topics
Introductory chapters	Chapter 4 The structure of industrial plant	6.1 Introduction
Maintenance objectives and task selection	Chapter 5 Maintenance objectives	6.2 Plant items and their failure characteristics
The top-down bottom-up approach	Chapter 6 Preventive maintenance decision-making Part 1: Principles, concepts and techniques	6.3 The preventive maintenance decision problem
Controlling plant reliability	Chapter 7 Preventive maintenance decision-making Part 2: Maintenance task selection	6.4 The maintenance actions
Exercises		
Case studies	Chapter 8 Maintenance task selection using reliability-centered maintenance	6.5 The timing of the maintenance action: maintenance policy

Key words

- Preventive maintenance
- Fixed-time maintenance
- Condition-based maintenance
- Design-out maintenance
- Opportunity maintenance
- Failure mode
- Hidden function
- Proof testing
- Rotables
- Maintenance-causing items
- *In-situ* repair

6.1 Introduction

Figure 6.1 – a reproduction, for convenience, of Figure 4.10 – is an outline of a typical life plan for a unit of plant. The crucial step in its formulation is establishing the level of preventive work that is needed if the maintenance objective is to be achieved, i.e. 'How much preventive work, and what type, will meet the user requirement at minimum cost?'

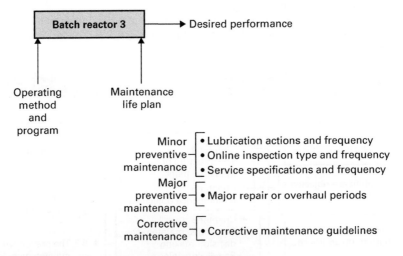

Figure 6.1 A typical unit and its maintenance life plan

Figure 6.2 shows the many factors that influence this decision procedure.

The various possible life plans will be made up of different proportions of preventive and corrective maintenance, ranging from 100% preventive (time-based or condition-based) to 100% corrective. Figure 6.3 (essentially a development of the model shown in Figure 5.3) shows the relationship, in a production-limited situation, between the level of preventive work and the total maintenance costs. It indicates that there is a level of

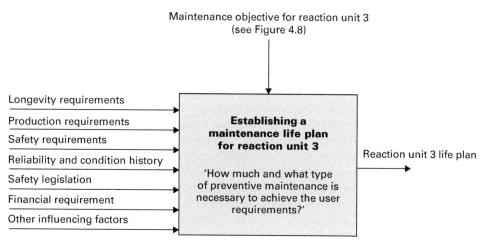

Figure 6.2 Factors affecting the maintenance life plan

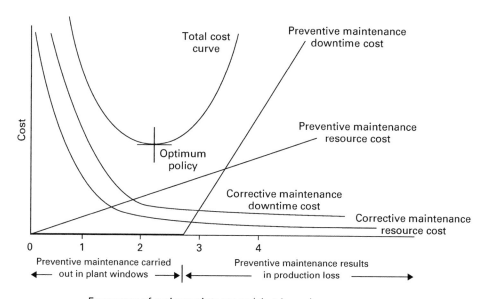

Figure 6.3 Relationship between preventive and corrective maintenance costs

preventive maintenance that minimizes the sum of the resource costs and the lost output costs. While it may be difficult to precisely locate this minimum it is usually not difficult to determine whether the plant is being under- or over-maintained.

In this case we are employing a policy of fixed-time overhaul on a large chemical plant. The problem is to decide on the optimum shutdown frequency. A shutdown frequency of once per year results in high corrective maintenance costs (not enough preventive work). A frequency of three times per year results in high preventive costs. In this case, it would appear that the best policy is to overhaul the plant twice per year (every 6 months). Note the shape of the corrective maintenance curve which has a major impact on the optimum frequency.

Models of this type have limited applicability, however. It is not just the frequency (or level) of preventive work that has to be decided but also its nature (time-based, age-based, inspection-based, etc.). In addition, the model assumes that the sales, production, or maintenance position is static, which is rarely the case. For example, the cost of lost output – and hence the optimum level of preventive maintenance – will vary from one time to another depending on whether the plant is sales limited or production limited. Finally, the model does not take into consideration the complexity of the plant. Some units might be more important than others (because of the greater impact of their failure on output or safety) and should attract more resources. Indeed, if the model has any applicability at all it is at unit level, e.g. deciding on the frequency of replacement of a reaction unit.

A procedure for formulating or improving a unit life plan should include the following steps:

(i) Identifying the maintenance-causing assemblies, sub-assemblies and components that make up a unit.
(ii) Determining the best 'maintenance task' for each of the above.
(iii) Assembling the unit life plan as an amalgam of the selected tasks.

> *This chapter* is concerned with identifying the array of maintenance tasks that might be used to maintain the parts of a plant unit. In addition the principles and the possible applications of each of the identified tasks are discussed.
>
> Chapters 7 and 8 use these principles, concepts and ideas to outline procedures for identifying the best maintenance task for each part of the unit.
>
> Chapters 7 and 8 will also show how the tasks are assembled into a unit life plan.

Exercise

E6.1   For the unit you identified in Exercise E4.1 write out the life plan in the tabular format indicated in Figure 6.1. *Note*: It is usual for the tasks making up the life plan for a particular unit to be embedded within a computerized maintenance schedule. In addition the tasks associated with the major maintenance may not be recorded at all. It is important that you extract/find this information in order to provide the best possible description of the life plan.

6.2 Plant items and their failure characteristics

6.2.1 The plan item: a definition

For our purposes we shall define *an item* as follows:

> An item can be considered as being any part of a unit that is likely to require *in situ* replacement or repair during the life of that unit.

For example, consider the hierarchical model of the chemical plant shown in Figure 6.4 (a reproduction, for convenience, of Figure 4.3). In this, the complete agitator assembly can be considered as an example of a *high-level item* because at some point in the life of the reaction unit it may be necessary to decide whether to repair or replace it. Conversely, the motor, gearbox, drive belts, coupling, agitator paddle and support frame can also be considered as items. All of these require an *in-situ* repair or replace decision to be taken in order to keep the reaction unit operating. As regards the gearbox shaft, however, the decision that is the most likely to have to be made – i.e. whether or not to replace it – will only arise when the box as a whole is in the workshop, so the shaft itself is *not* considered as an item.*

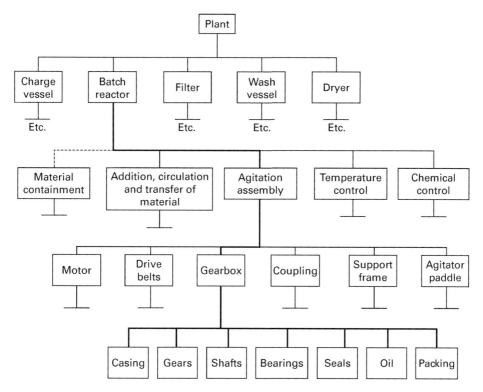

Figure 6.4 Hierarchical division of batch chemical plant

6.2.2 **Maintainability diagrams**

Replaceability and repair characteristics can be used to construct a *maintainability diagram* such as Figure 6.5, which refers to the chemical plant of Figure 6.4, and which

---

* Solid-state electronic equipment is customarily designed with a considerable degree of modularization. Mechanical plant on the other hand, is not often designed for ease of maintenance, and what modularization there is occurs only because of process function and manufacturing method.

locates the items in a plant hierarchy, i.e. according to their functional dependencies, and also employs a simple code to indicate their repair/replace characteristics. The following categories of item are then identifiable:

- *Simple replaceable* (SRIs, e.g. the drive belt): Likely to be maintained by replacement and discard.
- *Complex replaceable* (CRIs, e.g. the gearbox): Likely to be maintained by replacement and repair in workshop.

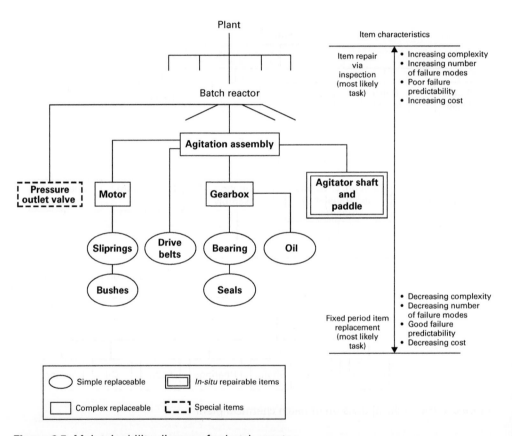

Figure 6.5 Maintainability diagram for batch reactor

- *High level* (e.g. the agitator assembly): Likely to be maintained by repair *in situ* (e.g. agitator shaft welding), but eventually by complete replacement.
- *Special* (e.g. relief valves): Likely to be maintained by periodic proof-testing *in situ* with adjustment, repair or replacement as necessary. These have an intermittent, particular, function only and are usually safety related. Failure is not observable under normal operation conditions because it has no immediate consequence, but makes

the plant's integrity seriously vulnerable to some other failure or process deviation, i.e. a consequence which falls in the *hidden function* category specified in reliability-centered maintenance (see Chapter 8).

Exercise

E6.2   Convert the hierarchical parts model of the unit you drew for Exercise 4.1(b) into a maintainability diagram (see Figure 6.5).

6.2.3   The items function, failure consequences and failure modes

Each of the items of Figure 6.5 has a *designated function*. When the item is unable, according to some predetermined criterion, to perform its designated function it can be said to have *failed*, and this could be a complete or a partial loss of function; i.e. the drive belts could fail completely or fail to transmit effectively due to slippage. The *consequences* of the *functional failure* will depend on whether the loss of function can be contained at unit level (temporarily, at least) or have consequences at plant level (lost production). The loss of function could also have safety or product quality consequences.

The functional failure of the item occurs because of one or more *failure modes*. In the case of the functional failure of SRIs (see Figure 6.5) this is most likely to be as a result of a single or dominant failure mode, e.g. drive belt slippage caused by wear. In the case of a CRI, it is likely that there is more than one failure mode, e.g. a gearbox could fail because of a 'serious oil leak' (caused perhaps by seal failure) or fail completely and suddenly through shaft failure. In the case of CRIs, irrespective of the number of modes of failure the most likely maintenance action will be to 'replace the gearbox' via some form of condition monitoring. It should also be noted that many CRIs may well have a dominant failure mode.

The higher-level items, e.g. the complete agitator system, will have numerous failure modes. Many of these will have been covered by analyzing the agitator system into its lower-level items. The most important reason for identifying failure modes at agitator system level, perhaps using failure modes and effects analysis (see Chapter 8), would be to identify the failure modes that might require complete agitator system replacement (e.g. an agitator shaft failure).

The point that is being made is that the definition of an item, and the analysis and categorization of a plant unit into its constituent items simplifies the process of building a unit life plan. *This pragmatic approach concentrates on deciding how to maintain the identified item (the hardware) rather than on how to deal with the myriad of failure modes.* However, it will be shown later in the course that for some critical items, e.g. the reaction unit steel casing (a pressure vessel) that might fail via a number of metallurgical mechanisms, this pragmatic approach will give way to a full blown failure modes and effects analysis.

Preventive Maintenance Guideline 1

For some non-critical units the life plan can be determined at unit level via manufacturers recommendations and local knowledge/experience	The life plan for most units require analysis of the unit into items and determination of the maintenance task at this level	The life plan for complex units/systems may require analysis down into failure modes and the determination of maintenance tasks at this level
Unit	Unit ↓ Items	Unit ↓ Items ↓ Failure modes

Review Question

R6.1   Define an 'item', functional failure and failure mode.

6.3 The preventive maintenance decision problem

It can be seen from Figure 6.5 that many maintenance decisions are needed to enable a life plan, of the type outlined in Figure 6.1, to be assembled. Table 6.1 shows the possible decision tasks for the gearbox of Figure 6.4. These are the building bricks of the maintenance life plan.

Table 6.1 shows that an item could be *adjusted, calibrated, repaired or replaced*, and that these actions could be *preventive* (action before failure) or *corrective* (action after failure). Alternatively, the need for such work could be *designed out*. The main alternative first-level tasks for maintaining an item are listed in more detail in Table 6.2, e.g. periodic repair, periodic visual inspection and replacement when necessary. Thus, each first-level maintenance task consists of:

(i) the maintenance action,
(ii) its timing (maintenance policy).

To complete this decision scenario Table 6.1 shows that additional decisions may be required at second (i.e. workshop) level (e.g. should the removed item be reconditioned or scrapped?). In addition third (i.e. stores) level decisions are required (i.e. regarding spares inventory policy).

Table 6.1 illustrates that decisions involving the maintenance life plans are closely linked with workshop reconditioning decisions and also with the spare parts inventory, e.g. when you set up a 'life plan' for a new equipment this directly influences stores inventory decisions.

Table 6.1 The preventive maintenance decision problem: What is the 'best way' to maintain the agitation system gearbox?

The alternative maintenance tasks	First-level decisions (plant level) Some combination of:		Second-level decisions (workshop level)	Third-level decisions (stores level)
	Action	Timing of the action		
	• Adjust or calibrate • Proof test • Always repair • Always replace • Repair vs replace on condition	• Action scheduled *before failure* on usage (hours, miles, etc.) or on calendar time (*FTM*) • Action scheduled *before failure* and on condition via inspection (*CBM*) • Action carried out *after failure*, either unplanned or planned (*OTF*)	• Workshop vs contract reconditioning • Repair vs recondition vs scrap, items and components	• *Decision to hold items or components* made by repair/replace decision. Stores decide on inventory policy, e.g. maximum and minimum stock holdings
	OR			
	Redesign, as indicated by failure cause investigation (DOM)			
Typical influencing information	• Failure characteristics of the item (statistics of failure) • Condition monitoring characteristics of the item • Consequences of failure of the item (in terms of safety, production and associated damage) • Resource cost characteristics • Stock holding cost of item compared to stock holding cost of component • Downtime cost saving via a replacement vs a repair		• Cost and quality of internal repair/reconditioning vs contract reconditioning • Conditioning of removal item/component and assessment of cost of repair/recondition/new	• Rate of demand for item/component which in turn is a function of number of such parts in use in plant. • Lead time of supply of part and/or is it being internally reconditioned? • Cost of holding the part vs cost of stock out

FTM: fixed-time maintenance; CBM: condition-based maintenance; OTF: operate-to-failure; DOM: design-out maintenance

Table 6.2 First-level maintenance tasks

Actions (first level)	Timing of the action

• Adjust/calibrate
• Proof test (for special items with a hidden function)
• Always repair
• Always replace
• Decide on repair vs replace after the failure-causing situation has been identified
	• Based on a policy of *FTM*. The action is scheduled on usage (hours, miles, output), calendar time, or some combination of these.
	• Based on a policy of *CBM* or *performance-based maintenance (PBM)*. The timing of the action is based on the condition of the item (or performance) as indicated via one or more of the following inspection methods:
	  – Operator functional monitoring
	  – Simple inspection (look, listen, feel, smell)
	  – Condition checking (against a limit)
	  – Trend monitoring:
	  (a) At fixed intervals or
	  (b) At variable intervals or
	  (c) Via continuous inspection or
	  (d) Via some combination of these.
	• Based on a policy of *OTF*. The action is carried out after failure. The action can involve considerable pre-planning (via spares, quick change), if the item is designated as critical.
	• Based on a policy of *OM*. The timing of the action is based on some other item's maintenance timing.

DOM, as indicated by failure-cause investigation after major or recurring failures	

OM: opportunity maintenance

Preventive Maintenance Guideline 2

The best maintenance task for an 'item' or 'failure mode' should be decided on after reviewing all of the maintenance actions, *viz.*:

- always repair;
- always replace;
- leave repair vs replace until the maintenance-causing situation has occurred;

and all of the effective policies, *viz.*:

- operate-to-failure (OTF);
- fixed-time maintenance (FTM);
- condition-based maintenance (CBM);
- design-out maintenance (DOM).

6.4 The maintenance actions

6.4.1 The alternative actions and their characteristics

Primarily these are as follows:

- *Adjustment (or calibration)*: Carried out with the aim of compensating for some age-ing mechanism (failure mode), bringing an item's function back within prescribed limits. Can be regarded as largely independent and complimentary to the main actions, and can be considered separately.

   In other words adjustment/calibrate are short-frequency actions that are carried out in addition to the longer-term actions of repair/replace.

- *Proof testing*: Checking the operational capability of special items or units. Also independent of the other actions and can be considered separately.

   This action is reserved for items (or units) with a hidden function (failure mode(s) not observable under normal operating conditions). Once again such actions are short frequency and are carried out in addition to the longer-term actions of repair/replace.

- *Replacement*: The maintenance of a unit by the replacement of its constituent items.
- *Repair*: The maintenance of a unit by the *in-situ* replacement or repair of the constituent components of an item.

6.4.2 The repair vs replace decision

It can be seen from Tables 6.1 and 6.2 that, in practice, the available decision options for an item of plant are:

(i) always repair the item *in situ* (online or offline and before or after failure);
(ii) always replace the item (online or offline and before or after failure);
(iii) leave the replace vs repair decision until item maintenance has been deemed necessary, e.g. the failure-causing event has occurred.

The main factors to be taken into consideration when deciding on which of these is the best are:

- the repair and replacement characteristics of an item as illustrated in Figure 6.5;
- the extra costs of holding both an item *and* its components (for replacement) rather than just the components (for repair);
- the possible saving in downtime costs if item replacement is speedier than item repair.

In most practical situations the comparison of these main factors, coupled with engineering judgment, allows the best of options (i)–(iii) to be identified. For example (see Figure 6.5), the obvious option for SRIs is to replace *in situ* and discard; the most likely option for many CRIs, such as electric motors, is to replace and send to internal or contract workshop for reconditioning. However, with high-level, high-cost items (such as the complete agitator assembly of Figure 6.5), the selection of the best action may not be straightforward. With such a complex item there are many possible modes of failure, some of which might be cheaper to put right by repair and some of which by agitator assembly replacement (e.g. shaft failure). The decision to hold the complete agitator assembly is a tradeoff of the cost of holding the complete system vs the time/cost saved by replacement rather than repair. The point being made is that even when the agitator assembly is held in stores the decision to repair or replace is best left until the failure-causing situation has occurred.

When considering the most likely actions for the items of Figure 6.5, it will be appreciated that in general the higher up the maintainability diagram, the more complex and expensive the item, and the more likely the action is to the *in-situ* repair 'rather than replace'.

Review Question

R6.2   In the case of CRIs (e.g. a gearbox), what factors have to be taken into consideration when deciding on whether to 'always replace' vs 'always repair'.

It will be instructive at this point to consider each of the main maintenance actions in more detail:

- *Always repair.* Where only *in-situ* repair is feasible the decision scenario is as shown in Figure 6.6. Item repair is only possible if a component is in stock or can be quickly bought in. Stores policy might be to hold any component that is likely to be required during the life of the plant. The rationale used for assessing the optimum number of components to hold and the optimum time and quantity for reordering is known as the *spares inventory policy*, which will take account of the rate of demand for the component (and therefore of the number of such components in use in the plant). In some situations it may well be economic to refurbish the component.

Preventive Maintenance Guideline 3
As already explained for *in-situ* repair to be the feasible maintenance action the cost of the repair of the item must be cheaper than the cost of replacement of the item; i.e. a trade off of the savings in downtime through an item replacement vs the extra costs of holding the complete item.

● *Always replace*: For this to be possible the item would need to be held in stores. If reconditioning were to be carried out internally the components also would have to be held. Where only item replacement is feasible as a first-level decision the scenario is as shown in Figure 6.7. Here it is assumed that the item repair is carried out internally and the workshop decisions involve choosing between repair, recondition or scrap, a decision to scrap having consequences for the stores inventory. Such items are sometimes referred to as *rotables*.

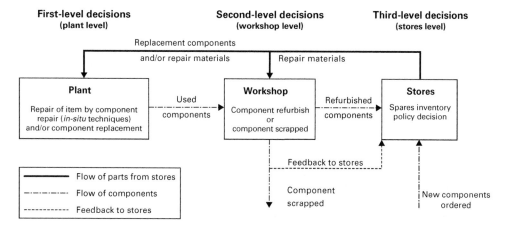

Figure 6.6 Decision scenario if the first-level decision is repair item

● *Repair vs replace*: The first-line replace/repair decision is sometimes left until the failure has occurred or is imminent. Such a policy would be adopted partly because of the high cost of the replacement work and partly because of the wide range of possibilities for the type of failure that would occur – each failure mode requiring a different action (see Figure 6.8). The decision would be influenced by such information as:
  – probable defective part and *in-situ* repair methods available;
  – time, labor and material cost of item replacement;
  – unit unavailability cost;
  – running time to next 'window of opportunity';
  – probable life of item after repair or temporary repair;
  – probable life of item after replacement;
  – condition and probable life of unit.

Clearly this is *dynamic* decision-making which would be aiming, as far as possible, at cost minimization but would also call for judgment of non-quantifiable factors. It is made much easier if some form of inspection procedure has provided prior warning of failure. If this is not possible and the item is considered critical then decision guidelines

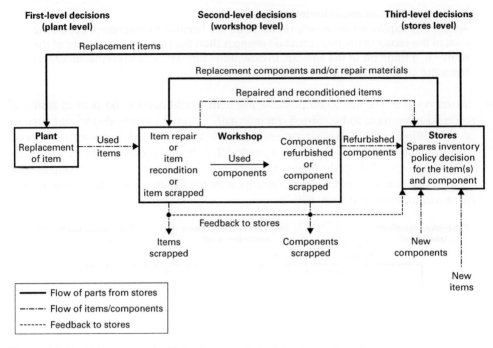

Figure 6.7 Decision scenario if the first-level decision is replace item

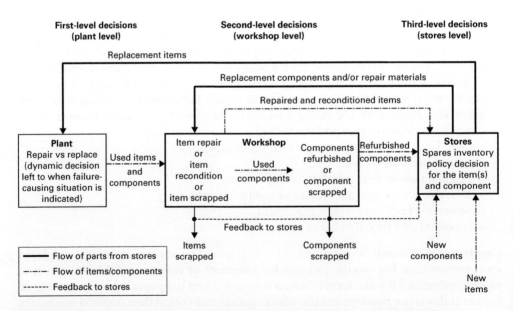

Figure 6.8 Decision scenario for a dynamic first-level replace vs repair decision

(with job procedures) must be established. *Choosing, in a dynamic situation, between the repair or replacement of a complex item is the most difficult, and the most commonly occurring, maintenance decision-making problem.*

It should be noted that the maintenance actions have been looked at separately to their timing (policy). The policies are looked at in Section 6.5. In practice, the 'action' and 'timing' (the maintenance task) would be determined together. There are a number of examples and an exercise in Chapter 7 to illustrate the 'maintenance selection procedure'.

Exercise

E6.3   For your own plant see if you can identify the following:

● Identify a CRI that is always (or mostly) replaced on failure.
● Identify a CRI that is always (or mostly) repaired on failure.
● Identify a CRI that requires a repair vs replace decision to be taken after (or shortly before) failure.

Review Question

R6.3   Explain why the decision scenario shown in Figure 6.8 is described as 'dynamic decision-making'. How does this differ from the decision scenario of Figure 6.7.

6.4.3 Reconditioning: internal vs contract

Although not indicated in Figures 6.6–6.8, an associated and secondary question is whether to maintain the repairable items and components internally – by setting up an in-plant workshop – or to use contract repair or exchange (or some combination of these). Although this would usually be decided on economic grounds there could well be other influencing factors, *viz.*:

● the availability of contractors,
● the complexity of the repair,
● quality assurance needs,
● security of supply.

Most companies have some combination of internal and contract repair. Controlling this can be one of the most difficult maintenance management problems. Figure 6.9 maps a typical system, for a large process plant, for dealing with repairable items (sometimes called *rotables*).

Exercise

E6.4   For your own plant draw a model to represent the flow of rotables between the plant and the stores (see Figure 6.9). Establish the percentage of rotables reconditioned externally and internally.

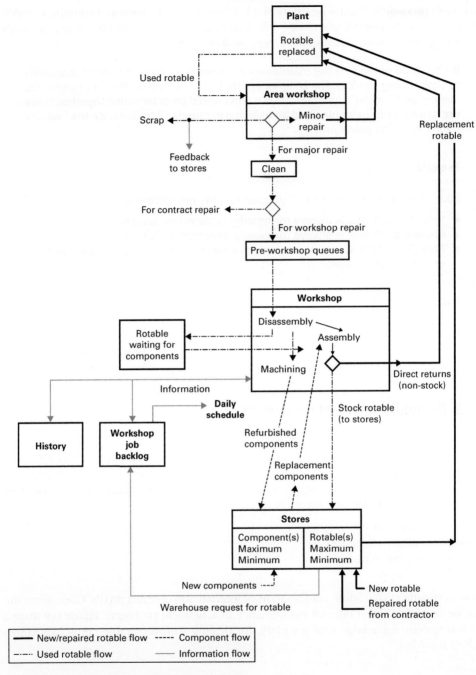

Figure 6.9 System for reconditioning rotables

6.4.4 *In-situ* repair techniques and the repair vs replace decision

In-situ repair techniques are to *corrective* maintenance what CBM techniques are to *preventive* maintenance, although the former have received far less attention in the open literature.

> For a maintenance repair technique to be considered as an *in situ* one, all phases of the repair process must be undertaken at the item's normal location.

In-situ techniques have major advantages where the cost of downtime is high. Their adoption can extend running times and improve availability via the reduction of unit outage times, and changes the balance of the tradeoff outlined in Section 6.4.2, many more items being repaired rather than replaced – or at least replaced less often.

Figure 6.10 details an online *in-situ* technique for valve replacement. *Appendix 2 lists the principal* in-situ *techniques.*

• The valve to be changed is closed and downstream piping is disconnected at the valve.
• The tool is attached to the valve.

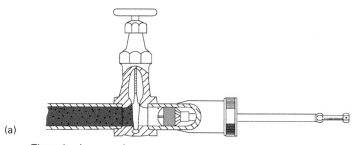

(a)

• The valve is opened.
• The tool is pushed through the open valve, and the seal is expanded until it presses tightly against the pipe wall and seals it.

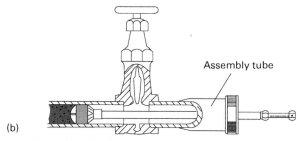

(b)

• Assembly tube A is removed, the pipe remains sealed.
• The faulty valve can then be removed for repair or replacement.

(c)

• A new valve is fitted and assembly tube A is reattached. The seal is released and the tool withdrawn. The valve is closed and the tool removed. The downstream piping is replaced.

Figure 6.10 Online valve replacement: principles of procedure

Review Questions

R6.4   Define an *in-situ* repair process. Can you describe (in outline) a true *in-situ* technique. How does the use of *in-situ* techniques affect the decision scenarios of Figures 6.6–6.8?

R6.5   A maintenance task is made up of an action and its timing (the policy). What are the alternative actions? What are the alternative policies?

6.5 The timing of the maintenance action: maintenance policy

The following is a description of the principles and concepts associated with the selection of alternative maintenance policies – 'the timing of the maintenance action' – see Table 6.2.

6.5.1 Fixed-time maintenance

These are first-level actions (repair or replace) carried out at regular intervals, or after a fixed-cumulative output, fixed number of cycles of operation, etc. They include item replacement, item repair and major strip-down for inspection (the author regards CBM as inspection carried out without major strip-down).

FTM will improve reliability only if the failure of the item concerned is clearly a result of some form of wear-out and if the useful life of the item is less than that of the unit in which it belongs. For example, consider the case modeled in Figure 6.11. The reaction

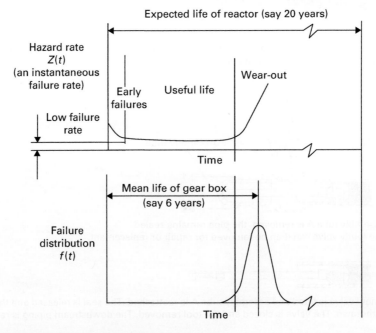

Figure 6.11 Reactor and gearbox failure statistics

vessel has a design life of approximately 20 years, while the gearbox of its agitator system is likely to wear out after about 6 years. FTM (i.e. replacement sometime before 6 years has elapsed) of the gearbox would be an effective policy for sustaining the reliability of the agitator system.

> This implies that the vertical axis of Figure 6.11 is a measure (f/t) of only those failure modes requiring gearbox replacement.
> The basics of failure statistics are covered in Appendix 3 to include a description of statistical failure models and their characteristics (e.g. mean, spread, standard deviation, etc.).

The cost-effectiveness of FTM will depend (among other things) on the predictability of the time-to-failure of the item concerned, i.e. on the dispersion, or spread, of the distribution of observed times-to-failure. The smaller the relative dispersion, the greater the predictability. For example, the time-to-failure of the motor in Figure 6.12 is much more uncertain than that of the gearbox and the FTM of the former would be more difficult to justify. In practice, of course, the big difficulty in applying this kind of analysis is that the statistical data is not often agitator available.

> In general, the lower-level items of Figure 6.5 (the SRIs) have good statistical predictability while the higher-level items, e.g. the agitator assembly, have poor statistical predictability. In other words, the statistical predictability decreases with complexity and the probable number of failure modes.
> It should be noted that in terms of deciding on complete agitator assembly replacement (rather than repair) the failure distribution should only include those failure modes that require agitator replacement.

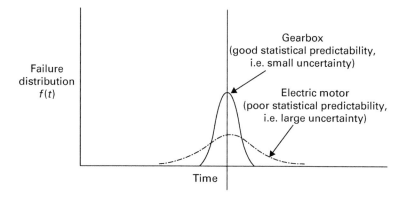

Figure 6.12 Statistical predictability

Figure 6.13(a) shows the failure distribution for an item whose useful life exceeds that of the system of which it is a part. Thus, the probability of its failure during the life of the system is low and the incidence of such failures random. FTM is therefore *not* an effective policy for improving reliability. If, in such cases, failure is unacceptable (or undesirable) then the alternative policies of Table 6.2 must be considered (e.g. CBM). The same

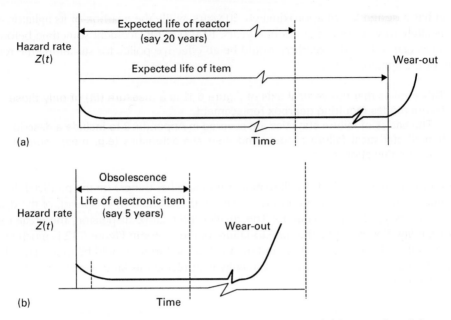

Figure 6.13 (a) Item in useful life stage during life of reactor, (b) Item replaced due to obsolescence before wear-out

can be said for the electronic item of Figure 6.13(b) that needs to be replaced (within its expected life) because it has become obsolete.

In spite of these limitations FTM, in one of the following forms, is often the most appropriate policy:

(i) *Group (or phased) replacement of large populations of identical (or similar) items (e.g. lamps, overhead cable supports, etc.).* For example, consider the maintenance, in a large building, of lamps the failure distribution of which might be as in Figure 6.14. One policy might be to replace them all annually, whether failed or not, and at worst only 10% of them would have failed before this renewal. Such a policy is usually much cheaper – in terms of the combined cost of labor and materials – than the alternative of replacing each lamp as it fails.

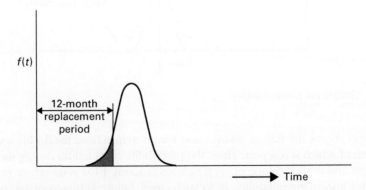

Figure 6.14 Lamp group replacement based on failure distribution

(ii) *Group replacement of dissimilar items (usually the SRIs; see Figure 6.5) in a service period or in a window of opportunity presented by a break in production.* The idea is indicated in Figure 6.15 where those simple items whose failure statistics show that they will last at least 12 months but probably not 24 months are replaced as a group at 12 months. Such a policy might well ensure that an acceptable plant reliability would be achieved at a more affordable cost.

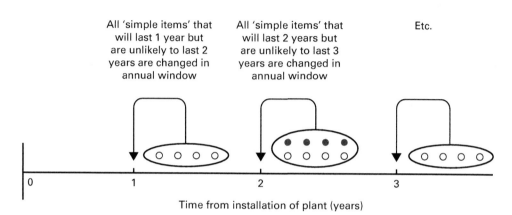

Figure 6.15 Group replacement of dissimilar items

(iii) *The replacement of safety-critical or production-critical repairable items (usually the CRIs, e.g. gearboxes; see Figure 6.5) where online inspection is not possible and the plant runs for long periods without shutdown.* The main difficulty is deciding on the item's replacement period. In most practical situations there is uncertainty caused by the lack of failure data. The best policy is probably to play safe and replace at cautiously short operating periods which can be extended with experience and in the light of information gained via inspection of any items removed for, say, reconditioning (see Figure 6.16).

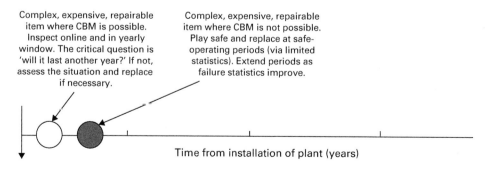

Figure 6.16 Policies for complex repairable items

(iv) *The shutdown of major process plant for overhaul*, where a large contract trade-force and other external resources are required. Note that one of the prime uses of CBM is to provide information to enable the shutdown workload to be predicted and planned in advance of the shutdown). In other words, the timing of the shutdown is fixed (in order to resource it) but much of the shutdown workload is condition based.

Preventive Maintenance Guideline 4
- FTM is only an effective policy if the item exhibits a time-dependent failure distribution and the mean life of the item is less than the expected life of the unit to which it belongs.
- FTM is not an effective policy if the item fails randomly.
- The greater the statistical predictability of an items failure distribution the more cost-effective FTM becomes.
- FTM always involves a degree of over-maintenance.
- FTM relies on failure data which is mostly absent.

Review Questions

R6.6 'The effectiveness of a FTM policy for an item depends on the shape of the items failure distribution'. Explain what this means by drawing a simple failure distribution.

R6.7 Describe two situations where FTM might be used as an effective policy.

6.5.2 Condition-based maintenance

An attractive idea is that the appropriate time for maintenance ought to be determinable by monitoring condition or performance – provided, of course, that a readily monitorable parameter of deterioration can be found.

For example, let us assume that the vibration level of the gearbox of Figure 6.11 can be monitored, and a failure event thus forecasted (see Figure 6.17), with a lead time of about 5 months. A monthly inspection interval will give adequate notice for planning and scheduling of the maintenance, thus minimizing the effect of lost production. The advantage of this over FTM is that it allows the operation of *individual items* up to nearly their maximum running time.

CBM is also the prime policy where an item exhibits little failure predictability (see Figure 6.12), *or fails randomly* (see Figure 6.13), or the statistical failure data is not available. It is particularly important for expensive repairable items (see Figure 6.16).

Clearly, the inspection interval adopted will be determined by the lead-time-to-failure. The effectiveness of CBM depends on no small measure on how reliably this can be determined from deterioration curves of the type shown in Figure 6.17.

The monitored parameter can provide information about a single component (e.g. about the wear of a brake pad) or about changes in any number of different components. The more specific the information provided, the better it is for maintenance decision-making.

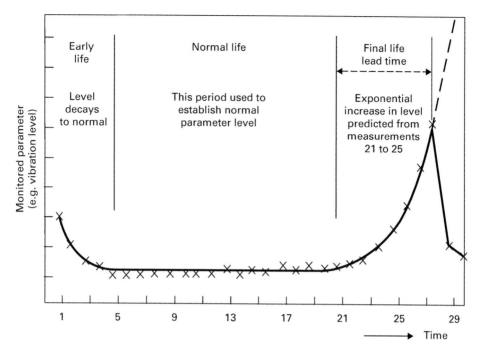

Figure 6.17 Vibration monitoring of gearbox

Condition monitoring can be accomplished in three main ways, *viz.*:

1. *Simple inspection*: Mainly qualitative checks based on looking, listening and feeling (e.g. to detect rope wear). The cost of this should be insignificant compared to the cost of replacement or repair. The period between inspections should be sufficiently short so that minor problems can be detected before they develop.
2. *Condition checking*: Done routinely by measuring some parameter which is not recorded but is used for comparison with a control limit. Such checking only has value where there is extensive experience of identical systems.
3. *Trend monitoring*: Measurement and graphic plotting of a performance or condition parameter in order to detect gradual departure from a norm (see Figure 6.17). This application is most effective where little is known about the deterioration character-istics. When enough knowledge of these has been acquired, condition checking can be substituted for trend monitoring.

The monitoring of performance and of condition is closely related. In the former case the parameter monitored would be some measure of a unit or item input or output, e.g. power consumed, pressure delivered. Changes in this might then be related to deterio-ration in some condition of concern. For example, Figure 6.18 shows how changes in per-formance of a pump can indicate a particular type of wear.

Where CBM is used extensively the high level of data collection renders mandatory the use of computerized systems of the type shown in Figure 6.19. These often have trend analysis capability. The extensive range of monitoring techniques available is indicated in Table 6.3.

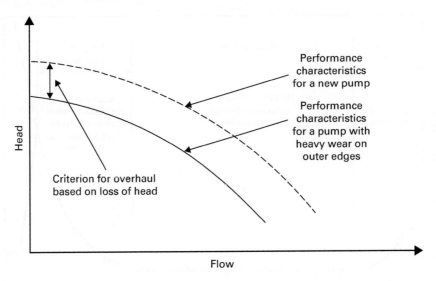

Figure 6.18 Performance monitoring criterion for centrifugal pump

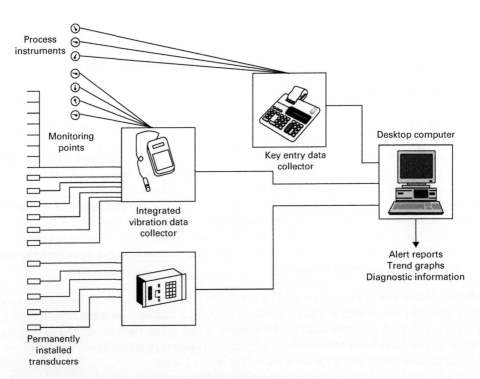

Figure 6.19 Collection of condition monitoring data

Table 6.3 Condition monitoring techniques

Type	Method	On/off line	Manual/ automated	Comments	Skill of operator	Equipment cost (£)
Visual	Human eye	On/off	Manual	Covers a wide range of highly effective condition checking and surface inspection methods.	Low/ average	0
	Optical probes	Off	Manual	Can be used for internal inspection of machines, good for detecting surface corrosion, wear and severe defects like cracks.	Average	50–1000
	Closed circuit television (CCTV)	Off	Manual	Permits detailed inspection of inaccessible/hazardous environment machine parts. Image recording and high-resolution analysis is a post-processing possibility.	High	1000– 10,000+
Temperature	Temperature crayons, paints and tapes	On	Manual	Simple and effective aids to visual inspection. Can resolve body temperature to within a few degrees and monitoring can be performed from a distance at a glance.	Low	10–50
	Thermometers, thermocouples	On	Manual/ automated	Range from stick-on thermometric strips to permanently installed thermocouple sensors. Can give visual temperature readout or an electrical input to a hard-wired monitoring system.	Average	20–500+
	Infrared meter	On	Manual	Non-contacting device which measures radiated body heat to estimate the	High	250–3000

(Continued)

Table 6.3 (Continued)

Type	Method	On/off line	Manual/ automated	Comments	Skill of operator	Equipment cost (£)
				surface temperature of a component. Covers a wide range of temperature but acts only on a small area.		
	Infrared camera	On	Manual	As above but can cover a much wider surface area. Can provide a detailed surface temperature picture and can be calibrated to give quantitative measurement.	High	1000–7500
Lubricant	Magnetic plugs and filters	On/off	Manual	Analysis of debris picked up by plugs or filter in an oil washed system. Mainly large debris picked up, 100–1000 μm.	High	50–1000
	Ferrography	N/A	Manual	Analytical technique used to separate ferrous debris by size to enable microscopic examination. Non-ferrous debris can also be separated but not graded. A wide range of debris size can be analyzed from 3 to 100 μm. A contract service is usually available.	High	12,000+ (for the machine)
	Spectroscopy	N/A	Manual	Analytical technique used to determine the chemical composition of the oil and debris. Generally for small debris size 0–10 μm. A contract service usually available.	High	14,000+ (for the machine)
Vibration	Overall vibration level	On	Manual/ automated	Represents the vibration of a rotating or reciprocating machine as a single number, which can be	Average	150–1000 (for a hand-held data

				trended and used a basis for the detection of common machine faults, but fault diagnosis is not possible and detection capability can be compromised.		collector)
	Frequency (spectrum) analysis	On	Manual/automated	Represents the vibration of a rotating or reciprocating machine as a frequency spectrum (or signature) which reveals the discrete frequency component content of the vibration. Provides the basis for fault detection, detailed diagnosis and severity assessment.	Expert	10,000+ (for a hand-held data collector)
	Shock-pulse monitoring (SPM), spike energy and kurtosis	On	Manual/automated	All of these techniques use high-frequency vibration signals to detect and diagnose a range of faults including rolling element bearing damage, lubrication failure and leak detection.	High	400–2500
	Structural monitoring	Off	Manual	A variety of vibration-based techniques exists for the detection and location of structural faults. The majority of such techniques involve imparting a known vibration into the structure and analyzing the resulting response.	Expert	15,000+
Crack	Dye penetrant	On/off	Manual	Detects cracks which brake the surface of the material.	Average	10–150
	Magnetic flux	On/off	Manual	Detects cracks at/near the surface of ferrous materials.	Average	100–500
	Electrical resistance	On/off	Manual	Detects cracks at/near the surface and can be used to estimate depth of crack.	High	200–1000

(Continued)

Table 6.3 (Continued)

Type	Method	On/off line	Manual/ automated	Comments	Skill of operator	Equipment cost (£)
	Eddy current	On/off	Manual	Detects cracks near to surface. Also useful for detection of inclusions and hardness changes.	Expert	250–5000
	Ultrasonic	On/off	Manual	Detects cracks anywhere in a component. Suffers from directional sensitivity, meaning that general searches can be lengthy. Often used to back up other NDT techniques.	Expert	500+
	Radiography	Off		Detects cracks and inclusions anywhere in a component, although access to both sides of component is necessary. Involves a radiation hazard.	Expert	8000+
Corrosion	Weight loss coupons	Off	Manual	Coupons are weighed and weight loss is equated to material thickness loss due to corrosion.	Low	25–100
	Incremental bore holes	On	Manual	A series of fine plugged holes of incremental depths which are periodically unplugged and scrutinized for leakage.		
	Electrical resistance	On	Manual/ automated	Electrical element and potentiometer are used to assess resistance change due to material loss. Capable of detecting material thickness reduction of less than 1 nm.	Average	100–750
	Polarization resistance	On		A good indicator of corrosion but is unreliable as a means of estimating material loss rate.	Average	150–500

N/A: not applicable; NDT: non-destructive testing

Preventive Maintenance Guideline 5
- CBM can be used as the maintenance task for randomly failing items if an inspection technique with a suitable lead time can be found.
- The inspection interval of a CBM task is a function of the inspection lead time.

Review Question

R6.8   CBM can be used effectively even where the items' failure distribution is random. Explain why this is so? What do you understand by lead-time-to-failure?

Exercises

E6.5   For your own company identify an electrical unit/system and a control system, see Figure 4.6, and write out the life plans in the tabular form indicated in Figure 6.1.

E6.6   Carry out a survey of the condition monitoring techniques used in your company and tabularize them as shown in Table 3 in Case study 1 of Chapter 12.

6.5.3 Operate-to-failure

No action is taken to detect the onset of, or to prevent, failure. The resulting demand for corrective work occurs with little or no warning. This will only be cost-effective if:

(i) the consequences of item failure in terms of lost production, or of danger or damage, can be regarded as negligible (or, alternatively, if the cost of letting the item fail is less than that of implementing alternative maintenance policies);

(ii) the consequences of item failure are serious but do not take effect for some time and it is possible to carry out the necessary repair within this period. (Obviously, such failures have to be identified and planned for in terms of decision guidelines, fault-finding and resources – *a kind of planned failure maintenance.*)

6.5.4 Opportunity maintenance

The timing is determined by that of some other action, e.g. much power station plant is maintained during the statutory boiler inspection.

This is more of a scheduling procedure rather than a maintenance policy. For example, opportunity maintenance (OM) could be employed in the case of the ammonia plant of course Case study 1 of Chapter 12. If there was a major failure within the normal 4-year operating period the company could 'take the opportunity' to carry out other work during the stoppage.

See Chapter 9 for a fuller discussion of 'opportunity scheduling'.

6.5.5 Design-out maintenance

By contrast with the previous policies, which are aimed at the avoidance or mitigation of failure, design-out aims to eliminate the cause of maintenance altogether. Clearly, this is a design problem but it is often part of the maintenance department's responsibility. In general, DOM only becomes an alternative after some experience of operation; i.e. if, in spite of carrying out the original maintenance tasks, the performance of the item remains unsatisfactory (exhibiting low reliability or high maintenance cost). Therefore, such a policy can only be implemented effectively if an information system exists which facilitates the choice (on cost and safety grounds) between the proposed redesign and the best of the various maintenance tasks (see Chapter 10). DOM is an area of maintenance management that benefits considerably from the application of failure modes and effects analysis (see Chapter 8).

Exercise

6.7   Now carry out Exercise 11.2 in Chapter 11.

6.5.6 Establishing the best maintenance policy

In the earlier part of this section we discussed the problem of deciding the best maintenance action. We now turn to the related question of timing.

Special items

These have to be treated separately to normal items because they have a hidden function, i.e. items that have an intermittent function and are usually safety related – failure is not observable under normal operating conditions because it has no immediate consequence, but makes the plants integrity seriously vulnerable to some other failure deviation. The most appropriate action is to *proof test* the item at fixed-time intervals. Assessing the appropriate duration of which is a complex problem which involves taking into account:

- Both the fail-to-danger and fail-safe rates of the item itself and the anticipated incidence of the process deviation (e.g. overpressure) which the item is protecting against.
- The time required to carry out the proof test (during which the item's protective function may be disarmed).
- The degree of item redundancy and 'majority voting' arrangements, and hence the possibility of staggered testing.
- The safety, environmental and economic consequences of an occurrence of the unprotected process deviation (i.e. of the feared accident).

In addition, each special item should be subject to the same decision logic (Figure 6.20) as normal items; e.g. a pressure relief valve may not only be tested fairly frequently (every few weeks say), but also replaced at longer intervals (e.g. every few years).

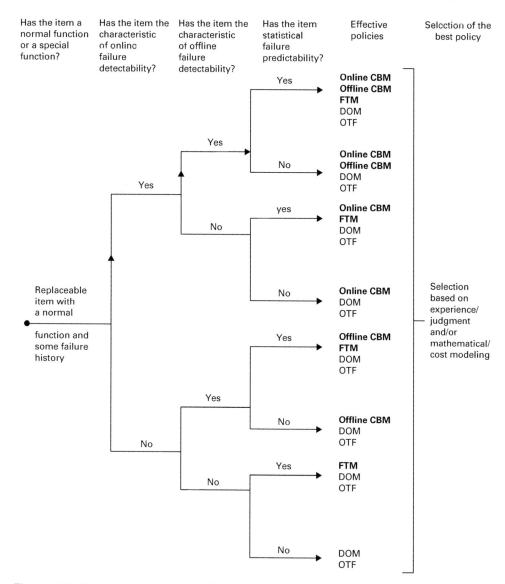

Figure 6.20 Decision logic for identifying the best maintenance policy

Normal items

For a normally operating item the decision logic shown in Figure 6.20, in conjunction with the failure and cost characteristics listed in Tables 6.4(a) and 6.4(b), lead firstly to the identification of the various *effective policies* and then to the identification of the *best (most cost-effective)* of these:

An 'effective policy' is a policy if used will help in controlling the reliability of the items (and hence the unit), e.g. see Figure 6.11 – a fixed-time replacement of the gearbox at 5 years is an effective policy.

Asking the three questions along the top of Figure 6.20 identifies whether FTM and CBM are effective in controlling the reliability of the item. DOM and OTF are possible policies, and are always considered alongside the effective policies.

The 'best policy' is the most 'cost-effective' policy available within the various constraints (e.g. safety).

Table 6.4(a) The main failure characteristics of an item

> - Useful life
> - Mean life
> - Uncertainty of item life (Is the statistical predictability good? See Figure 6.12.) as measured by range, standard deviation
> - Detectability of the onset of failure (Is inspection possible?): parameter to be monitored, techniques available, lead-time-to-failure
> - Mean replacement time
> - Reparability (Can the item be reconditioned?)

In the majority of cases the best procedure can be identified via engineering judgment of the main influencing factors and application of the logic of Figure 6.20. For example, the initial ranking given in the figure is as follows:

1. CBM (online)
2. CBM (offline)
3. FTM
4. DOM
5. OTF

Table 6.4(b) The main cost and safety characteristics

> - Consequence of failure in terms of cost output, poor product quality, gearbox running costs, associated damage, increased maintenance resource cost.
> - Consequence of failure in terms of actual or potential hazards to personnel and or general public.
> - Consequence of failure in terms of environmental damage.
> - Statutory safety requirements.
> - Direct costs of maintenance, including:
>   - Cost of item (to purchase and to hold a spare)
>   - Cost of labor to replace and/or repair
>   - Cost of the best inspection technique (if any)
>   - Cost of redesign (if possible)
>
> Requires an understanding of:
> - the item's function;
> - the ways in which the item's functional performance can lost or reduced.

This can be justified on the following grounds:

- If an effective online condition-based procedure can be found it is normally the best one to adopt, especially in process plants, where downtime cost is usually very high.
- CBM is usually cheaper and more effective than FTM because of the inherent variability of the item time-to-failure or lack of knowledge about it.

- FTM is normally cheaper than OTF because of the high cost, in the latter case, of the lost production or the consequent damage.

In only a few situations will the maintenance manager need to employ statistical reliability or cost analysis to determine the optimum procedure.

Preventive Maintenance Guideline 6
- The maintenance task for SRIs is usually fixed-time replacement and discard.
- The maintenance task for CRIs is usually condition-based replacement and recondition.
- The initial maintenance task for 'special items' is to proof test.

Exercise

6.8   Now carry out Exercise 11.1 in Chapter 11.

Review Questions

R6.9   Identify the main failure characteristics of an item, i.e. the failure information needed to decide on the optimum maintenance task.

R6.10   Classify items according to their maintenance characteristics and show how the categorization aids the determination of a maintenance task.

Review Questions Guidelines

R6.1   An item can be considered as being any part of a unit that is likely to require replacement or repair during the life of that unit.
A 'functional failure' occurs when an item is unable to perform its designated function.
A complex item like a gearbox might fail because of a number of failure modes (e.g. an oil leak, a shaft failure, etc.).

R6.2   The cost of the extra production loss caused by unit downtime (if repair takes longer than replacement) vs the extra cost of holding the replaceable item.

R6.3   In the case of Figure 6.7 the decision to replace or repair the item is taken at the beginning of the life of the unit and thereafter always used (it can be reviewed periodically).
In the case of Figure 6.8 the decision to replace or repair the item is not taken until the maintenance-causing situation has occurred – perhaps with the aid of decision guidelines.

R6.4   *In-situ* repair – all phases of the repair must be undertaken at the items normal location – a truc *in-situ* technique would avoid production loss (e.g. the furminite process – see Appendix 2).

R6.5   See Table 6.1.

R6.6   FTM is only an effective task if the failure distribution exhibits a wear-out characteristic (see Figure 6.14). The idea is to replace the item before the wear-out phase is reached.

R6.7 (i)   Group replacement of large populations of identical (or similar) items (e.g. lamps).

      (ii) The shutdown of major process plant for overhaul (e.g. the ammonia plant of Case study 1 of Chapter 12).

R6.8 The condition monitoring 'lead-time-to-failure' is the time from when the monitored parameter starts to deviate from normal to the time of failure (see Figure 6.17). CBM monitors individual items to pick up deviations which might lead to failure. Thus, the technique is independent of the type of failure distribution.

R6.9 See Table 6.4.

R6.10 Explained in Section 6.2.2, Figure 6.5 and Section 6.5.6.

7 Preventive maintenance decision-making Part 2: Maintenance task selection

'For the wheels were just as strong as the thills
And the floor was just as strong as the sills,
And the panels just as strong as the floor,
And the whipple-tree neither less nor more,
And yet as a whole it is past a doubt,
In another hour it will be worn out!'

Oliver Wendell Holmes

Chapter aims and outcomes

To explain the principles and concepts of maintenance task selection procedures.

On completion of this chapter you should be able to:

- understand the principles underlying the procedure for selecting the best maintenance task for a plant item or a failure mode;
- appreciate the use of 'universal maintenance task' catalogs;
- understand how the individual maintenance tasks can be assembled into a life plan for a unit.

Chapter route map

Book divisions	This chapter in the division	Chapter topics
Introductory chapters	Chapter 4 The structure of industrial plant	7.1 Introduction
Maintenance objectives and task selection	Chapter 5 Maintenance objectives	7.2 Examples of maintenance task selection
The top-down bottom-up approach	Chapter 6 Preventive maintenance decision-making Part 1: Principles, concepts and techniques	7.3 Assembling the maintenance life plan for a unit
Controlling plant reliability	Chapter 7 Preventive maintenance decision-making Part 2: Maintenance task selection	7.4 Standby units and the life plan
Exercises		
Case studies	Chapter 8 Maintenance task selection using reliability-centered maintenance	

7.1 Introduction

This chapter is concerned with showing how the principles, concepts, procedures and guidelines of the last chapter can be used to select the best 'maintenance task' for each identified item in order to build a unit life plan.

Ideally, the manufacturer of the 'plant unit' should specify a maintenance task(s) for each item as part of a manufacturer unit life plan. Alternatively, he should provide the 'maintenance failure characteristics' (see Table 6.4) of his products so that the user may himself establish the best maintenance tasks. In practice, manufacturers mostly supply limited information on unit life plans (mainly for short-life simple items, lubrication and servicing) and even less on failure characteristics.

The author has come across an example of what can be called 'universal maintenance tasks' for many of the commonest items that can be found in industrial plant (see Table 7.1). It can be seen that this provides much useful information for determining the best maintenance task [1].

The maintenance manager, more often than not, has to develop his own unit life plans with limited information about the failure characteristics of plant items. *Taking into consideration the size and complexity of industrial plant, i.e. the total number of items that have to be dealt with, the procedure(s) used to select the best maintenance task must have incorporated into them a degree of pragmatism.* The procedures listed below (to select the best maintenance task for an item) all follow the principles and guidelines of the previous section. The main difference between the procedures is in the level of detail and analysis:

(a) For *standard items* (simple replaceable items (SRI), complex replaceable items (CRI), special items, etc.), *use the items maintenance characteristics* coupled with experience and judgment (see Section 6.2.2 and **Preventive maintenance guideline 6**). Also use where possible maintenance task catalogs (see Table 7.1).

(b) For *uncomplicated situations*, use the *principles and guidelines of Chapter 6 coupled with experience and judgment*. This approach is illustrated in Section 7.2 using a series of examples.

(c) For *complex and/or high cost and consequence of failure items*, use where necessary *cost and statistical modeling*. This approach is illustrated in Exercise E7.2 (at the end of this section).

(d) For *complex high-level items* and/or technically sophisticated items, *use failure modes and effects analysis to identify the items failure mode* and then the approach outlined in (b) or (c) to identify the best maintenance task. This approach is outlined in Chapter 8 via the use of reliability-centered maintenance.

Table 7.1 Universal maintenance tasks, an example

Item	Classification: Brake; mechanical friction; operated by mechanical link mechanism; strongly corrosive surroundings; operated more than five times per shift; sudden breakdown may cause fatal accident or damage exceeding £1500 (treat separately: lifter 3)		Universal maintenance item guide list
Standard defects	Defective components	Description of defect	MTTF*
	Steel parts	Corrosion	4 yearly
	Link bearings	Wear	4 yearly
	Nuts, other fastening elements	Loosening	Never
	Operated braking element, friction area	Wear	3 monthly
	Braked element, friction area	Wear, grooved	4 yearly
Universal maintenance procedures	Description		Frequency
	Activate. Measure time taken to stop (maximum $a =$ ____ s, 0.5 s + operating time of mechanism)		8 hourly
	Watch out for wear on braking element (thickness of lining minimum $b =$ ____ mm, 70% of new thickness); watch out for grooves on braked element (depth maximum $c = 0.5$ mm); watch out for corrosion, lubricate $d =$ ____ (general specification M.38)		Monthly
	Watch out for loose bolts; check play of link bearings (total free movement should not exceed 30% of normal lifter travel, i.e. maximum $e =$ ____); watch out for wear of braked element (wall thickness minimum $f =$ ____ mm, minimum 70% of original).		Yearly
Remarks	Component break-down: 1. Mechanism 　　1.1 Levers 　　1.2 Links and bearings 　　1.3 Bolts 2. Friction elements 　　2.1 Braking element (shoes, etc.) 　　2.2 Braking element (drum, disk, etc.) 3. Lifting elements (not included) 4. Closing elements 　　4.1 Spring, weight, etc.		

*MTTF: mean time to failure

7.2 Examples of maintenance task selection

7.2.1 Example 1: The rubber lining of a chemical reaction vessel

(see Figure 6.4: the material containment leg of the diagram)

The main work needed on these vessels is the repair (needing 2½ days work) or replacement (needing 10 days work) of the rubber lining, which is subject to permeation by chemicals and which can eventually deteriorate to failure. It has been found that because this process can be accelerated by accidental damage the time-to-failure of the lining can be anything from 3 to 9 years, with a mean value of 6 years. The deterioration is, however, slow and gives about a year's notice of failure. It is important not to allow the rubber to deteriorate too far. Penetration of the steel vessel is hazardous and also necessitates a long and expensive repair. If the deterioration of the rubber lining can be detected at an early stage it can be repaired *in situ* using a cold bonding process (see Appendix 2), a task which takes 2½ days, as compared with complete replacement (which takes 10 days). Extensive deterioration can contaminate the product, causing a diminution in customer confidence in product quality.

A simple maintainability diagram for the vessel assembly and lining is shown in Figure 7.1. The cost of relining is high, both as regards material and labor; an *in situ* repair is by far the cheaper action. Thus, the *repair vs replace* decision is left (see Figure 6.8) until the lining is inspected (the inspection history also being used as the basis for guidelines for making this decision).

For safety reasons, among other things, operate-to-failure is not an acceptable policy. Thus, the range of effective policies is as follows:

(i)   Fixed-time maintenance (vessel isolation, visual and tactile internal inspection then repair vs replace as necessary).

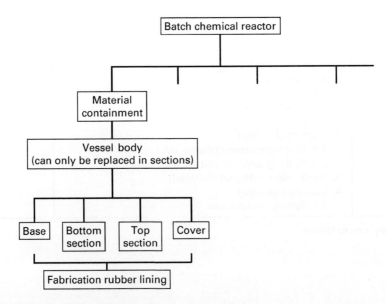

Figure 7.1 Maintainability diagram for vessel and lining

(ii) Condition-based maintenance via:
   (a) online fiber-optical or televisual inspection through the manhole (without isolation),
   (b) electro-chemical monitoring,
   (c) product sampling for contamination.

Option (ii) (b) is only possible if the rubber has been penetrated, allowing a current to flow; this is not acceptable so the option is only available as a safety device to give warning of such penetration. Option (ii) (c) has been investigated but rejected because of the high rate of deterioration once contamination has begun; it also could be used as a shutdown warning but each batch of product would need to be sampled. The choice is therefore between option (i) and option (ii) (a).

There are clear advantages in online inspection because of the considerable time needed to isolate and wash the reactor before internal inspection and repair can be undertaken. Online inspection, however, needs optical aids because it is impossible to see or touch enough of the lining from the manhole. Fiber optical methods have been tried but are of limited use due to their small field of vision. Television did prove better but was considered insufficiently reliable without a tactile inspection backup. Online inspection is still being investigated but in the meantime *fixed-time internal inspection, with repair or replace on-condition, remains the selected procedure* (see Table 7.2). Using the limited data available the optimum interval between such inspections appears to be 12 months, but this can be reviewed as more data is collected.

Table 7.2 Maintenance task for the vessel lining

Item	Timing	Online or offline	Frequency	Time and labor	Maintenance action	Online or offline	Frequency	Time and labor	Secondary action
Reaction vessel rubber lining	Visual inspection and touch	Off	Annually at agreed shutdown	3 days 2 fitters	Replace as necessary	Off continuation of shutdown	2 yearly	1 day 2 men	Replace lining 8 days 4 fitters 2 men

7.2.2 Example 2: The rotary joint of a paper machine

The dryer section of a large paper machine is made up of some 22 steam-heated rotating cylinders of the type shown in Figure 7.2. The paper is dried as it passes over each cylinder. The machine is operated continuously and its unavailability cost is high. Each cylinder has a rotating joint, the function of which is to allow steam to enter the cylinder and condensate to exit, while the cylinder is in motion.

Steam enters the joint (see Figures 7.2 and 7.3) via a flexible hose and passes through the joint on the outside of an siphon pipe. It then condenses in the cylinder, returns to the joint via the siphon, and leaves it through the condensate head, a flexible hose carrying it to sink. The rotating part of the joint is made up of a quick release mechanism, shank, spherical washer and gland assembly. During operation, seals A and B (see Figure 7.3) wear, but it has been found that seal A fails first, allowing steam to escape, damaging the paper and therefore precipitating machine shutdown. A spring provides the sealing force

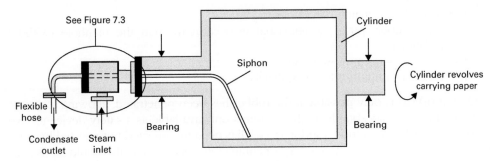

Figure 7.2 Rotary joint and heated cylinder assembly

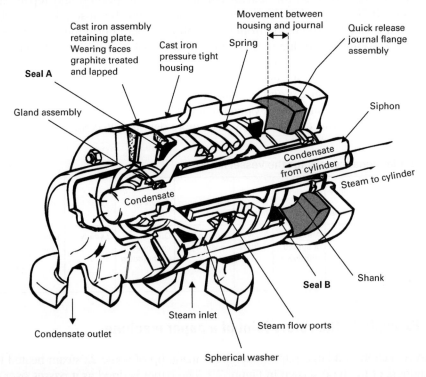

Figure 7.3 Rotary joint

between the shank/seal-B and washer/seal-A interfaces and also promotes self-adjustment of the joint as the seals wear. Steam leaks often require the machine to be taken offline. Replacement of the joint after failure or for seal inspection takes about 2 hours of offline work. The time-to-failure of the joints ranges from 6 to 20 months, with a mean value of about 13 months.

A simple maintainability diagram for the cylinder assembly is shown in Figure 7.4. The rotary joints are costly but repairable. It is much quicker to replace than to repair

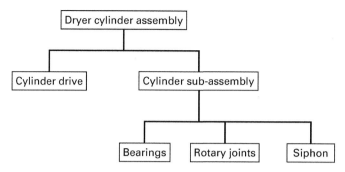

Figure 7.4 Maintainability diagram for dryer cylinder assembly

them *in situ*. Thus, bearing in mind the high cost of machine unavailability and the large number of rotary joints in use, the best maintenance action is *replace and recondition* (see Figure 6.7).

The effective maintenance policies are:

(a) *Fixed-time replacement*: Because of the poor statistical predictability and the high-unavailability cost the interval between replacements might need to be as short as 6 months and would therefore carry very high direct maintenance.
(b) *Operate-to-failure*: Would be far too expensive as regards maintenance costs (but should be considered).
(c) *Online condition-based maintenance*: Using a simple visual means of inspecting the wear of the joint seals. This has been proposed after careful consideration of Figure 7.3. It can be seen that the spring takes up wear by pushing the housing and condensate head away from the rotating part of the joint, the flexible hose on the steam inlet and condensate outlet allowing this movement. Therefore, the wear on the seals can be monitored by measuring the movement of the housing relative to the rotating part of the joint.

In this case, option (c) *online condition-based maintenance* is by far the most economic. It is outlined in detail in Table 7.3.

Table 7.3 Maintenance tasks for rotary joint

Item	Timing	Online or offline	Frequency	Time and labor	Maintenance action	Online or offline	Frequency	Time and labor	Secondary action
Rotary Joint (22 off)	Visual condition checking	On	Monthly online maintenance routine for 22 joints	1 h for routine 1 fitter	Replace joints (about 1 per month)	Off	About once per month on agreed shutdown	2 h per joint (1 fitter)	Recondition

Note that the timing of the offline procedures must take into consideration the operational scheduling characteristics of the plant and unit.

7.2.3 Example 3: The roller element bearings of a paper machine

The machine of the previous example contains many roller element bearings, including the two main ones on each of the heated cylinders (see Figure 7.2). It has been in use for some time and the available data suggests that the mean time to failure (MTTF) of the bearings is about 5 years, although some fail within months while others last many years. The lost-production cost of bearing failure is high.

The maintenance action is *replacement of the bearing* (see Figure 6.7). The effective policies to be considered are condition-based maintenance, using shock pulse monitoring, and operate-to-failure. Operate-to-failure is unacceptable because of the high unavailability and repair costs. The economically appropriate policy is *condition-based maintenance based on monthly inspections and trend monitoring* (see Table 7.4).

Table 7.4 Maintenance task for cylinder bearings

Item	Timing	Online or offline	Frequency	Time and labor	Maintenance action	Online or offline	Frequency	Time and labor	Secondary action
Bearings	SPM* trend monitoring	On	Weekly as part of a running maintenance routine	4 h for routine (1 fitter)	Replace bearings (≈2 bearings per month)	Off	6 monthly at wire belt shop	2 h (1 fitter 1 rigger)	None

*SPM: shock pulse monitoring

7.3 Assembling the maintenance life plan for a unit

We have now reached the point where we need to consider the best way of assembling the various identified maintenance tasks into a complete maintenance life plan for the unit. To illustrate how this might be done, let us look again at our example, the chemical reactor (see Figure 6.4).

The determination of the task for the reactor rubber lining was explained earlier (see Table 7.2). Employing a similar analysis tasks would need to be identified for the other reactor items (gearbox, motor, bearings, etc.) and listed in a similar way. It must be emphasized that the tasks and, in particular, their timing are decided in the light of the operational scheduling characteristics of the reactor (see Figure 7.5). This facilitates the selection of periodicities that are compatible with plant-wide scheduling.

An extract from the reactor life plan is shown in Table 7.5. The frequency of the major offline *preventive work* is based on the agreed yearly shutdown of the reaction streams. The replacement of the lining and overhaul or replacement of the vessel are condition based. The minor preventive work is undertaken online (or can be carried out in windows of opportunity resulting from the pattern of production) and at intervals of one or more months.

> This must only be regarded as an introduction to the procedure for assembling a life plan. A full analysis is given in Chapter 9 under the top-down bottom-up approach (TDBUA).

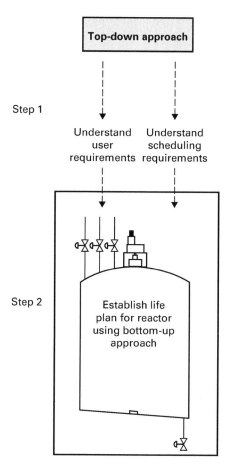

Figure 7.5 Reactor scheduling characteristics

Exercise

E7.1   Senior management have asked you to revise the existing maintenance life
plan that you identified in your answer to Exercise 6.1. In order to do this,
they want you to use the approach outlined in this section (see Table 7.5 as
a guideline) and the information you have already gathered as a result of
answering Exercises E4.1 and E6.2.

Review Questions (the following questions refer to Case study 1 of Chapter 12)

R7.1   What were the main factors involved in determining a 4-year operating
period for the ammonia plant?

R7.2   Explain in a few lines the basis of the syn-gas compressor life plan.

Table 7.5 Extract from reactor life plan

Item	Timing	Online or offline	Frequency	Time and labor	Initial maintenance action	Online or offline	Expected frequency	Time and labor	Action
Material containment Rubber lining	Visual inspection and touch	Off	Y (at agreed shutdown)	3 days 2 fitters	*In situ repair*	Off	2Y (WO*)	1 day 2 trade assistants	Replace lining 8 days 4 fitters + 2 trades assistants
Steel casing (pressure vessel)	Statutory inspection	Off	2Y (at agreed shutdown)	2 days 2 fitters 1 inspector	*In situ repair of jacket and joints as necessary*	Off	4Y (WO)	2 days 2 fitters	Replace vessel on-condition
Agitation system AC motor Bearings	SPM+ trend monitoring	On	2M	Minutes 1 inspector	Replace motor on condition	Off	4Y (R*)	1 h 1 fitter 1 electrician	Recondition motor
Greasing	Fixed-time	On	2M	Minutes 1 greaser	–	–	–	–	–
Gearbox Bearings	SPM trend monitoring	On	2M	Minutes 1 inspector	Replace box on condition	Off	4Y (R)	4 h 2 fitters 2 riggers	Recondition gearbox
Greasing	Fixed-time lubrication	On	2M	Minutes 1 greaser	–	–	–	–	–
Gears	Lubrication, oil trend monitoring	On	2M	Minutes 1 inspector	Replace box on condition	Off	?	4 h 2 fitters 2 riggers	Recondition gearbox
Gland	Visual inspection	On	1M	Minutes 1 inspector	Adjust gland	On	6M	1 fitter minutes	Repack gland on condition

Weigh vessel system									
Weighing mechanism	Visual condition checking	Off	6M	1 h 1 inspector	Calibrate mechanism	Off	1Y	30 min. 1 inspector	Recondition mechanism on condition
Powder feeder	Visual condition	Off	6M	1 h 1 inspector	Calibrate mechanism	Off	1Y	30 min 1 inspector	Recondition mechanism on condition
Hydraulic drive	Lubrication, oil trend monitoring	Off	2M	Minutes 1 inspector	Replace drive unit	Off	3Y	1 h 1 fitter	Recondition drive unit
Valves									
Type A (5 off)	Fixed-time	Off	2Y	1 h 1 fitter (per valve)	Replace valve				Recondition valves (internal)
Type B (10 off)	Fixed-time	Off	5Y	1 h 1 fitter (per valve)	Replace valve				Recondition valves (internal)
Type C (pressure relief)	Fixed-time	On	1M	Inspection (minutes)	Proof test				Replace and recondition as necessary

Y: yearly; M: monthly; +: shock pulse monitoring; *WO: wear out; *R: random.

7.4 Standby units and the life plan

The milling system of Figure 7.6 is a part of an alumina refinery and is an excellent example of the use of standby units to improve the reliability and maintainability of process plant. In this particular case, production required that any two of the three mills should be available continuously. The third mill could therefore be regarded as a standby unit (i.e. available in the event of one of the operating mills unexpectedly failing) other than when it was the one which was undergoing its scheduled major offline maintenance (during which time there would be no standby, of course). The following are some guidelines for its operation and maintenance:

- The system user-requirement must be clearly specified.
- The life plan for each unit should be determined using the approach outlined in this chapter. When on standby a unit can be considered to have a hidden function, so its life plan should incorporate some form of proof testing, which might be inspection and checking by the operator.

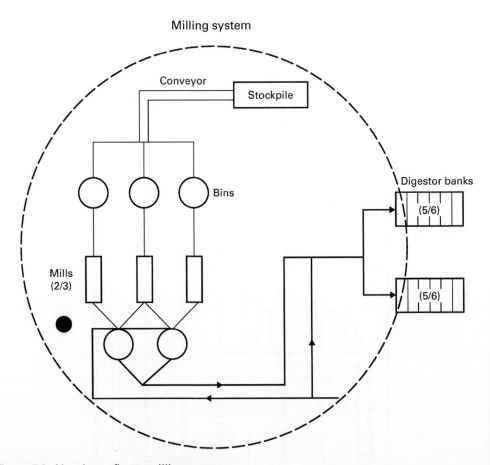

Figure 7.6 Alumina refinery milling system

● The units should be operated in a way which reduces the likelihood of:
  (a) several running-units at a time being in a poor condition, i.e. of simultaneous failures creating a demand for replacements greater than the number of standbys – which, of course requires the operating histories (e.g. running times since last maintenance) to be noted;
  (b) running-unit failures when a standby is in maintenance – the units that will be running throughout this period should be inspected at the start of it.

Exercise

E7.2 Examine your own plant to see if you can find examples of standby units. Identify the way the units are operated and maintained. How does this compare with the guidelines given in Section 7.4.

E7.3 The wear plate of a chipping machine[1]

The chipping machine of Figure 7.7 is part of a series structured continuously operated saw mill (see Figure 7.8). The customary maintenance period for the saw mill is a 2 week long annual shutdown. Outside of this window production is lost if the mill is stopped.

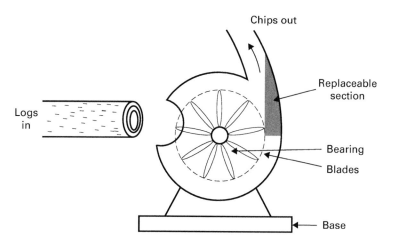

Figure 7.7 Schematic of chipping machine

The main major maintenance task associated with the chipping machine is the replacement of the wear plate. (Minor maintenance tasks associated with the machine can be fitted into the short production stops. The other major task is associated with the blades which have a longer life than the wear plate.)

Failure characteristics of the wear plate
The life of the wear plate is time dependent (see Figure 7.9). The mean life of the plate is 18 months with a range of ±3 months.

[1]Guideline solution at the end of this chapter.

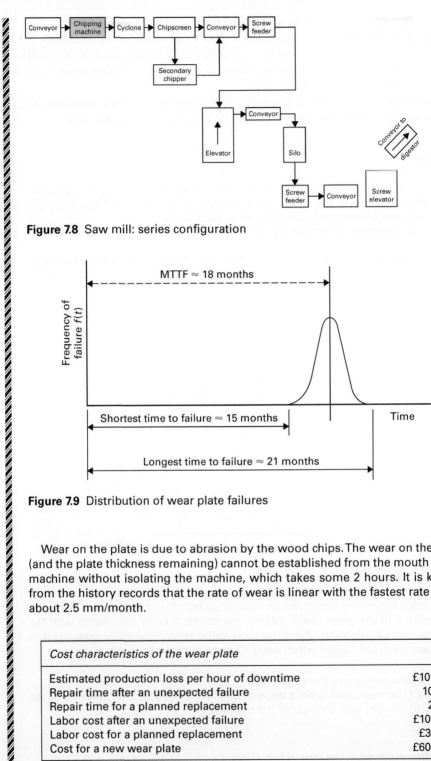

Figure 7.8 Saw mill: series configuration

Figure 7.9 Distribution of wear plate failures

Wear on the plate is due to abrasion by the wood chips. The wear on the plate (and the plate thickness remaining) cannot be established from the mouth of the machine without isolating the machine, which takes some 2 hours. It is known from the history records that the rate of wear is linear with the fastest rate being about 2.5 mm/month.

Cost characteristics of the wear plate	
Estimated production loss per hour of downtime	£1000
Repair time after an unexpected failure	10 h
Repair time for a planned replacement	2 h
Labor cost after an unexpected failure	£1000
Labor cost for a planned replacement	£300
Cost for a new wear plate	£6000

The problem
The management of the mill considers the present maintenance task of 'operate the wear plate to failure and replace' is too expensive. They have asked you to investigate the alternative maintenance tasks and compare their costs against the existing policy. They have pointed out that the mill has about 9 years of operational life left to run.

Question A
Establish the estimated cost of the existing task of 'operate-to-failure and replace' over the next 9 years (the life of the mill), use Table 7.6 as a guide.

Table 7.6 Cost of operate-to-failure and replace over 9 years

Maintenance task	Average number of replacements over 9 years	Expected production lost cost (£)	Labor cost (£)	Materials cost (£)	Total cost (£)
Operate-to-failure and replace plate					

Question B
Management feel that some form of fixed-time replacement policy would be better than operate-to-failure – establish the cost and frequency of such a task:

(i) Would fixed-time replacement of the wear plate be *effective* in controlling the reliability of the chipping machine?
(ii) If the failure distribution was as shown in Figure 7.10 (rather than as shown in Figure 7.9) would fixed-time replacement still be *effective*?

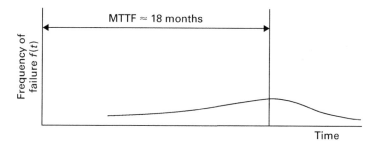

Figure 7.10 Alternative failure distribution of wear plate

(iii) Suggest two possible periods for fixed-time replacement of the plate using Figure 7.9 as a guide. Estimate the cost of each of these policies over the next 9 years. Use Table 7.7 as a guide. How do the costs compare to your answer in Question A?

Table 7.7 Estimated cost of a fixed-time replacements over 9 years

Maintenance task	Average number of replacements over 9 years	Expected production lost cost (£)	Labor cost (£)	Materials cost (£)	Total cost (£)
Fixed-time replacement at ? months					
Fixed-time replacement at ? months					

Question C

Having seen the cost of the fixed-time policy management have asked you to establish a maintenance task based on condition-based maintenance and to cost this over 9 years using Table 7.8 as a guide.

Ultrasonic techniques could be used, but a far less sophisticated procedure would be to drill one, or more small-diameter holes (where the wear is likely to occur) and check periodically with wire to see whether the hole has been penetrated:

(i) Establish the depth of the holes in the wear plate and the periodicity of checking (if the hole has been penetrated) to ensure the policy is effective in controlling chipping machine reliability.

(ii) The technique outlined in (i) is called condition checking. A much more widely used technique of condition monitoring is called 'trend monitoring'. Can you think of a technique for trend monitoring the wear plate?

(iii) Estimate the cost of the technique outlined in (i) and compare it with Questions (A) and (B). (Assume the cost of the inspection is negligible.)

Table 7.8 Estimate of the costs of a condition-based task

Maintenance task	Average number of replacements over 9 years	Expected production lost cost (£)	Labor cost (£)	Materials cost (£)	Total cost (£)
Condition-based maintenance and replace					

Question D

The way the question has been structured has led you to consider only 'replace' as the maintenance action. In actual fact, the first decision should have been the replace vs repair decision. Use Table 7.9 (as a guideline) and the following information to compare 'plate repair' and 'plate redesign' against the procedures of Tables 7.6–7.8:

● Hard coating welding techniques could be used to replace the material worn off the plate and return it to an 'as new' condition at a cost of £2000. The welding takes approximately 24 hours.

- It has been estimated that redesigned wear plate with improved wear-resistant material would cost £20,000, and would have life in excess of 9 years.

Table 7.9 Estimated cost of plate repair and redesign

Maintenance task	Average number of replacements over 9 years	Expected production lost cost (£)	Labor cost (£)	Materials cost (£)	Total cost (£)
Fixed-time repair at 12 months					
Redesign	—	—	—	—	—

Question E
Enter your selected procedure onto Table 7.10.

Table 7.10 Selected maintenance task for the wear plate

Item	Timing	Online or offline	Frequency	Time and labor	Initial maintenance action	Secondary action	Spares requirement
Wear plate							

Question F
If the cyclone (see Figure 7.8), needed to go offline for cleaning every 3 months for about 3 hours, how would this affect your selected maintenance task for the wear plate?

Reference

1. Grothus, H., Plant Engineering Institute, D-427, Dosten 2, Wettring 4.

Review Question Guidelines

R7.1   The factors are listed on page 229 of Case study 1 in Chapter 12.
R7.2   The life plan is based on a 4-year fixed-operating period before major mainte-nance. The work scope for the compressor at overhaul is based mainly on infor-mation obtained from previous shutdowns (offline inspection) and from online monitoring over the operating period. Some fixed-time replacement of items is also used at the shutdown. In addition, the extensive online condition monitor-ing also protects against catastrophic failure.

Exercise Guideline Solutions

E7.3
Question A

Maintenance task	Average number of replacements over 9 years	Expected production loss (£)	Labor cost (£)	Materials cost (£)	Total cost (£)
Operate-to-failure and replace plate	6*	6 × 10 × 1000 = 60,000	6 × 1000 = 6000	6 × 6000 = 36,000	102,000

*Probabilistic based on $\dfrac{\text{Remnant life of mill}}{\text{Mean life of plate}} = \dfrac{9}{1.5} = 6$ years

Question B
(i) Yes since the failure distribution is age related.
(ii) Not really because the 'statistical predictability' is very poor, i.e. there is a major random element involved in the failure.
(iii)

Maintenance task	Average number of replacements over 9 years	Expected production loss (£)	Labor cost (£)	Materials cost (£)	Total cost (£)
Fixed-time replacement at 12 months	8*	0	2400	48,000	50,400
Fixed-time replacement at 15 months	7+	12,000	2100	42,000	56,100

*Replacement is timed for the annual shutdown. The last replacement at the end of 9 years is unnecessary because the mill is at the end of its life.
+One of the 15-month plate replacements coincides with the annual shutdown. This saves the production lost cost

Question C
(i) If the holes are 5 mm deep and the inspection period 1-month this will ensure at least 1-month notice of replacement (the maximum rate of wear is 2.5 mm/month).
(ii) Although, unlikely holes of different depth could be drilled and monitored for penetration. Alternatively a threaded hole could be tapped and a bolt inserted. This could be taken out periodically and checked for wear.

(iii)

Maintenance task	Average number of replacements over 9 years	Expected production loss (£)	Labor cost (£)	Materials cost (£)	Total cost (£)
Condition-based maintenance and replace	6[+]	12,000	1800	36,000	49,800

[+]Assumes plate goes almost to the end of its life and no replacement coincides with the annual shutdown

Question D

Maintenance task/ redesign	Average number of repairs over 9 years	Expected production loss (£)	Labor cost (£)	Materials cost (£)	Total cost (£)
Fixed-time repair at 12 months	8	0	2400	16,000	18,400
Redesign	—	—	—	—	20,000

Note: Select fixed-time repair at 12 months as least cost solution. In practice many maintenance managers would select redesign

Question E

Item	Timing	Online or offline	Frequency	Time and labor	Initial maintenance action	Secondary action	Spares requirement
Wear plate	Fixed-time	Offline	12 months at annual shutdown	2 h 1 fitter 24 h 1 welder	Repair wear plate	None	Welding rods (spare plate?)

Question F
Possibility of carrying spare wear plate and replacing (for repair) at 15 months.

8 Maintenance task selection using reliability-centered maintenance

'What we anticipate seldom occurs; what we least expect generally happens.'
Benjamin Disraeli

Chapter aims and outcomes

To explain the basic concepts, procedure, uses and limitations of reliability-centered maintenance (RCM).

On completion of this chapter you should be able to:

- understand the classical RCM procedure;
- understand how failure modes, effects and criticality analysis (FMECA) is used within the RCM procedure;
- appreciate the uses and limitations of RCM decision tree logic;
- use RCM to determine a maintenance task for an item and a life plan for a unit.

Chapter route map

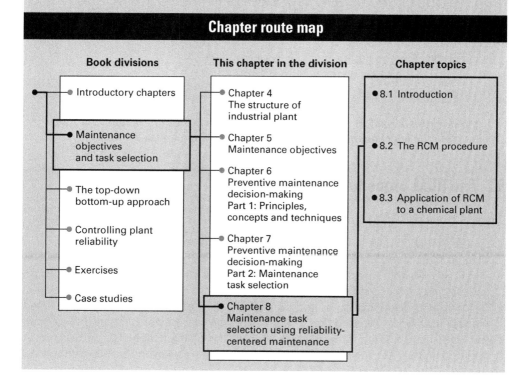

Book divisions	This chapter in the division	Chapter topics
Introductory chapters	Chapter 4 The structure of industrial plant	8.1 Introduction
Maintenance objectives and task selection	Chapter 5 Maintenance objectives	8.2 The RCM procedure
The top-down bottom-up approach	Chapter 6 Preventive maintenance decision-making Part 1: Principles, concepts and techniques	8.3 Application of RCM to a chemical plant
Controlling plant reliability	Chapter 7 Preventive maintenance decision-making Part 2: Maintenance task selection	
Exercises	Chapter 8 Maintenance task selection using reliability-centered maintenance	
Case studies		

Key words

- Reliability-centered maintenance
- Failure modes and effects analysis
- Maintenance significant items
- Maintenance steering group (MSG)
- Block diagram analysis
- Fault tree analysis
- Consequence analysis
- Criticality analysis
- Decision tree analysis
- Hidden function

Further reading

Reading 8.1

8.1 Introduction

Reliability-centered maintenance (RCM) evolved in the airline industry during the 1960s and 1970s from the original work of the methods originators – F. Stanley Nowlan and Howard F Heap [1]. Nowlan and Heap stated that the logic of RCM is based on three questions, *viz.*:

1. How does a failure occur?
2. What are its consequences for safety or operability?
3. What good can preventive maintenance do?

And they further emphasized that, in RCM:

> 'the driving element in all maintenance decisions is not the **failure** of a given item, but the **consequence** of that failure for the equipment as a whole'.

8.2 The RCM procedure

Figure 8.1 outlines firstly, in Steps 1–4, the basic structure of RCM analysis, *viz.*:

1. system definition and acquisition of operational and reliability information;
2. identification of *maintenance significant items (MSIs)*, i.e. items the failure of which would significantly threaten safety or increase cost (because of loss of production and/or high direct repair cost);
3. for each MSI, determination of the significant failure modes, their likely causes, and whether they can be detected (and if they can be, the ways in which this might be done);
4. for each significant failure mode, selection of the maintenance task, or tasks most appropriate for reducing its likelihood of occurrence or mitigating its consequences.

The analysis has then to be followed by:

5. the formation of the task list into a workable plant-wide schedule;
6. implementation of the schedule and sustained feedback of in-service data for periodic review and update.

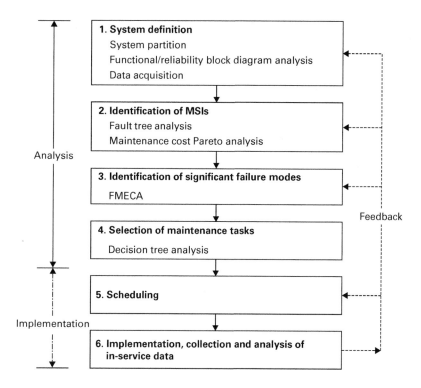

Figure 8.1 Basic structure of RCM

It can be seen that Steps 1–4 is a similar procedure to that used in Chapters 6 and 7. The main difference is that failure modes and effects analysis (FMEA) is used in Step 3 to analyze the item into its failure modes.

Much of the analysis is a rational ordering of techniques that have long been well established and routine in reliability engineering. For example, Step 1 is basically system partitioning (separation into identifiable units) and reliability block diagram analysis.

The authors' approach deviates from RCM in Step 1 because he puts emphasis on the use of 'process flow diagrams' (see Figure 4.7), which allows an understanding of the way the plant is used to satisfy its market. This provides essential information for the scheduling steps, RCM Steps 5 and 6 (see also Chapter 9).

Although Step 2, identification of the MSIs, might well be accomplished just by reviewing history records, operator's logs and cost data to pick out the unreliable or maintenance-costly items (an activity facilitated by 'Pareto analysis', which is little more than sorting out the worst performers into a ranked list, e.g. of the 'top ten'). Fault tree analysis might be needed, if the plant is a complex one.

It is important that any RCM procedure used should clearly define MSIs in terms of their size and complexity. If the MSIs are too large the myriad of failure modes become unmanageable.

Step 3 is nothing more than a failure mode, effect and criticality analysis (FMECA), a step-by-step procedure – (based on documentation of the type illustrated in Table 8.1) for the systematic evaluation of the failure effects and the criticality of potential failure modes in equipment and plant.

To these are added, in Step 4, the logical task-selection decision tree which has been specially developed for RCM and is regarded by some as the kernel of the whole approach. In this, the question repeatedly posed, in order to filter out the various maintenance options, is as follows:

Is the task under consideration both *applicable* (Could it be done? Would it work?) and *worthwhile* (Would its cost, direct and indirect, be less than that of just allowing the failure to occur?)?

A similar approach to the authors' definition of EFFECTIVE and COST-EFFECTIVE used in Chapters 6 and 7.

The decision tree begins, however, with a *consequence analysis*, typically along the lines of the one displayed in Figure 8.2, which is based on the particular form recommended by Nowlan and Heap. By its means, significant failure modes are categorized according to their consequences, which, as regards their processing in the subsequent *task analysis* part of the tree (see Figure 8.3), are prioritized (in this version), as below:

1. *Hidden (or unrevealed)*: Increase risk from other failures (applies mostly to non-fail-safe protective equipment).
2. *Safety-related or environmental*: Threaten life, health or environment.
3. *Operational*: Threaten output, or quality of service.
4. *Non-operational*: Incur only *direct* cost of repair.

Having been categorized by consequence in the upper part of the task selection tree, each failure mode is then subject, in the lower part, to a decision logic along the lines of Figure 8.3. This leads to identification of an appropriate maintenance task or, if none can be found, to the suggestion that redesign be considered.

Figure 8.3 highlights the branch of the tree that is followed for a failure with *safety* consequences; for the other categories of failure the final, or lowest, questions are different, as indicated (e.g. for a hidden failure a *failure-finding* task, or *proof test*, should be considered before turning to possible redesign).

Note that the effect of the decision tree is to rank the task options in a definite order of preference. The analyst is directed to look firstly for a condition-based task, only secondly for a restoration (repair) task, and so forth. Implicit in the method is therefore the assumption that, where both of these options are viable, the condition-based one will be the more appropriate (and likewise the repair option as compared with replacement, etc). Now, while this may well be true in *most* practical cases it is by no means obvious

Table 8.1 Extract from a typical FMECA worksheet

LUBRICATION SYSTEM

REF. DRAWING – XYZ 123
OPERATIONAL STATE – Normal

Date:
Originator:
Approved:

Item identity/ Description	Function	Failure mode	Failure cause	Failure detection method	Failure effect		Compensating provisions	Severity	Loss frequency, λ_0			Data source	Remarks
					Local effect	System effect			λ_p	α	β	λ_0		
22.2 Oil heater	Maintain lube oil temperature	22.2/1 Heater unit failure	Open circuit	Oil temperature gauge	Violent foaming of oil during start-up	Low lube oil temperature – fluctuating oil pressure	Pre start-up checks include oil temperature readings	2	73	0.4	1.0	29.2	Reliability Data Handbook	Heater maintains lube oil temperature during S/D
		22.2/2 External leak	Seal/ flange leak	Visual level gauge on oil reservoir	Loss of lube oil from system	Bearing or seal failure on drive unit	Bearing temperature high alarm. Automatic drive unit S/D on HH alarm.	2	73	0.6	0.3	13.1		

Notes: λ_p, failures per million hours of operation; α, proportion of total failures caused by this failure mode; β, probability that this failure mode will proceed to system failure; $\lambda_0 = \lambda_p \times \alpha \times \beta$.

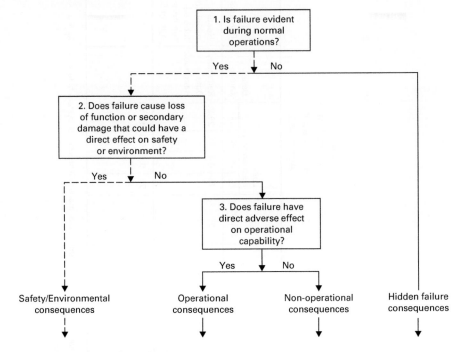

Figure 8.2 Consequence analysis

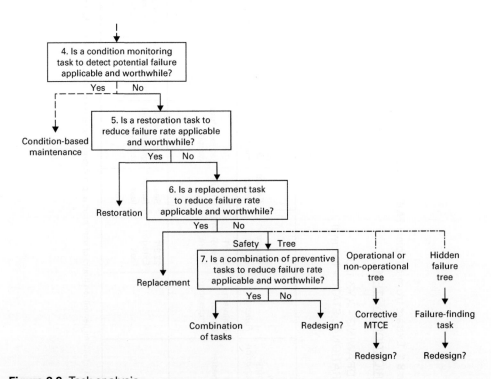

Figure 8.3 Task analysis

that it will be in *all* of them. In some forms of the decision tree that have been developed the analyst (before making his final selection) is, in fact, directed to finish with a comparison of all the types of tasks that have been identified as viable.

> Although, the logic decision diagram of RCM uses the same principles and concepts outlined in Chapter 6 it is much more detailed and less flexible than the 'task selection procedure' outlined in Section 6.5.6. The classic RCM procedure is also expected to cover all units/items of the plant.
>
> Rather than use this classic RCM approach the author prefers a more pragmatic approach *viz.* use FMEA to identify failure modes then the decision logic illustrated in Section 6.5.6 to identify the best maintenance tasks.
>
> This is the approach that will be used in Chapter 9 as a part of the top-down bottom-up approach (TDBUA) to establish a maintenance strategy for a complex industrial plant.

Exercises

E8.1   Carry out an Internet search to establish the recent developments of RCM which claim to make the procedure more suitable for industrial plant. Identify the key differences between these recent RCM developments and the 'classic RCM procedure' outlined in this section.

E8.2   Identify a unit of plant from within your own company that is regarded to be in the top ten in terms of high maintenance costs and/or in terms of low reliability. Carry out a FMEA for a critical item/system of this unit. (This unit may, or may not, be the unit used in Exercise E4.1.)

8.3 Application of RCM to a chemical plant[1]

8.3.1 Background

The case study is based on a chemical plant manufacturing specialty polymers. Figure 8.4 shows a process flow diagram of one of three production lines. The raw materials are delivered by road and stored in silos and tanks. The raw materials are then pumped and pneumatically conveyed to the mixing tank. The materials are mixed together at ambient temperature before being pumped to the primary reaction vessel where the reactants are heated to temperatures around 270°C. This is where the chemical reaction is initiated. The reaction continues through another three reactors to the final reaction stage. At each stage the reaction is controlled via electronic monitoring and adjustment of the temperatures and pressures. The final product viscosity is advanced by progressively increasing temperature and vacuum through the five reaction stages. The differential pressure between the reactors maintains flow. Five of the six vessels (including the first mixing tank) are agitated. From the final reactor the product is pumped through filtration and pelletized by an extension head.

---

[1] Based on a case study contributed by Ian Bendall (former student of the Manchester University, M.Sc. in Maintenance Engineering).

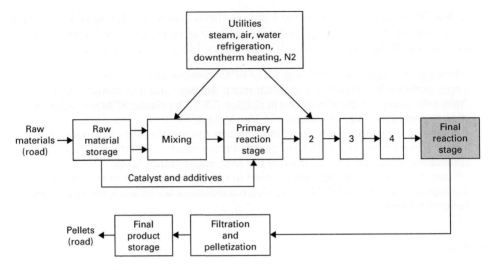

Figure 8.4 Process flow diagram

The cool, solid pellets are pneumatically conveyed to finished product silos from where it is shipped by road to customers.

Between the mixing vessel and pelletization the units are in series and operate as a continuous chemical process (there is no redundancy at unit level or inter-stage storage). Because of the high operating temperatures, shutdown and start-up of any of the lines take several days and none of the reactors can be shutdown or isolated for intrusive maintenance without a full line shutdown. The plant utilities, steam, compressed air, nitrogen, cooling water and hot oil heating (downtherm) are common to all production lines, but each line can be safely isolated from these supplies for maintenance. A full site shutdown occurs after 24 months, this period has been determined by statutory inspection requirements, and plant operating experience.

The turnaround lasts for 5 days, but because of the staggered shutdown and start-up of the lines there is up to 21 days between full production.

8.3.2 Final reaction stage: the process and equipment

The final reaction stage (see Figure 8.5), is concerned with achieving the final product viscosity within specified limits. This is achieved by heating the product up to the desired temperature (via the heating jacket[2]) but also by agitating the product to expose large product surfaces to the vacuum. This is achieved via a shaftless agitator cage[2]. The cage is driven by a variable speed (inverter controlled) 9 kW motor through a cycle-type gearbox[2]. Bearing housings[2] (oil cooled) are mounted at each end of the reactor body to carry the agitator cage steel shafts – the housings also contain the sealing arrangement.

The vapors and gases (carrying some solids) rising from the product are drawn off into the vacuum line[2], spray condenser[2], mist separator[2] and ejectors[2]. The solids are extracted and settled in the hot well. The liquid is filtered in the hot well and returned

---

[2]A description of these parts is given in the appendix to this chapter.

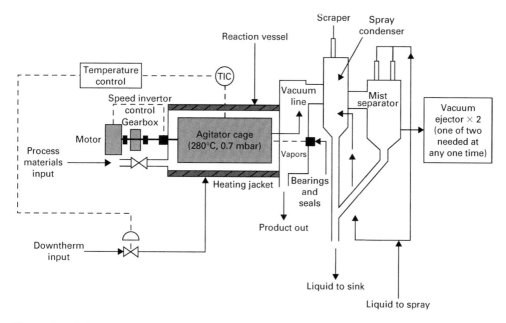

Figure 8.5 Schematic model of final reactor stage

to the condenser/separator. From the mist separator the vapors (now clean from solids) flow to one of the two steam ejectors.

8.3.3 RCM analysis of the final reactor

The equipment making up the final reaction stage is shown in Figure 8.5. This can be considered to be made up of the reaction unit (casing, agitator, vacuum line, spray condenser, mist separator and support frame) and the vacuum ejectors. The subject of this study is the reaction unit.

A criticality ranking in conjunction with previous reliability history was used to decide which units (and in which order) should be subjected to RCM analysis. The reaction unit was ranked one and was considered as one of the most critical units in the process. The vacuum ejector has redundancy and was ranked three and not considered at this stage of the analysis.

All of the equipment/subsystems associated with the reaction unit were subjected to a FMEA. Tables 8.2 and 8.3 show examples of the FMEA for the vessel shell and the agitator system.

Failure mode 3.A.5 (see Table 8.3), in conjunction with Table 8.4 can be used to illustrate the logic used in the 'consequence of failure analysis' and in the 'selection of the maintenance task'. The consequence of failure analysis is aided by a decision tree of the kind shown in Figure 8.6 (see also Figures 8.2 and 8.3). In the case of agitator seizure (bearing failure) the failure would be evident and cause operational loss (see Table 8.4). In order to identify the maintenance task, a number of questions are asked in the order

Table 8.2 FMEA for material containment

			System: Final reactor unit Subsystem: Material containment	
Failure modes information sheet				
Identifier	Function	Functional failure (loss of function)	Failure mode	Failure effect
1	To contain product flow through vessel, under vacuum conditions with no air leakage or leakage from heating jacket.	A. Loss of containment	1. Vessel fractures	Failure of vessel weld due to thermal or other stresses, causes air leaks, possible loss of vacuum and product leakage, or vacuum system fails. Time to repair, several weeks.
			2. Gasket/joint leakage	Failure of door or nozzle joints causes air leaks, possible loss of vacuum and product/vapor leakage if vacuum system fails. Time to repair, several days.
			3. Agitator bearing failure	If agitator bearing collapses, agitator drops and rubs on reactor bottom. Wears through reactor wall. Downtherm vapor into system and product leakage if vacuum system fails. Time to repair, 2 months.
2	To be able to indicate and control the level of product in the vessel.	A. Loss of indication	1. Radioactive shield not open properly	No or false indication of level causing process upsets.
			2. Failure of radioactive sensor	Causes process upset.
		B. Incorrect-level indication	1. Loss of strength of radioactive source	False-level indication will give process upset.
			2. Sensor out of calibration	False-level indication will give process upset.
		C. Loss of Control	1. Control valve fails to respond due to seizure	High/low-inconsistent-level control gives flood forward and process upset.
			2. Control valve diaphragm holed	High/low-inconsistent-level control gives flood through causing loss of Class I product.

Table 8.3 FMEA for agitation system

System: Final reactor unit
Subsystem: Agitation system

Failure modes information sheet

Identifier	Function	Functional failure (loss of function)	Failure mode	Failure effect
3	To agitate product within the vessel, increasing surface area of product exposed to vacuum system.	A. Complete loss of agitation	1. Power failure	Agitator drive stops. Loss of agitation. Loss of flow out of vessel. Breakdown of control system. Full system shutdown.
			2. Motor failure	Motor fails either electrically or mechanically causing loss of drive to agitator. Offclass product produced. Time to replace motor, 6 hours.
			3. Gearbox failure	Gearbox fails mechanically, causing loss of drive to agitator. Offclass product produced. Time to replace gearbox, 9 hours.
			4. Coupling failure	Coupling fails, causing loss of drive to agitator. Offclass product produced. Time to replace coupling, 6 hours.
			5. Agitator seizes	Agitator support bearings seize. Offclass product produced and cooldown required to replace bearing assembly. Time for repair including startup, 5 days.
			6. Failure of interlock system	If interlocks fail, shutdown agitation. Alternatively interlocks could fail to shutdown agitation, leading to secondary damage.
		B. Partial loss of agitation	1. Internal failure of agitator cage	Agitator cage is in two halves, coupled at center by ring of bolts. If bolts fail, then half of agitator does not turn. Likely to cause quality parameter problems, the estimate time to repair is 6 weeks.
			2. Agitator bearing failure	If agitator bearing collapses, agitator drops and rubs on reactor bottom. Wears through reactor wall. Downtherm vapor into system and product leakage if vacuum system fails. Time to repair, 2 months.

(Continued)

Table 8.3 (*Continued*)

Failure modes information sheet

System: Final reactor unit
Subsystem: Agitation system

Identifier	Function	Functional failure (loss of function)	Failure mode	Failure effect
4	To control agitation speed to set point I 0.1 rpm	A. Loss of control of agitation speed	1. Inverter failure to change speed	Inverter fails to change speed. Likely to cause some quality parameter problems. The estimate time to repair is 6 hours.
			2. Inverter fails to zero speed	Agitator stops. Offclass product produced, time to repair, 6 hours.
			3. Control is not accurate due to inverter problem	Line upsets, and poor quality parameters. Likely to cause some offclass product. Time to repair, 6 hours.
			4. Over-speed trip operates	Agitator stops. Offclass product produced, time to repair, 6 hours.
5	To seal vessel/agitator against full vacuum 0.1 mbar	A. Total loss of seal	1. Agitator shaft cracked or weld failure	Vacuum on vessel pulls cooling oil into vessel. Loss of vacuum, poor quality and contaminated product. Time to repair is about 5 days (line shutdown).
		B. Partial seal loss	2. Seal leaks so much vacuum cannot be maintained	Difficult to control vacuum, so poor quality parameters on product. Time to replace seals is about 5 days (line shutdown).
			3. Gasket leaks so much vacuum cannot be maintained	Difficult to control vacuum, so poor quality parameters on product.
			4. Seal liquid low causing leakage	Liquid seal is lost, causes some offclass product. Time to top-up seal liquid, ½ hour.
			5. Loss of oil cooling to shafts	Shaft overheats, seals burn and wear quickly. Eventually total loss of sealing will occur. Time to replace seals is 5 days (line shutdown).

Table 8.4 Failure consequence and maintenance task analysis

Failure consequence and maintenance task analysis

System: Final reactor unit
Subsystem: Agitation system

Identifier	Failure consequence				Maintenance task			Defaults			Identified maintenance task	Interval
	Evident	Safety	Environment	Operation	On-condition	Rest	Replace	Rail find	Redesign	Run to fail		
3.A.1	Y	N	N	Y	N	N	N	N	N	Y	No scheduled maintenance.	
3.A.2	Y	N	N	Y	Y						Vibration monitor motor. Look for bearing and rotor faults. Motor current analysis to monitor condition of motor.	Monthly
3.A.3	Y	N	N	Y	Y						Vibration monitor gearbox, look for gear and bearing problems.	Monthly
3.A.4	Y	N	N	Y	Y						Vibration monitor looking for coupling faults.	Monthly
3.A.5	Y	N	N	Y	Y						Vibration monitor drive and non-drive end bearings.	Monthly
3.A.6	N				N	N	N	Y			Proof check all interlocks.	Yearly
3.B.1	Y	N	N	Y	Y						Vibration monitor looking for looseness.	Monthly
3.B.2	Y	N	N	Y	Y						Vibration monitor of drive and non-drive end bearings.	Monthly

Notes: N: no; Y: yes.

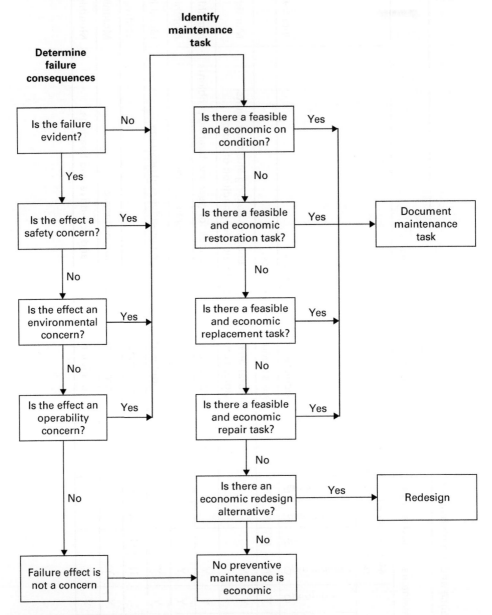

Figure 8.6 Maintenance task selection decisive diagram

shown in Figure 8.6. In our case, condition-based maintenance is feasible and economic (vibration monitoring) and this is the 'selected maintenance task' – the remainder of the questions are not asked (even though it may be more feasible and economic). The identified maintenance task is then documented for scheduling. Once all of the mainte-nance tasks are identified the maintenance life plan is assembled (see Table 8.5).

Table 8.5 Life plan for final reaction unit

	Craft	Operator	Eng/Tech/ Cont
Online maintenance			
Daily			
Check			
Barrier fluid level and usage		1 × 30 minutes	
Level/pressure/temperature of cooling oil system			
Pressure drop across steam strainers cooling water filters			
Glycol flow			
Weekly			
Monitor frequencies of scraper operation		1 × 30 minutes	
Carry out visual check of insulation		1 × 30 minutes	
Monthly			
Vibration monitor the motor, gearbox and agitator bearings	1 × 115 minutes		
Look for bearing and gear faults including misalignment	1 × 30 minutes		
Motor current analysis	1 × 120 minutes		
3 monthly			
Ultrasound monitor steam traps			
Yearly			
Check radioactive source strength		1 × 20 minutes	
Check and calibrate level indicator	1 × 60 minutes		
Check and tighten holding down bolts	1 × 4 hours		
2 yearly			
Crack detection of support frame			1 × 6 hours
OffLine Maintenance			
Yearly			
Proof check interlocks, over-speed trip and relief valve	1 × 4 hours	1 × 2 hours	
2 yearly			
Video/visual inspection of reaction intervals, vessel jacket steam pipework, downtherm pipework, cooling water pipework	2 × 4 days		3 × 3 days
Overhaul steam control valve, level control valve, temperature control valve	1 × 2 days		1 × 3 days
Overhaul scraper mechanism	2 × 2 days		

Review Questions

R8.1 List the main advantages and disadvantages in using RCM to establish the unit life plans and preventive schedule for an ammonia plant of the type featured in Case study 1 in Chapter 12.

R8.2   Compare the RCM procedure of Figure 8.1 with the TDBUA of Table 9.1 and Figure 9.5. Explain how the TDBUA attempts to overcome the disadvantages you may have listed in Question R8.1.

Exercise

E8.3   Use the RCM analysis of the final reactor as a 'guide' to extend your answer to Exercise E8.2 into a life plan for the selected unit.

Reference

1. Nowlan, F.S. and Heap, H., *Reliability Centred Maintenance*, National Technical Information Service, Springfield, Virginia, 1978.

Review Questions Guidelines

R8.1   *Advantages*: The RCM procedure is detailed, comprehensive and systematic. It uses the ideas of FMECA to identify failure modes, and the principles and concepts of preventive maintenance to identify the effective maintenance tasks.
Disadvantages: It is extremely 'resource hungry' even for a relatively small project. Thus, it is best used for the critical items of plant. It would not be realistic to use RCM to establish the maintenance life plans for all the units and systems of a large and complex industrial plant, it was never designed to do this. The decision-making procedure of RCM to determine the effective maintenance task is based on asset/reliability-oriented objectives rather than business-oriented objectives.

R8.2   The TDBUA is business centered and via Step 1 brings down business-centered objectives to the preventive maintenance decision-making of Step 2. Step 1 also provides information on the scheduling characteristics of the plant to enable Step 2 and Step 3 to work towards a cost-effective preventive maintenance schedule. It will be noticed that Step 2 of the TDBUA is much more pragmatic than RCM in that it ranks units in order of importance and concentrates the analytical resources on the most critical units. At item level the TDBUA as far as possible uses concepts, principles and experience to decide on the maintenance procedures (tasks) and reserves a FMECA for only the most complex of items. This saves considerable analytical resource.

Appendix for RCM example

Final reaction stage: equipment description (see Figure 8.5)

Agitator system drive train

The drive train consists of a variable speed, inverter controlled 9 kW motor, a speed reducer and agitator cage. The cage speed is around 2.5 rpm and there are couplings between motor and speed reducer, and speed reducer and agitator. The agitator cage has a stub shaft at either end and each stub shaft is supported in two rolling element bearings.

The gear reducer is a 'cyclo'-type gearbox. There are four major components to the gearbox, these being:

1. High speed shaft with eccentric bearing.
2. Cycloid disks.
3. Ring gear housing with pins and rollers.
4. Slow speed shaft.

The gearbox has two reduction stages, and each stage employs two cycloid disks displaced through 180° to balance centrifugal forces. As the input shaft rotates, the eccentric bearing rolls the cycloid disks around the internal circumference of the ring gear. If this travel is in a clockwise rotation then the disks rotate about their own axis in a counterclockwise direction, the lobes of the disks 'engage' successively with the pins on the ring gear producing an output that is reversed and reduced in speed to the input. The reduction ratio is determined by the number of lobes on the disks, for one revolution of input the disks rotate one lobe in the opposite direction. The transmission from the disks to output shaft is via pins and rollers projecting through holes in the disk.

Agitator cage

The horizontal cylindrical reactor has a shaftless agitator cage with disks in a spiral arrangement. The bore of the disks increase from inlet to outlet. Weirs are installed between the disks in the outlet half of the reactor, these 'scrape' the disks in order to limit the amount of product picked up by the agitator cage. Bearing houses are mounted externally on each end of the reactor, these contain the bearings and sealing arrangement. A two-stage sealing arrangement is used at either end, the first stage consists of scraper rings and a vacuum trap and is situated in the high temperature zone close to the reactor end cover. The second-stage sealing is achieved by using radial sealing rings which are flooded with a glycol head. Both the stub shafts and the housings are cooled with oil, fed from an external system.

Vacuum line

Connects the main reactor body to the spray condenser. The line has a 300 mm stainless steel vertical section connected to the reactor body, which is heated by downtherm circulating in limpet coils, and a horizontal section connected between the vertical section and the spray condenser.

Spray condenser

A stainless steel section of the vacuum train where a liquid is sprayed into the vapor to remove solid conveyor. There is a pneumatically operated scraper at the top of this section. This operates timer and keeps the inlet nozzle clear of solid build up.

Reading 8.1 An introduction to RCM

M.J. Harris, Honorary Fellow, Manchester School of Engineering, Manchester, UK

Introduction

The first thing to get quite clear is that RCM is not just a portmanteau term for those maintenance procedures which have been *scheduled* via some kind of operational research analysis using cost and reliability data: e.g. calculations of the optimum frequencies for given preventive tasks, proof tests, or inspections. In fact, such optimums exist only for rather infrequently occurring, rather special cases and searching for them is usually not all that productive. The author has encountered, in a major company, the use of the term RCM to refer to just that kind of activity, and this is quite misleading. RCM is much more than that.

In RCM the life plan for a unit (or system) is formulated via a structured framework of analysis aimed, in principle (but see later), at ensuring the attainment of the unit (or system) inherent reliability, i.e. the reliability that it was designed to attain (it was a fundamental, starting-point assumption of the method's originators – F. Stanley Nowlan and Howard F. Heap of United Airlines in the USA – that this was the maximum level of reliability that could be attained). The method incorporates several of the basic techniques of reliability engineering which will be touched on in the reliability engineering unit.

In the 1950s, airlines in the USA (and elsewhere) were finding that as they introduced bigger aircraft, with more complex systems, their customary policy of periodically overhauling all systems – in the belief that each system would eventually deteriorate unless renewed – was generating an excessive, totally unachievable, workload. Indeed, they also suspected that safety and operational reliability were being threatened by unnecessary interference with satisfactorily running systems. A joint task force, comprising representatives of the civil airlines and of the regulatory Federal Aviation Authority (FAA), was therefore convened to study this problem. Significant among its many revealing findings, reported in 1960, was that over 80% of aircraft items showed no evidence at all of age-related deterioration in function. The task force therefore concluded that:

(i) scheduled overhaul had little effect on the reliability of complex items, unless wear-out was dominant (which was rarely the case);
(ii) for many items there was no effective form of preventive maintenance.

During the 1960s further work carried out by a maintenance steering group (MSG), comprising representatives of the FAA, the airlines and the manufacturers, showed that more efficient maintenance programs could be developed using logical decision processes, progressively more refined formulations of which were eventually recommended in the handbooks MSG-1 (1968), MSG-2 (1970) and MSG-3 (1980). The first of these was used with great success to develop the maintenance program for the new Boeing-747, the later versions being applied equally successfully to the DC-10, A-300, Concorde, etc. The most significant outcome of this was probably the considerable shift from scheduled overhaul to condition-based maintenance (with great savings in maintenance man-hours and spares holding). The name 'RCM' for the new approach was coined by its moving spirits, Nowlan and Heap, shortly after the publication of MSG-2, and was the title of the definitive handbook on the topic which they published at about that time [1]. Most of the variants of RCM that have since been developed for general industrial, as opposed to aviation, application (e.g. that of Moubray [2]) have, in fact been based on MSG-2.

Nowlan and Heap stated that the logic of RCM is based on three questions, *viz.*:

(i) How does a failure occur?
(ii) What are its consequences for safety or operability?
(iii) What good can preventive maintenance do?

And they further emphasized that, in RCM . . .

'the driving element in all maintenance decisions is not the **failure** of a given item, but the **consequence** of that failure for the equipment as a whole'.

RCM in civil aviation

The benefits of RCM in its industry of origin have been outlined by Moubray [2]. For example, before its introduction the initial maintenance program for the Douglas DC-8 specified scheduled overhaul of 339 items; that of the later DC-10, which was based on MSG-2, of only seven items, an improvement which led, among other gains, to a reduction in the spares inventory of more than 50%. In addition to such organizational and economic gains, the resulting better understanding of failure processes has improved reliability by enabling preventive tasks to be directed at specific evidence of potential failures.

Various factors have contributed to this success:

● The RCM program has had one clear objective, safety and technology driven, *viz.* achievement, as mentioned earlier, of 'the inherent reliability capabilities' of the equipment concerned (and Nowlan and Heap also added 'and to do so at minimum cost')
● Aircraft systems are clearly specified and standardized, with much system redundancy. Also, they all have to fulfill a similar, mission-based, duty (for any one design, at least). The collection of data on reliability, availability and maintainability can therefore be relatively rapid.
● Much basic benchmark information for initial, design stage, RCM assessment can be 'borrowed' from the history of already functioning similar systems.
● As in other high technology sectors (e.g. nuclear power), there is a firmly established prescriptive culture and hence an acceptance of strategy directives produced by specialists.
● The work has been 'zero-based', i.e. applied at the design stage with little reference to resource constraints, provided it is effective in controlling reliability.
● Last, but by no means least, the considerable cost of the program can be spread over the total fleet.

In industry at large, however, the situation may be very different.

RCM in industry

Over the past 10 years or so RCM analysis – broadly of the kind that has been described but, as explained, with occasional modification to suit a particular technology – has been tried in many different industries. The author and various of his colleagues have studied its application in a wide selection of these, *viz.*, food processing, pharmaceuticals, offshore extraction, petrochemicals, steel production, metal forming, automobile manufacture, fossil-fired power generation, hydro and nuclear power generation. We have found that, with notable exceptions – where RCM has been demonstrably beneficial and has become part of the company's culture – the success attained has not been of the level achieved in aviation. Indeed, in some cases RCM has been tried and abandoned, the company concluding that, for little and slow return, it demanded much greater resources of time and manpower than they had anticipated. There are several reasons for this, most of which arise because the maintenance management problem in these industries is, in many aspects, fundamentally different from that in the aviation business.

Although, 'achieving the inherent reliability' is always adopted as the *de jure* objective of all RCM analyses and implementations, the *de facto* objective for most industrial plant (i.e. in the power, process, manufacturing and extractive sectors) may be rather different. More often than not, the plant concerned will already have been operating for some time, many years even. The level and mix of resources will have been set by custom and usage but will be perceived as being in need of reduction and rationalization. So the RCM exercise will not be 'zero-based' and the dominant maintenance management objectives will be financial rather than technological. The aim will be to decrease maintenance costs, e.g. by justifying moving to contract rather than in-house arrangements.

A typical industrial installation will often be a unique design assembled to meet a wide range of output requirements. There will be few standard systems. Collection of the necessary information on plant design and operation, and of data – whether generic or experiential – on reliability and maintainability will therefore be no small task and the high cost of the whole RCM exercise cannot be shared among similar plant.

Operation will frequently be via a single stream of diverse units run either on a batch basis, or continuously between major (often statutory) overhauls, features which may dominate maintenance decision-making, e.g. there may be clear windows of opportunity for preventive work at zero indirect cost. In such circumstances, there may be relatively little that can be gained from a costly RCM exercise. A salutary illustration of this was recently encountered by the author. A major pharmaceutical company had embarked on RCM in order to improve the generally poor availability of their plant. Although some small gains did indeed result, these were achieved only by putting a disproportionate effort, in time and manpower, into the study. Closer examination revealed that the greater part of the company's operation involved batch processing (with product changes) and that the dominant contribution, by far, to extended downtime was likely to be caused by delays in wash down and changeover. Effort devoted to improving the planning of these latter activities would clearly have been far more cost-beneficial, in the first instance, than the RCM exercise.

Unless special steps are taken (see later) there can be such a long delay between launching the RCM exercise and implementing its recommendations (intervals of 2 years or more have been recorded) that the latter can be overtaken by other changes – in plant, operating policy, sales requirement, and so on. A significant factor here is that, translating the results of the RCM analysis into a workable maintenance schedule is invariably just as complex and demanding a task as the RCM analysis itself.

As explained, a number of the applications of RCM which have been studied by the author have, however, been successful, and this can be attributed to several features which they tended to have in common. Firstly, although achieving inherent reliability was always the notional working objective of the exercise, as it must be, other achievable objectives were identified, clearly defined and established as being primary, and were not part of a hidden agenda. For example, several companies had taken their main objective to be an educational one, to make production and maintenance aware of each other's needs and problems as part of fostering a self-managing, culture. Such an aim is usually very achievable because RCM, in most industries, is almost always undertaken not prescriptively, i.e. by specialist analysts issuing directives, but co-operatively and in-house, by facilitator-led operator–maintainer teams – an arrangement which can stimulate information exchange (and also, incidentally, the flow of previously unavailable reliability and maintainability data).

Secondly, a limited pilot exercise was invariably undertaken – checking preconceptions regarding the time and resources needed, revealing potential difficulties, and undertaking a critical and representative subsystem. (This last point is an important one. Enthusiasm for, and commitment to, the study has been vitiated when an unimportant area of plant has been misguidedly selected.)

Thirdly, although when applied successfully to new plant RCM was carried out across the board (as an integral part of the design process) when applied to existing plant steps were taken to ensure that the analysis was only undertaken on those units where there were clear economic or safety benefits to be gained, i.e. on units critical to overall plant availability (identified by, say, reliability block diagram analysis) or on units exhibiting disproportionately high maintenance cost. In a study on an offshore oil and gas extraction platform, e.g. the whole operation was analyzed into just over a hundred subsystems. It was then found that just 24 of these accounted for over 80% of total maintenance man-hours expended (a classic case of Pareto's 'Law of Maldistribution'). Furthermore, the maintenance regime for half of these last 24 was already dictated by either legislative or Code-of-Practice mandatory requirements and could not easily have been changed. The RCM exercise was therefore confined to the remaining dozen subsystems, which accounted for approximately 50% of the man-hours. A halving of the predicted workload for these was achieved – giving a reduction in the total expected maintenance workload for the platform of rather more than 25%.

The benefits of RCM

Where it has been successful the benefits of RCM in general industry have been much the same as those claimed in the aviation (and military) sectors, *viz.:*

(i) *Traceability*: In the long term, the most important of the virtues of RCM. All maintenance policy decisions (and the information, assumptions and reasoning that led to those decisions) are fully documented. In the light of this, subsequent plant reliability can be periodically audited, maintenance experience reviewed and strategy updated (where necessary) on a rational basis.

(ii) *Cost saving*: As with aviation the overall maintenance workload is reduced, due to a general shift away from time-based or usage-based preventive work (such as regular major overhauls) and towards condition-based work – with a consequent reduction in spares holding.

(iii) *Rationalization*: By identifying unnecessary preventive work, unachievable, and therefore uncontrollable, maintenance workload is eliminated. In one section of a food plant, e.g., the total scheduled preventive workload before the introduction of RCM was 25,000 man-hours – of which, typically, only 12,000 was completed, with no guarantee, of course, that it had all been directed at the more needful work. Under the RCM-determined regime it was established that the really necessary preventive work actually amounted to an achievable 12,000 man-hours.

(iv) *Plant improvement*: Redesign eliminates recurrent failures or poor maintainabilities.
(v) *Education*: The whole exercise raises the workforce's overall level of skill and technical knowledge. As mentioned earlier, this is a natural consequence of the operation of the facilitator-led study teams. Also, the actual existence of an RCM regime will itself tend to attract better-skilled personnel into maintenance.

RCM and the TDBUA approach

If the ideas that underlie RCM are to be more widely accepted in industry, and the benefits of its rational approach fully realized, two fundamental aspects must be addressed:

(i) its strongly 'asset-centered' approach which, as explained at the start of this chapter, takes insufficient account of resource, operating pattern and market factors;
(ii) the resource-hungry nature of its implementation (2000 man-hours of team effort can be needed for even a quite modest project).

A consequence of the first of these is that operational and resource considerations are only fully addressed at the later, task selection, stage of the analysis and then only separately for each task, i.e. each time the question – 'Is the task worthwhile?' – is asked. It is therefore no great surprise that the analysis is rather inefficient, i.e. resource-hungry (aspect (ii) above) if applied in its full form to a typical industrial plant where, as has been explained in Sections 6 and 7, almost every aspect of maintenance strategy formulation will probably be dominated by plant-wide considerations, such as operational availability for maintenance.

The TDBUA approach eases the above difficulties by providing an initial 'broad-brush' reliability, availability, maintainability and safety (RAMS) assessment of the plant concerned. An assessment which relatively quickly identifies firstly, the operationally determined maintenance constraints and opportunities and then the maintenance-significant items. The in-detail core of RCM analysis, FMEA identification of significant failure modes followed by decision tree selection of appropriate tasks for reducing their incidence or mitigating their effect can then be restricted to the most critical of the MSIs. The TDBUA approach has the additional advantage of providing a structure for systematically incorporating all the task recommendations, for non-critical as well as critical items, into a workable schedule for the whole plant.

References

1. Nowlan, F.S. and Heap, H., *Reliability Centred Maintenance*, National Technical Information Service, Springfield, Virginia, 1978.
2. Moubray, J., *Reliability Centred Maintenance*, Butterworth-Heinemann, Oxford, 1991.
3. Sandtorv, H. and Rausand, M., Closing the loop between design reliability and operational reliability, *Maintenance*, 6(1) pp. 13–21, March 1991.

PART 3

The top-down bottom-up approach

9

Determining the life plan and schedule: The top-down bottom-up approach

'If a window of opportunity appears, don't pull down the shade.'

Tom Peters

Chapter aims and outcomes

To outline a systematic and pragmatic procedure, the top-down bottom-up approach (TDBUA), for establishing the maintenance life plan for each plant unit and a preventive maintenance schedule for the complete plant.

On completion of this chapter you should be able to:

- understand the TDBUA for establishing a maintenance strategy;
- understand the procedure for establishing life plans for plant units (a summary of Chapters 6–8) and a preventive maintenance schedule for the plant;
- understand the principles and concepts of preventive maintenance scheduling, including the ideas of opportunity scheduling;
- appreciate that with most existing plants a 'catch-up' corrective strategy comes before a preventive maintenance strategy.

Chapter route map

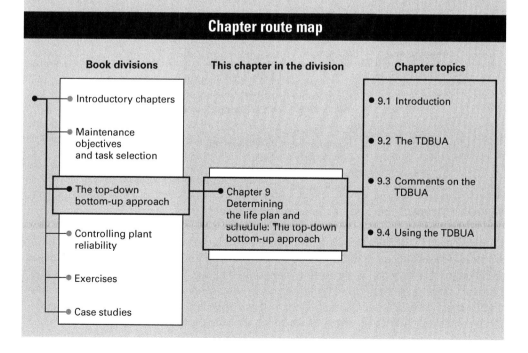

Book divisions	This chapter in the division	Chapter topics
Introductory chapters		9.1 Introduction
Maintenance objectives and task selection		9.2 The TDBUA
The top-down bottom-up approach	Chapter 9 Determining the life plan and schedule: The top-down bottom-up approach	9.3 Comments on the TDBUA
Controlling plant reliability		9.4 Using the TDBUA
Exercises		
Case studies		

Key words

- Preventive maintenance schedule
- Opportunity scheduling
- Top down bottom up approach
- Plant criticality
- Catch-up maintenance
- Risk/probability matrix

9.1 Introduction

In the previous chapters we explained how a life plan for a single unit of plant can be systematically determined. The next step is to consider how to incorporate this into a procedure for formulating the maintenance strategy for the whole plant, which may well be large and complex.

In accomplishing this the procedure will involve:

(a) formulating a *maintenance life plan* for each unit of plant (see Figure 9.1);
(b) formulating guidelines for setting up a plant-wide *preventive maintenance schedule* (see Figure 9.2);
(c) ensuring that the resulting workload can be properly resourced.

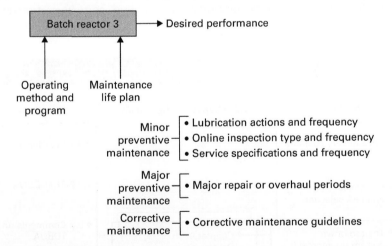

Figure 9.1 A typical unit and its maintenance life plan

In theory, task (a) should be straightforward; for each unit, some form of life plan should be provided by its manufacturer. However, manufacturers' life plans vary from the excellent to the abysmal; at worst they may only be lists of lubrication routines. In addition, in a large plant there may be hundreds of units each with a different manufacturer and in most cases the life plan will be written for general use, e.g. the recommended job frequencies will not be appropriate to a particular plant's scheduling characteristics.

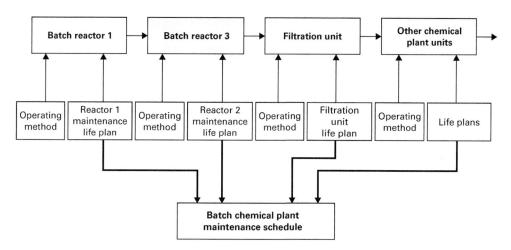

Figure 9.2 Assembling a maintenance schedule

The determination of a preventive maintenance schedule for the whole plant (see Figure 9.2) is an inherently difficult task. The schedule is the sum of the multitude of maintenance procedures contained in the unit life plans and is impacted by many factors prominent among which are:

• the plant structure, e.g. the level of redundancy at plant stream, unit and item level;
• the capacity for inter-stage and final-product storage;
• the level of occurrence of unscheduled corrective maintenance;
• the incidence of planned outages, e.g. for catalyst changes or statutory safety work.

Perhaps the most important factor is the relationship between the product and its market. In some cases, the demand for a product can be constant and stable – such as is placed on a generator required to supply base-load power to the distribution grid, while in others it may be variable and uncertain, in which case the maintenance schedule must be dynamic, i.e. responsive to production needs.

> The food processing plant of Chapter 3 produced numerous product varieties each to a varying market (often varying in the short term). This required a flexible production program and a corresponding flexibility with the preventive maintenance schedule.

Resourcing the schedule can be difficult if the maintenance workload has major peaks, e.g. during petroleum refinery turnarounds, because the required contract labor may be of limited availability. In other situations resources have to be provided not only for the preventive but also for corrective work, the latter often taking priority (leading inadvertently to changing from a preventive strategy to one based on operation-to-failure).

In short, the formulation of a maintenance strategy for a large plant is an involved and complex problem, the resolution of which requires a systematic, and pragmatic, approach. Such an approach – which the author calls *top-down bottom-up approach* (TDBUA) – is an integral part of business-centered maintenance. It is outlined in Table 9.1 and Figure 9.3.

Table 9.1 The TDBUA

Step 1 *(Top-down)*	*Understand the plant structure and the characteristics of its operation* *(see also Figure 9.3)* (a) Construct a process flow diagram and establish a plant inventory. (b) Understand the plant-operating characteristics and the production policy. (c) Rank units in order of their importance (criticality). (d) Establish the user requirements for the plant, plant sections and units (maintenance cost vs output/safety/longevity). (e) Understand the maintenance scheduling characteristics of the plant (using information from 1(a) and 1(b)).

Step 2
(Bottom-up)
	Establish a maintenance life plan for each unit
	(a) Identify the manufacturer's unit life plan (new plant) and/or the existing unit life plan and establish if they are likely to meet the requirements of 1(d) and (e) in a cost-effective way. If yes, record it as the unit life plan. If no, move to 2(b) for units with a low criticality ranking and to 2(c) for units with a medium/high criticality ranking.
	(b) For non-critical units establish a revised life plan based on previous experience and manufacturer's recommendations. The life plan should be based on essential maintenance only (lubrication and inspection) — a wait and see policy.
	(c) For units with a medium/high criticality ranking establish a revised life plan via the following procedure:
	    (i) Analyze the unit into its maintenance-causing items.
	    (ii) Determine the maintenance tasks for each identified item. Use analysis appropriate for the importance/complexity of the item, *viz.*:
	        ● For standard items (SRIs, CRIs, special items, etc.) use the items' characteristics coupled with experience and judgment.
	        ● For uncomplicated items (or uncomplicated situations within which the item is used) use — preventive maintenance principles and guidelines coupled with experience and judgment (see Section 7.2).
	        ● For complex and/or high cost and consequence of failure items use statistical cost modeling (see Exercise E7.3).
	        ● For complex high-level items and/or technically sophisticated items use FMEA to identify the items' failure modes and then the decision logic of Figure 6.20. Alternatively use RCM (see Chapter 8).
	    (iii) Assemble the maintenance tasks in the form of a unit life plan (see Tables 8.5 and 9.3). As far as possible the list should identify jobs with frequency, resource and method.
	(d) Identify the need for spare parts and/or repairable items for each unit. Link such requirements to the overall spares inventory policy.

Step 3 *(Bottom-up* *continuation)*	*Establish a maintenance schedule for the plant (see Figure 9.9)* (a) Prepare a plant listing of maintenance work by unit (based on the inventory of 1(a)). (b) Establish the minor preventive schedules. (c) Establish the major preventive schedules. (d) Estimate from 3(b) and (c) the resource requirements for the scheduled workload. Forecast from experience the expected non-schedulable workload. Consider the effect that resourcing the workload might have on the maintenance schedule, in particular, the shutdown schedule. Change the schedule as necessary.

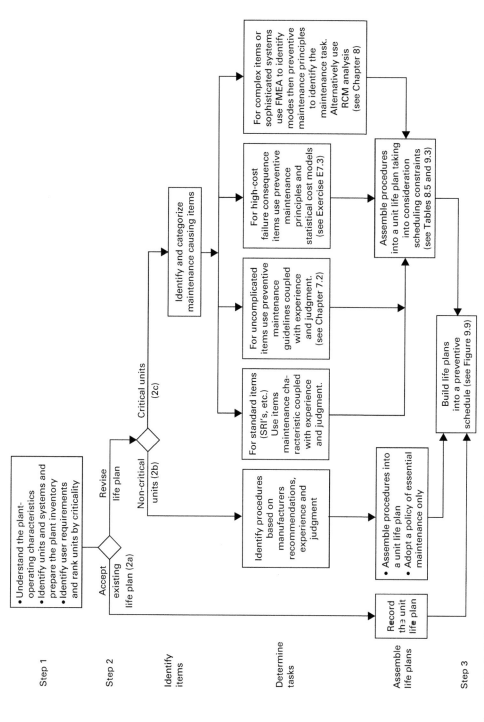

Figure 9.3 Building a life plan for a plant unit

R9.1   Refer to the aluminum smelter of Case study 2 of Chapter 12. It was established that a condition-based maintenance policy for the ring furnace pits was cost-effective but caused a scheduling/resourcing problem. Explain why? Outline the solution to this problem.

9.2 The TDBUA

9.2.1 Outline of TDBUA

The iterative approach outlined in Table 9.1 and Figure 9.3 encapsulates the *top-down* analysis of Chapters 4–6 and the *bottom-up* analysis of Chapters 6–8.

In *Step 1* – in which the relative importance (to safety and economics) of the constituent units of the plant is established – those units are first identified and then a process flow diagram of the plant drawn up. *User requirements* are identified using the approach outlined in Chapter 5 (see Figures 5.9 and 5.10) and the *maintenance scheduling characteristics* of the plant studied.

In *Step 2* maintenance tasks are identified and assembled into *unit life plans.* Much of the information derived during Step 1 is used for decision-making in Step 2.

In *Step 3* the information derived during Step 1, e.g. scheduling characteristics, is used in assembling the *preventive maintenance schedule.*

It must be emphasized that this approach should be regarded as a *guideline* – for assisting the maintenance department to formulate a new strategy or to revise an existing strategy. *Because of the large differences, in structure and in operating characteristics, between one physical asset system and another the approach might well need some modification in any particular case.*

Review Question

R9.2   Draw a single logic diagram to represent the TDBUA for reviewing the life plans and preventive schedule for an industrial plant.

9.2.2 Step 1: Understanding the structure and characteristics of operation of the plant (the 'top-down' stage of the analysis)

(a) Construct process flow diagrams and draw up a plant inventory
Construct process flow diagrams such as those of Figure 4.7 (modeling the complete system) and Figure 4.8 (modeling its subsystems). The process flow diagrams should indicate plant production rates, raw material storage capacity; inter-stage storage and final-product(s) storage capacities; the latter the way the units have been structured to perform process functions – e.g. at least one of the filtration units is needed to operate to fully meet the requirements of the reaction stream (see Figure 4.8). The process flow diagrams should also identify unit production rates,

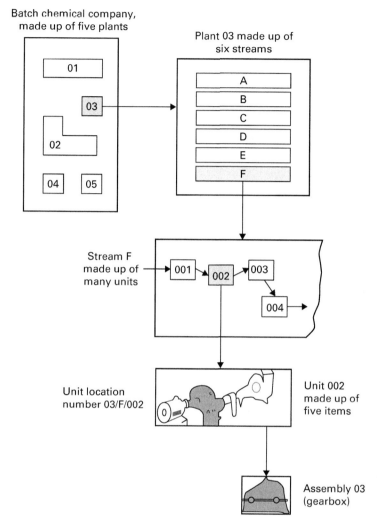

Figure 9.4 A simple hierarchical coding system

product-quality requirements and unit-operating patterns. Use the process flow diagrams to make up an inventory of the plant at unit level, tying up with the documentation system and essentially a list of units, with a description and an identity code (see Figure 9.4).

(b) *Understand the plant-operating characteristics and production policy*

Identify the production-operating policy for the plant (arriving, through discussion and investigation, at a description which is not disputed by any of the parties concerned). This should include the process relationship between all the plants making up the operation. In each case, it is necessary to identify the plant-operating pattern (shifts per day, days per week, weeks per year, with seasonal variations) and the expected product output, mix and quality.

Determine how other production factors (such as raw materials supply) and any external factors (such as safety regulations) influence the operating pattern of the plant and/or unit(s). Estimate the lost-production costs for the plant and for its units. Determine whether these are constant or variable (e.g. in power generation, they might depend on the time of day; in agrochemical production on the time of year). It will be instructive to use the batch chemical plant throughout this section to illustrate each of the steps of the procedure.

The batch chemical plant, which manufactures a wide range of similar organic chemicals, comprises six reaction streams, three making soluble products and three making insoluble ones. Each stream is dedicated to a specific range of chemicals and the streams are not inter-changeable. The finishing streams are also divided into those processing soluble and those processing insoluble products, and are only inter-changeable within these groupings. A plant path (as indicated in Figure 4.7 by the bold line) is a complete path through the plant from reaction process to packaging. A typical reaction stream, indicating the interrelationship of the units, is shown in Figure 4.8. The reaction process operates on a 48-hour batch cycle while the finishing process operates on a 168-hour semi-continuous cycle. A number of reaction cycles have to be completed before enough chemical is stored to allow the finishing process to begin.

In addition to the main product flows, the plant is supported by a full range of chemical and engineering services, i.e. primary and intermediate chemical supplies, salt, flake ice (not shown). The reaction streams are computer controlled and the rest of the plant is remotely controlled, hence the plant can be operated by a small production staff.

The production plan is complex because of the many products manufactured, but there is a balance throughout the plant which means there is little or no spare capacity in the finishing streams if all the reaction streams are in use. At present the plant is production limited.

(c) Rank the plant units in order of their criticality

It is important to rank the identified units (or systems) according to the impact of their failure on production and safety. Such a ranking is best based on the consequences of unit failure multiplied by the likelihood of unit failure:

Ranking of units by failure consequence		
Level 1	Failure causes an immediate and high production loss	Failure causes an immediate and high-risk safety hazard
Level 2	Failure causes an immediate but low production loss	Failure causes an environmental pollution hazard
Level 3	Failure causes a potential production loss	Failure causes a potential safety hazard
Level 4	Failure causes no immediate or potential production loss	Failure causes no safety hazard

A number of companies have constructed their own consequence/risk probability matrix. Figure 9.5 shows an example of such a matrix used by Woodside energy. Such a matrix would be suitable for ranking the units for the batch chemical plant.

Risk probability/consequence matrix

	People	Assets/production	Environment	Reputation	Probability					Action priority rating
					1	2	3	4	5	
					Never heard of in industry	Occurs in industry	Occurs in WEL	Occurs several times/ years in WEL	Occurs several times/ years at location	
F	No injury	No damage	No effect	No impact	Low					C4
E	Slight injury	Slight damage	Slight effect	Slight impact						C3
D	Minor injury	Minor damage	Minor effect	Limited impact		Medium				C2
C	Major injury	Local damage	Local effect	Considerable impact			High			
B	Single fatality	Major damage	Major effect	National impact						C0/1
A	Multiple fatality	Extensive damage	Massive effect	International impact				Intolerable		

(Consequence axis on left, Probability axis arrow pointing right)

Figure 9.5 Woodside consequence — risk probability matrix

(d) Identify the user requirement for each unit

Using the information gathered in (a) and (b), identify the plant user requirement. User requirements are identified via the approach outlined in Figures 5.9 and 5.10. The information derived at this stage ((b) and (c)) is essential for formulating, in Step 2, the unit life plans.

> The batch chemical plant can be considered as being made up of six mostly independent plant paths. Up until now an average availability level, for a plant path, of 92% has been achieved. Because of the demand for the product the maintenance objective for the next 2 years is to increase this figure to 96% at no extra maintenance cost. The plant is about 10 years old and has an expected life of 30 years or more, given appropriate life-extension work. The plant can be regarded as hazardous because of its employment of corrosive chemicals at high temperature and pressure. The company is safety conscious and has recently introduced Du Pont safety procedures and standards.

> The user requirements for the individual units are determined as outlined in Figure 5.10. This will be illustrated using reaction unit 3 as an example. This is a production-critical unit from which production want 100% reliability of operation over its 51-week operating period (i.e. 98% annual availability) and high product quality (i.e. conforming to written quality standards). In addition they have stated that the reactor should be maintained in such a way that it will operate safely for its expected life.

(e) Understand the maintenance scheduling characteristics of the plant (using information from (a) and (b))

(i) Identify the opportunities, the production windows, for offline maintenance. These may result from seasonal, monthly, weekly or daily variations in demand for the product. Some of these windows may be well defined in terms of frequency and duration, e.g. those arising from statutory pressure vessel inspection. In other cases, they may occur with much less certainty, e.g. due to fluctuating demand for the product. This is one of the most important characteristics influencing *opportunity scheduling*, such as may be desirable for a power station on two-shift operation tending to generate windows of up to 1-week duration, which occur with random incidence.

Production-related windows can arise:

- for a unit, or a group of units, because of production scheduling, e.g. in a multi-product plant where a given product mix does not require a particular production line;
- for the plant, or for units, because of production changes, e.g. catalyst changes;
- for a unit, or a group, because of the availability of redundant or standby equipment;
- for a unit, or a group, because of the availability of inter-stage storage and excess capacity;
- for the whole plant, or for units, because of statutory safety work.

  (ii) Identify 'domino' situations, where the effects of offline maintenance on a unit propagate along a batch process. Inter-stage storage prevents the whole line coming off and spreads the maintenance for the line over a longer period, i.e. it smooths peaks.

  (iii) Identify 'process chains' where, in order to maintain a single unit, a whole process involving many units needs to be taken offline. This either causes maintenance resource peaks or excessive planned downtime for maintenance.

Information from this step is essential to setting up the maintenance schedule (part of Step 3).

> The batch chemical plant is operated on a full-time basis, i.e. 168 hours per week. During the Christmas week, however, the plant is not used by production but the chemicals are held in process to minimize the effect of the holiday loss. There are no windows for long-term maintenance scheduling. There is an agreed maintenance shutdown of 1 week per plant path. Closer investigation shows that over any monthly period all the units in a plant path become available for maintenance, at short notice, for periods of between 2 and 8 hours. These windows arise randomly because of the batch nature of the process and the various washing-out procedures that are required between different products. They can be used for small offline jobs if there is good communication between production and maintenance.
>
> It will be instructive at this point to consider how the batch nature of the process influences the scheduling of the major offline maintenance. Because of the short cycle time (48 hours) of the reaction process each reaction stream has to be considered as a whole when major maintenance work needs to be carried out. In other words, if a single reaction unit is taken offline for 1 day, then the whole reaction stream has to be taken offline. This is not the case with the units in the finishing stream because the cycle times are much longer. Thus, if a reaction stream is taken offline for, say, 3 days, this window of maintenance opportunity moves down the finishing stream unit by unit, the 'knock-on' principle. The inter-changeability between finishing streams makes the scheduling of maintenance in this window a straightforward exercise.
>
> Because there is a little inter-changeability between reaction streams, and no spare capacity in a normal sales market, failure of the plant means high down-time cost.

Exercise

E9.1   Outline the maintenance scheduling characteristics for a plant within your own company. If possible use the process flow diagram of your answer to E4.2 to carry out this exercise. You should give particular attention to influence that the market demand for the product has on the production and maintenance schedules.

Review Questions

R9.3   Refer to the ammonia plant of Case study 1 of Chapter 12 and discuss in outline the maintenance scheduling problem. Do you consider there were any maintenance windows at plant level or at unit level?

R9.4   Refer to the bus fleet of Case study 6. Can you explain maintenance windows in this fleet situation? How were they used for scheduling maintenance work?

9.2.3 Step 2: Establishing a maintenance life plan for each unit of plant (the 'bottom-up' analysis)

Step 2 uses the information from Step 1, in particular from Part 1(c)–(e), in order to decide on the amount of preventive maintenance that can be justified for each unit (see Figure 9.6). Part 1(c) and (d) identifies critical units and provides essential economic

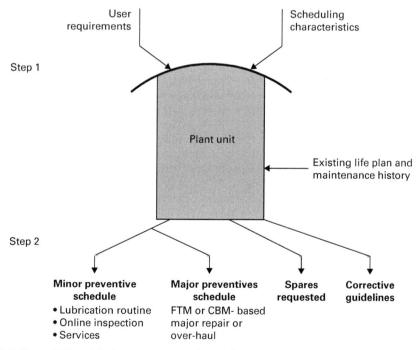

Figure 9.6 The relationship between steps 1 and 2

and safety information, Step 1(e) the essential scheduling information, e.g. in the case of the filtration system of Figure 4.8, the frequency of offline maintenance can be decided at unit level – taking a filtration unit offline does not affect other units. In other cases, Part 1(e) will have identified the incidence and duration of windows for individual units.

Step 2 now proceeds as follows (see Figure 9.3):

(a) Identify the manufacturer's (or the existing) life plan

Identify the life plan recommended by the manufacturer (or the existing life plan) and establish whether it is likely to meet the *user requirements* and can be carried out within the *scheduling opportunities*.

If the answers to these questions are yes, *record it as the current unit life plan.*

If the answer is no, move to 2(b) for units with a low criticality ranking and to 2(c) for units with a medium/high criticality ranking.

> Reaction unit 3 will be taken as the illustrative example so some information about its construction is now needed, i.e.:
>
> - *Material containment*: 1000 gallon mild-steel rubber-lined vessel built in ring sections.
> - *Agitation system*: DC variable-speed motor, worm reduction gearbox, mild-steel rubber-lined paddle agitator.
> - *Weigh vessel system*: Mild-steel rubber-lined vessel (300 gallon) – not shown, weighing mechanism, weigh scale instrumentation.
> - *Pumping system 1 (recirculation and filter press feed)*: DC variable-speed motor, monopump, pump protection instrumentation, mild-steel rubber-lined pipework, GRP/PVC line pipework, valves and fittings.
> - *Pumping system 2 (filter press feed)*: As for pumping system 1.
> - *Instrumentation and controls*: DP cell (level), thermocouple in tantalum clad pocket, steam injection posts (temperature), pH probe (chemical).
>
> The vessels are considered as pressurized because of the steam injection and are subject to a 2-yearly pressure vessel inspection.
>
> Considerable information is available on the failure and deterioration characteristics of the pumps, motors, gearboxes, etc., but this is not the case with the rubber lining, for which the most that can be said is that it has a life which can be as little as 3 and as large as 9 years, with a mean value of 6 years, and that the only method of monitoring its deterioration is by a combination of visual and tactile inspection (see Chapter 7, Example 1 under the Section 7.2.1). The time to onset, and the subsequent rate, of deterioration are also uncertain but it is known that the rate is slow and the lead time to eventual failure exceeds 1 year. A lining inspection and repair takes 2½ days and a replacement of 10 days.
>
> The existing life plan was not documented; it was based on performing the essential lubrication online and undertaking major maintenance in the 7-day annual shutdown, when the main job was the inspection and repair of the rubber lining. Apart from this the work was carried out on an *ad hoc* basis and there had been a considerable level of corrective work – some of which had caused unavailability. The current reactor availability is around 90% and many of the failures cause considerable disruption. It has also been noted that the condition of the reactor is below specification.
>
> *Clearly, the existing life plan of the reactor is in need of radical review.*

(b) Establish a revised life plan for units with a low criticality ranking
   The less important units of plant (low criticality ranking – which in some situations could well be the majority) might only require a minimum level of maintenance (servicing and simple inspection tasks, i.e. minor maintenance) – a *'wait and see' policy*. Such information will mostly be provided by the manufacturer or will be decided on from engineering experience.

(c) Establish a revised life plan for units with a medium/high criticality ranking
   The principles associated with this step were outlined in Chapters 6 and 7, using the example of a chemical reactor. The same example will therefore be used here:

   (i) Analyze the units into their maintenance-causing items An example of this is outlined in Figure 9.7. A more pragmatic approach might be to identify the maintenance-causing items via the manufacturer's manuals or drawings.

   (ii) Determine the best maintenance task for each identified item It can be seen from Table 9.1 and Figure 9.3 that a number of approaches/techniques can be used to determine the best maintenance task:

   ● For standard items (simple replaceable items, SRIs; complex replaceable items, CRIs; special items; etc.) the maintenance task can be identified using their category characteristics (see Figures 6.5 and 9.8) coupled with experience and judgment, e.g. the maintenance task for the gearbox of Figure 9.8 might be, 'replace and recondition' via some form of vibration monitoring and/or oil monitoring.

   ● For uncomplicated items and situations use preventive maintenance guidelines coupled with experience and judgment. For example, see the rubber-lining analysis of Section 7.2 resulting in the maintenance task reproduced here as Table 9.2.

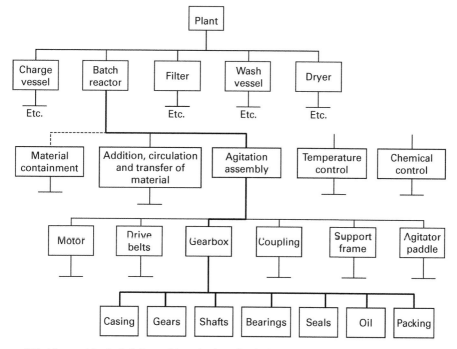

Figure 9.7 Hierarchical division of batch chemical plant

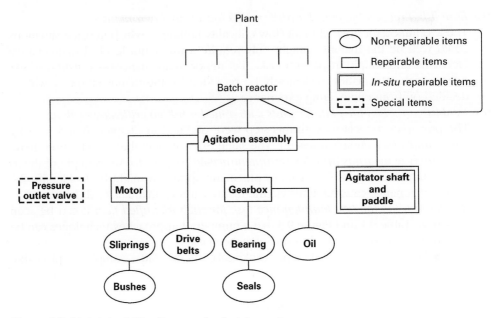

Figure 9.8 Maintainability diagram for batch reactor

Table 9.2 Maintenance task(s) for the vessel lining

Item	Timing	On/offline	Frequency	Time and labor	Action
Reaction vessel rubber lining	Visual inspection and touch	Offline	Annually at agreed shutdown	3 days 2 fitters	*Maintenance action:* Repair as necessary
		Offline Continuation of shutdown	2 yearly	1 day 2 men	*Secondary action:* Replace lining 8 days 4 fitters 2 men

- For complex and/or high-cost and consequence items use statistical cost modeling (see Exercise E7.3) the wear plate of the chipping machine.
- For complex high-level items and/or technically sophisticated items use some form of failure modes and effects analysis (FMEA) to identify failure modes and then the decision logic illustrated in Figure 6.20 (or the reliability-centered maintenance (RCM) decision logic used in the example of Section 8.3) to identify the best task.

(iii) *Assemble the maintenance tasks into a unit life plan*

One way of recording a unit life plan would be in the form of the listing shown in Table 9.3. *This is a statement of the maintenance work required on the reactor over its expected lifetime.* The list should also be in a form suitable for assimilation

Table 9.3 Extract from reactor life plan

Item	Timing	On/offline	Frequency	Time and labor	Initial maintenance action	On/offline	Expected frequency	Time and labor	Action
Material Containment *Rubber lining*	Visual inspection and touch	**OFF**	Y (at agreed shutdown)	**3 days** 2 fitters	*In-situ* repair	**OFF**	2Y (WO)	**1 day** 2 trade assistants	Replace lining 8 days 4 fitters + 2 trades assistants
Steel casing (pressure vessel)	Statutory inspection	**OFF**	2Y (at agreed shutdown)	**2 days** 2 fitters 1 inspector	*In-situ* repair of jacket and joints as necessary	**OFF**	4Y (WO)	**2 days** 2 fitters	Replace vessel on condition
Agitation System *AC motor* Bearings	SPM trend monitoring	On	2M	Minutes 1 inspector	Replace motor on condition	Off	4Y (R)	*1 hour* 1 fitter 1 electrician	Recondition motor
Greasing	Fixed time	On	2M	Minutes 1 greaser	—	—	—	—	—
Gearbox Bearings	SPM trend monitoring	On	2M	Minutes 1 inspector	Replace box on condition	*Off*	4Y (R)	*4 hours* 2 fitters 2 riggers	Recondition gearbox
Greasing	Fixed-time lubrication	On	2M	Minutes 1 greaser	—	—	—	—	—
Gears	Lubrication, oil trend monitoring	On	2M	Minutes 1 inspector	Replace box on condition	*Off*	?	*4 hours* 2 fitters 2 riggers	Recondition gearbox

(Continued)

Table 9.3 (Continued)

Item	Timing	On/offline	Frequency	Time and labor	Initial maintenance action	On/offline	Expected frequency	Time and labor	Action
Gland	Visual inspection	On	1M	Minutes 1 inspector	Adjust gland	On	6M	Minutes 1 fitter	Repack gland on condition
Weigh vessel system *Weighing mechanism*	Visual condition checking	*Off*	6M	*1 hour 1 inspector*	Calibrate mechanism	*Off*	1Y	*30 minutes 1 inspector*	Recondition mechanism on condition
Powder feeder	Visual condition	*Off*	6M	*1 hour 1 inspector*	Calibrate mechanism	*Off*	1Y	*30 minutes 1 inspector*	Recondition mechanism on condition
Hydraulic drive	Lubrication, oil trend monitoring	*Off*	2M	*Minutes 1 inspector*	Replace drive unit	*Off*	3Y	*1 hour 1 fitter*	Recondition drive unit
Valves *Type A (5 off)*	Fixed time	*Off*	2Y	*1 hour 1 fitter (per valve)*	Replace valve				Recondition valves (internal)
Type B (10 off)	Fixed time	*Off*	5Y	*1 hour 1 fitter (per valve)*	Replace valve				Recondition valves (internal)
Type C (pressure relief)	Fixed time	On	1M	Inspection (minutes)	Proof test				Replace and recondition as necessary

SPM: shock-pulse monitoring; WO: wear-out; R: random; Y: yearly; M: monthly; On: online schedule; *Off*: window schedule; **OFF**: shutdown schedule.

into the overall *plant maintenance schedule*, so it will be necessary to adopt standardized frequencies (based on calendar or running time) for maintenance work – in particular for offline work which should link with the information coming through from Step 1(e). Referring to the reactor example, the following actions might also be helpful:

- Divide the maintenance tasks listed in Table 9.3 into online and offline. Online tasks, by definition, are independent of production, and should be considered for scheduling on a plant- or area-wide basis.
- As far as possible, group the offline tasks (including inspection-based ones) by trade and periodicity into 'jobs', and formulate the instructions and times for them, e.g.:
  - Mech. A Service, monthly 5 hours, job code 125M;
  - Elect. B Service, 3 monthly (inspection-based), 8 hours, job code 127E; etc.

  For convenience of work planning a 'job' can be regarded as any maintenance task (or combination of tasks) taking, say, less than 24 hours (three shifts) and needing no more than a few artisans. A 'job' can be handled on a single work order card. Work taking longer than 24 hours and/or requiring many artisans can be classified as a major repair, reconditioning or overhaul, and can be made up a number of 'jobs' – perhaps arranged into a standard package with bar chart.

  It is also useful to identify the 'jobs' that could be carried out in the *opportunity* created by the failure of a particular item.

  The unit life plan should be reviewed periodically in the light of maintenance cost and reliability performance (see Chapter 10).

(d) *Identify the need for spare parts and repairable items*

The analysis of Step 2(b) and (c) identifies the need for spare parts and for reconditioning. Such information can also come direct from the manufacturer's manual.

In general, the maintenance engineer decides what spare parts are to be held and their specifications.

The spares inventory policy is a function not only of demand for the various parts but also of such factors as the opportunity for inter-changing parts. In general, this task is the responsibility of the 'stock controller'.

> For the reactor, we extend analysis such as that of Table 9.3, i.e. repair and/or replace decisions lead to the need for spare items or components. For example, in the case of the AC motor of the agitation assembly it is necessary to hold the complete motor. The spare components would be held only if the motor is to be reconditioned in-house.

The factors influencing reconditioning policy are also complex. For example, deciding whether to recondition or to replace with new may be based on a type of life-cycle analysis of the alternatives. Once again, an influencing factor is the rate of demand for an item and, therefore, it will be necessary to determine the number of identical items on site (see Figure 6.9). Using this information the design of the reconditioning cycle should address such aspects as:

- the determination of the reconditioning facilities needed;
- the determination of the manpower needed;

- the determination of the spare parts needed;
- the total number of floating items;
- the inventory policy for the reconditioned parts, the logistics of moving reconditioned parts around the cycle.

9.2.4 Step 3: Establishing a preventive maintenance schedule for the plant (*putting it all together*)

This step is concerned with deciding on the best way to schedule the hundreds (perhaps thousands) of individual tasks/jobs identified in the unit life plans, taking into consideration the maintenance scheduling characteristics identified in Step 1(e), i.e. the effect that offline work might have on production and on maintenance resources. The scheduling procedure is shown in Figure 9.9 (see also Table 9.1 and Figure 9.3).

(a) Prepare a listing, by unit, of maintenance work for the plant
    Prepare a list (the *Main List*) of all the maintenance work identified for every unit of plant, arranging the list in the order of process flow. This should tie up with the plant inventory of Step 1(a) (see also Figure 9.4).

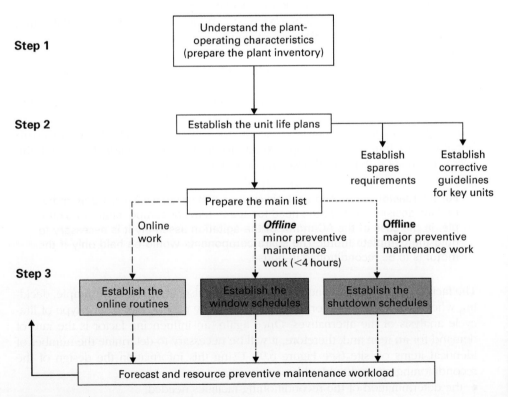

Figure 9.9 Step 3: The scheduling procedure

For the reaction stream F of Figure 4.8 the main list would be made up of the life plans of each of the items listed below:

Reaction stream F	
03F001	Reaction unit 1
03F002	Reaction unit 2
03F003	Reaction unit 3
03F004	Preparation unit
03F005	Filtration unit 1
03F006	Filtration unit 2
03F007	Dispersion unit
Etc.	

(b) Formulate the minor preventive maintenance schedules

This is made up of the online work and minor offline preventive work:

(i) Extract the online work (mainly inspection tasks) and group the jobs according to trade, geographic area or plant type, and frequency. Prepare job instructions for these routines. Such work can be scheduled independently of production and is made up of:

- operator monitoring routines;
- trade-force inspection routines (line patrolling);
- instrument-based routines (undertaken by specialist internal or contract resources).

Such work is particularly important because it often leads to the identification of the need for major offline work.

For the reaction stream online routines can be extracted from the main list and classified by trade and frequency. In the case of the reactor this would be as follows:

Fitter	Inspector		Greaser
M Visual inspection and adjustment of agitation system gland	M Proof test type C pressure relief valve		2M AC resistor bearings Gearbox bearings
	2M SPM AC motor bearings SPM gearbox bearings Lubrication monitor gearbox Lubrication monitor hydraulic drive		

M: monthly; Y: yearly.
Inspection and lubrication routines are established from this list.

(ii) The remainder of the work in this category is made up of simple offline inspection or lubrication and the replacement of *simple items* (i.e. routine services). It is undertaken frequently and is of short duration and can almost always be fitted into production windows. *It is essential that such work is carried out because it is directed at controlling the reliability of the complex items.*

In this the reaction stream, window maintenance jobs can be classified as those that can be carried out in the production windows (i.e. jobs of less than 4-hour duration) and those that do not require the plant to be taken offline. The procedures that can be carried out in windows of opportunity are also listed by unit, and are grouped by trade and frequency, e.g.:

03F001   REACTION UNIT 1

6M Inspection   Inspector, 2.5 hours
    Visually inspect weighing mechanism, and adjust and calibrate as necessary
    Visually inspect powder feeder and adjust and calibrate as necessary, etc.
2Y Valve replacement   Fitter, 5 hours
    Replace type A valves (5 off)

The identified jobs are then scheduled for each trade and for a complete year. A bar chart as in Figure 9.10 is often used to assist this last process. Where there is a definite production window the job can be scheduled to the day. If the timing of the window is not know with certainty the job can be scheduled to the nearest week and fitted in when the window occurs. Offline window work that is triggered by the output from condition monitoring routines, e.g. gearbox replacement, is not scheduled until the need has been thus indicated.

(c) *Formulate the major preventive maintenance schedules*
    This is a complex problem the solution of which will be different for different plant. The following pragmatic approach attempts to identify the key points of scheduling:
    (i) Where the required frequency of occurrence and duration of the work are less than those of the expected windows (e.g. see the machine shop case, Figure 9.11). This is by far the easiest situation for scheduling. The offline work can be scheduled at

Reaction stream weekly workload

Figure 9.10 Extract from reaction streams preventive maintenance schedule

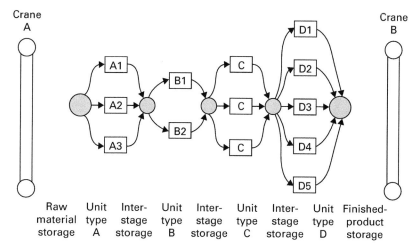

Figure 9.11 Scheduling characteristics of a machine shop

Plant structure:
Units in parallel/series structure with spare capacity
at unit level plus inter-stage storage. Many unit windows.

Plant-operating pattern
Single shift 5 day-week (sales limited). Many plant windows.

Planned maintenance can be scheduled at unit level,
smoothing the workload over a long period.

unit level and spread out in order to smooth the workload. *This in turn makes for easier work planning and provides the opportunity for better resource utilization.*

(ii) Where the required frequency of occurrence and duration of offline work are greater than those of the expected windows (e.g. see the base-load power station case, Figure 9.12). Identify and schedule the work from the main list that can be carried out in the maintenance windows (in this case windows occurring because of the presence of standby or redundant units, e.g. as with most pulverizing mills). The remaining offline work can only be carried out with the plant shut down.* The most straightforward situation is where most of the offline jobs are time based. *The time between plant shutdowns can be based on the shortest unit running period* (in our example the time between statutory safety inspections of the boiler). As far as possible, other jobs are fitted into this period and into multiples of it.

Scheduling the plant shutdown on a time basis has considerable advantages for organizing the labor to match large work peaks.

There are numerous variations that can complicate this situation. For example, it is often possible to extend the shortest running period by applying condition-based

*In this case 'plant' means a boiler-turbine-alternator stream or 'set'.

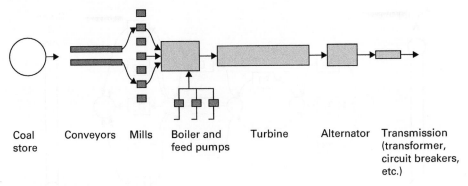

| Coal store | Conveyors | Mills | Boiler and feed pumps | Turbine | Alternator | Transmission (transformer, circuit breakers, etc.) |

Plant structure
Units in parallel/series structure with spare capacity on parallel sections, e.g. mills, feed pumps. No inter-stage storage.

Plant-operating pattern
Continuous except for maintenance (production limited) – no plant windows. Back up plant to cover but much less efficient.

Planned maintenance scheduled by category
(i) online inspection schedule at item level (since independent operation) into a smooth workload over long period.

(ii) Window schedule at unit level (e.g. mills) into a smooth workload over long period.

(iii) Shutdown schedule at plant level based on safety inspection of boilers (3 years). Workload dominated by shutdown peaks (up to 1300 men).

Figure 9.12 Scheduling characteristics of a power station

maintenance to the critical items. However, this might shorten the planning lead time. A major shutdown is often chosen to coincide with, and be an extension of, a major window.

For the batch chemical plant an extract from the maintenance shutdown plan for a reactor stream is shown in Table 9.4. The initial running time is based on the shutdown work for reaction unit 3 and the preparation unit. In subsequent years the longer-term maintenance will be fitted into this shutdown, giving the following major shutdown schedule:

Yearly	Shutdown list A (reaction and preparation unit)
2 yearly	Shutdown list B (list A plus lining repair, plus statutory inspection)
4 yearly	Shutdown list C (list B plus steel casing repair)

Other work is fitted into the shutdown as necessary.

The yearly shutdown of the reaction stream also determines the plant path shutdown, which starts with the reaction stream shutdown (typically of 4-day duration). Work on the remaining plant sections and units is carried out as the window is 'knocked down' the path.

The plant comprises six 'plant paths' and in order to spread the load evenly over the year (to make the best use of in-house labor), there should be a

Table 9.4 Extract from the shutdown plan for a reaction stream

Unit	Item	Timing	On/offline	Frequency	Time and labor	Initial maintenance action	On/offline	Expected frequency	Time and labor	Secondary maintenance action
03F003	Rubber lining	Fixed time (visual inspection and touch)	Offline	Y (At agreed shutdown*)	3 days 2 fitters	Repair lining as necessary	Offline	2Y	1 additional day (4 days total) 2 fitters	Replace in-situ on condition
03F004	Rubber lining	Fixed time (visual inspection and touch)	Offline	Y (At agreed shutdown of unit 3)	3 days 2 fitters	Repair lining as necessary	Offline	2Y	1 day 2 fitters	Replace in-situ on condition
03F001	Steel casing	Statutory inspection	Offline	2Y (At agreed shutdown of unit 3)	2 days 2 fitters 1 inspector	Repair jacket and joints as necessary	Offline	4Y	2 days 2 fitters	Replace vessel on condition
03F002	Steel casing	Statutory inspection	Off	2Y (At agreed shutdown of unit 3)	2 days 2 fitters 1 inspector	Repair jacket and joints as necessary	Offline	4Y	2 days 2 fitters	Replace vessel on condition

Y: yearly.
*Schedule other maintenance work (window and deferred) into this shutdown as convenient.

major shutdown of a plant path every 2 months; the flexibility of the finishing stream aids such scheduling.

(iii) *Opportunity scheduling*

Because of the uncertainty associated with both the frequency and duration of windows (and sometimes of the incidence of the offline work) it is inevitable that the scheduling of the offline work will involve a considerable level of opportunity taking, e.g. taking advantage of failure occurrences, or of unexpected windows, to carry out planned preventive and/or corrective maintenance. Perhaps the most difficult situation to schedule for is where plants generate a considerable level of major offline work due to randomly occurring failure – despite the application of preventive maintenance.

In such situations opportunity scheduling is perhaps the most important policy. The more recent computerized work planning and scheduling packages greatly facilitate this.

(d) Resourcing the workload

The ability of the organization to resource the maintenance workload has been surveyed in the discussion of Step 3(a)–(c). The principal factors affecting this are the planning lead time, the size of resource peaks and the availability of contract labor. Thus, where the resources are unable (or cannot be afforded) to meet the major outage demand the schedule would need to be revised. In the case of a power station example (see Figure 9.12), this would depend on the ability to use contract labor. If that was inhibited by industrial relations factors the shutdown schedule would need modification.

The larger the work peaks the longer needs to be the planning lead time. In the case of a typical power station, planning a shutdown takes 12 months – so fixed-time shutdowns are invariably used.

Scheduling Guidelines

1. When the maintenance windows provide more time than the planned offline preventive maintenance work requires, the aim of scheduling is directed at smoothing the workload.
2. When the planned offline preventive maintenance work requires more time to carry out than the maintenance windows provide, the aim of scheduling is directed at minimizing lost-production costs.
3. When the planned offline preventive maintenance work requires more time to carry out than the maintenance windows provide, opportunity maintenance should be used (where possible) to reduce the shutdown workload.

Exercise

E9.2   Use the principles and concepts of Section 9.2.4 to revise the existing maintenance scheduling procedures for your plant which were identified in Exercise E9.1.

Review Questions

R9.5   In terms of scheduling explain the difference between a plant where the duration of offline work is less than frequency and duration of windows and a plant where the duration of offline work is more than the frequency and duration of windows.

R9.6   The ammonia plant in Case study 1 of Chapter 12 was some 30 years old and had not been maintained well for at least 10 years. Use this case study to explain what is meant by a 'catch-up policy'.

9.3 Comments on the TDBUA

The TDBUA was used to revise the existing life plans and preventive schedule in order to achieve the maintenance objectives, e.g. to improve plant output at reduced maintenance cost (see Chapter 5).

A way of representing the situation for an existing plant is shown in Figure 9.13. The plant has been operated for a number of years and the maintenance strategy had become reactive, point 1.

An additional problem is that plant that has been maintained reactively will be 'out of condition', i.e. there will be a considerable level of catch-up maintenance necessary to bring the plant back up to an acceptable level (to say, the original equipment manufacturers' specification). Any revision of maintenance strategy should be preceded by a plant condition audit, i.e. a ranking of units by their condition.

The maintenance manager is faced with two interrelated problems. He needs a catch-up strategy to bring the plant back up to condition, i.e. to get from points 1 to 2 in Figure 9.13. He also needs to revise the life plans and preventive schedule to hold the condition of plant from point 2 into the future.

The catch-up strategy could be carried out over a short period (see Figure 9.13) by using high levels of contract labor – perhaps as part of a major shutdown (see Case study 7 of Chapter 12). Alternatively, it could be spread over a much longer period by using a priority system based on the 'unit condition ranking' in conjunction with the criticality ranking of the TDBUA (see Figure 9.14).

The main use of the TDBUA is to revise the life plans and preventive schedule in order to operate a proactive maintenance strategy from point 2 into the future.

The batch chemical plant example did not consider the catch-up problem. The following comments related to whether the revised life plans and preventive schedule (established via the TDBUA) are an improvement over the former? Will the availability, product quality and equipment condition improve at no increase in resource cost? This is best answered by reference to the reactor and reaction stream examples.

The maintenance strategy has moved away from 'annual shutdown with ad hoc planning' to 'condition based' founded on the following three interrelated preventive schedules:
 (i) Online lubrications and inspections.
 (ii) Services and minor maintenance undertaken in production windows.
 (iii) A major plant shutdown.

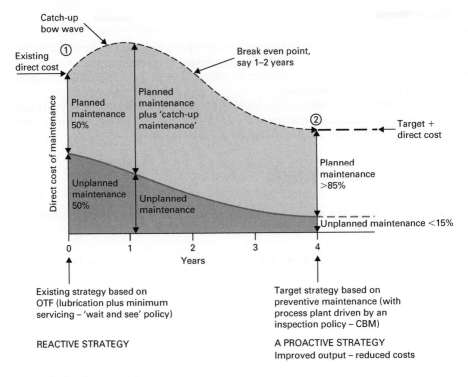

Figure 9.13 Catch-up strategy

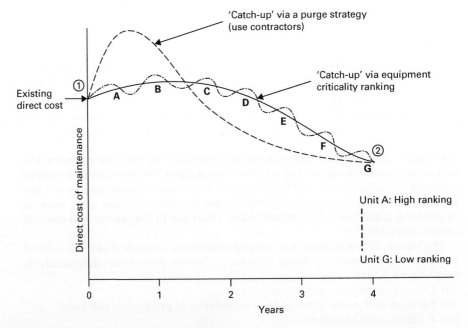

Figure 9.14 Alternative catch-up strategies

Although the expected level of improvement is not easily quantified it is clear that the emphasis on condition-based maintenance should both minimize unexpected failures and improve the efficiency of shutdown planning. What should result from the new strategy is a movement from situation (a) of Figure 9.15 to situation (b).

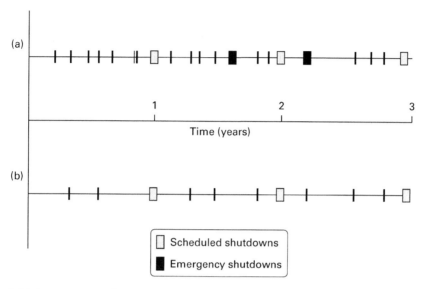

Figure 9.15 Improvement in operating pattern: (a) existing operating pattern and (b) operating pattern after strategy revision

It should also be emphasized that documenting the life plans as in Table 9.3 greatly facilitates the application of opportunity maintenance. This is especially so if the documentation is computerized. In the advent of an unexpected maintenance window (or a failure of some other part of the reaction stream) the maintenance schedules can be used to extract the maintenance jobs for the reactor that are outstanding at that time.

Review Question

R9.7   By using the ammonia plant in Case study 12 explain what you understand by 'opportunity scheduling'. What are the difficulties in using opportunity scheduling? Why has modern computer planning software made opportunity scheduling easier?

9.4 Using the TDBUA

To date, perhaps the most successful application of this was to an up-rated and modernized blast furnace which was part of an integrated steelworks. The main lessons learned were the following:

- Such a project is best initiated and co-ordinated by a small inter-disciplinary project team with a project leader.

- Step 1 must involve the senior levels of production and maintenance management. Perhaps the most important part of this is 1(c) – *Determining the user requirements*. There is a sense in which the result of this step should be regarded as a *contract* between maintenance and production.
- The bottom-up phase – in particular Step 2 *(Formulating a life plan for each unit)* – must involve maintenance supervision, artisans and plant operators who are concerned with the particular units of plant under scrutiny. *This is essential for benefiting from 'local knowledge' and for promoting future commitment to the life plan.* It is important that maintenance supervision (and, to a lesser extent, artisans and operators) is regularly updated on the principles, concepts and techniques of preventive maintenance.

Review Question Guidelines

R9.1   There were over 1000 pits in total most of which had started life at the same time. The failure distribution of the pits time-to-failure (need for relining) was time dependent. Thus, a condition-based maintenance policy would generate a workload that was also time dependent and would peak as shown in Figure 9.9. The company would be unable to resource such a peak — manpower and materials. For this reason a fixed-time repair policy was used and the pits scheduled to smooth the workload.

R9.2   Use a combination of Figure 9.3 (Table 9.1) and Figure 9.9.

R9.3   The ammonia plant has no plant-level windows. (The catalyst life has been extended past 5 years.) The only windows available are at item level, i.e. there are numerous duplicate pumps. A decision had been taken to run the plant as long as possible before major maintenance. In order to do this all the pressure vessels had been analyzed via FMEA to identify failure modes and failure consequences, i.e. to ensure they would operate safely for a designated operating period of 4 years. The life plans for the individual units of plant was based on this operating period. Thus, the total workload for the plant was divided into offline routines (inspections and services on duplicate pumps, etc. and control loops) and a major 4-yearly shutdown of the complete plant.

R9.4   In the case of the bus fleet windows were available in a number of forms. The excess number of buses over maximum demand created windows for major maintenance. There was also an excess of major assemblies in the reconditioning loop (e.g. engines). Finally, the demand for buses over the week created windows over the weekend and during the lower demand periods during weekdays (see Figure 9.3).

R9.5   Where offline work is less than the duration of the windows (see Figure 9.11) scheduling is relatively straightforward. In general, the scheduling aim is to smooth the workload.
    Where offline work is greater than the duration of the windows (see Figure 9.12) scheduling becomes more difficult. A decision has to be taken about when (FTM, CBM or opportunity) and for how long the plant needs to be taken offline. As far as possible all work that can be carried out outside these shutdowns is identified and carried out in windows. In such situations the aim of scheduling is to minimize unavailability costs.

R9.6   Some 8 years before the audit was carried out a decision had been taken by the ammonia plant management to shut down the plant after 4 more years of operation. As a result of this decision maintenance was neglected for a number of years. At the time of the audit this neglect was obvious and much of the plant was below an acceptable condition. For example, the syn-gas compressor was way out of manufacturers' specification, see my comments in Case study 1 of Chapter 12. This plant had to be brought back up to specification, i.e. a catch-up strategy otherwise a preventive maintenance regime would not be effective.

R9.7   If the ammonia plant fails unexpectedly (or comes offline for production reasons) the *opportunity* is taken to carry out offline maintenance on other areas of the plant. This should improve availability in the long term. The main difficulties associated with opportunity scheduling is the discipline required to ensure that outstanding work is pre-planned. In addition, it may be difficult to resource the work (in particular man power) at short notice. Modern computer planning software has made opportunity planning more viable. All outstanding jobs can be pre-planned and held on the computer against the units they are associated with. They can be pulled off at short notice.

PART 4

Controlling plant reliability

10 Controlling plant reliability

'To make a mistake is only human; to persist in a mistake is idiotic.'
Cicero, 106 bc Roman philosopher

Chapter aims and outcomes

To describe a maintenance management system that can be used to monitor and control the reliability of an industrial plant.

On completion of this chapter you should be able to:

- understand the concepts and principles of plant reliability control and be able to draw a schematic diagram to model its operation;
- appreciate that poor maintenance is only one of the three main causes that adversely affect the reliability of equipment, the other two being maloperation and poor design;
- understand the systems that promote the proactive control of equipment reliability and the reactive control of equipment reliability.

Chapter route map

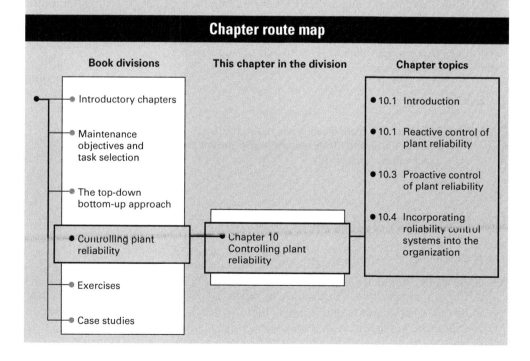

Book divisions	This chapter in the division	Chapter topics
Introductory chapters		10.1 Introduction
Maintenance objectives and task selection		10.1 Reactive control of plant reliability
The top-down bottom-up approach		10.3 Proactive control of plant reliability
Controlling plant reliability	Chapter 10 Controlling plant reliability	10.4 Incorporating reliability control systems into the organization
Exercises		
Case studies		

10.1 Introduction

The previous chapters have dealt with the task of formulating the life plan for each of the units that make up a plant (see Figure 9.1) and a maintenance schedule for the plant as a whole (see Figure 9.2). Little has been said, however, about reviewing the performance of the 'plant units' to determine whether the life plan is effective, i.e. whether the life plan is providing the desired output as regards all its various aspects (plant availability, product quality, safety, etc.). This, *the control of plant reliability*, is probably the most important maintenance control activity. Once again, the batch chemical plant will serve as the vehicle for explaining it (see Figure 4.7).

Figure 10.1 outlines the mechanisms for controlling the reliability of one of the refinery units, and illustrates the classic ideas of *reactive* control – using the feedback of operational and maintenance data – and also highlights *proactive* control via the feedforward of ideas for reliability and maintenance improvement.

Exercise

E10.1   Select a unit from your own plant (perhaps the unit you selected to answer E4.1) and draw a schematic model that illustrates the idea of 'plant reliability control'.

10.2 Reactive control of plant reliability

The requirements of the systems (see Figure 10.1), are to:

(a) monitor the output parameters of each unit (e.g. reliability (mean time to failure (MTTF)), maintainability (mean time to repair (MTTR)), plant condition, etc.) and some of the input conditions (e.g. whether the unit life plan is being carried out to specification and at anticipated cost);

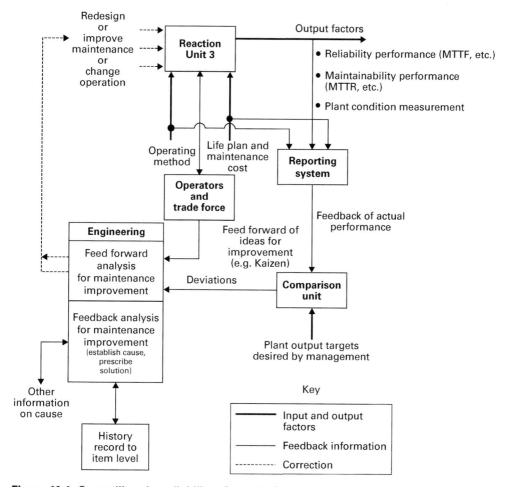

Figure 10.1 Controlling the reliability of a unit of plant

(b) determine the root cause of any failure [*note that a control system for this must encompass several departments because the cause could originate in production (maloperation), in engineering (poor design) or in maintenance*];
(c) prescribe the necessary corrective action.

At plant path level of the batch plant, control can be envisaged as in Figure 10.2, i.e. each unit having its own control system. Once again, the difficulty is caused by the multiplicity of units which make up a major industrial plant, and therefore of control systems needed. The consequent data processing has been made manageable by modern computer technology which can easily handle the many independent control mechanisms. The difficulty, however, usually lies not in the processing but in the acquisition of the data. Company management may therefore need to concentrate control effort on selected units, those which they deem critical; for the rest they may use the maintenance costing system

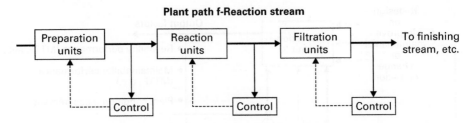

Plant path f-Reaction stream

Figure 10.2 Controlling the reliability of a plant

to identify the most troublesome, e.g. those of highest high maintenance cost, poorest product quality, highest downtime, and so on.

10.3 Proactive control of plant reliability

Figure 10.1 also illustrates the proactive approach, which differs from the reactive in that it does not wait for failures or for high-cost problems to occur before taking action. The basic idea is that all members of the organization (but especially the shop-floor) should continuously seek ways of improving unit reliability, and hence output, safety, and so forth.

The Japanese call this *kaizen*. The shop-floor form small inter-disciplinary (but plant-orientated) teams to improve the reliability of selected units. (Preventive maintenance is interpreted literally – to prevent the need for *any* maintenance, by design-out and other actions.) Upper management circles ensure that the idea is promoted and accepted throughout the organization. This ensures that middle management circles give assistance and advice to the shop-floor teams as necessary.

Review Question

R10.1 Use the model you developed in Exercise 10.1 (or Figure 10.1) to explain the difference between proactive and reactive control of plant reliability.

10.4 Incorporating reliability control systems into the organization

Although, Figures 10.1 and 10.2 are useful for understanding the mechanisms of reliability control, it still remains to incorporate these ideas into a scheme for a working maintenance organization. This is shown in the general model, Figure 10.3, and the application of this to a chemical plant organization, which is outlined in Figure 10.4.

It can be seen that there are several interrelated levels of plant reliability control in an organization, each with its own responsibilities and roles. The first operates between

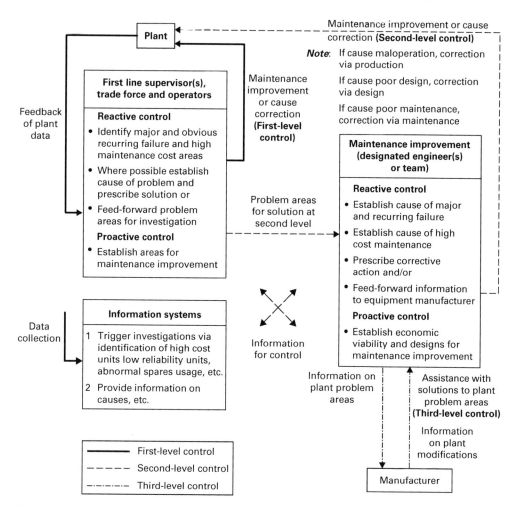

Figure 10.3 General model of reliability control within an organization

the shop-floor and supervisors, and to a large extent is independent of the information systems – however a history record can be important here. This level of control is particularly useful because there is a quicker reaction to problems. As the personnel involved may be present at a repair, and can discuss it with operators and artisans, there is likely to be first-hand knowledge of the cause of failure. In addition, it is at this level that the main thrust of proactive control operates; if the personnel involved cannot establish the cause and/or prescribe and implement a solution, then the problem is passed up to the second level.

The second level of control operates through designated engineers and/or a maintenance investigation team. To be effective, this requires the integration of information systems and engineering investigation. The information system (computerized) should be designed around the ideas illustrated in Figure 10.5, and should therefore be capable of identifying problem units, and hence triggering corrective investigation within

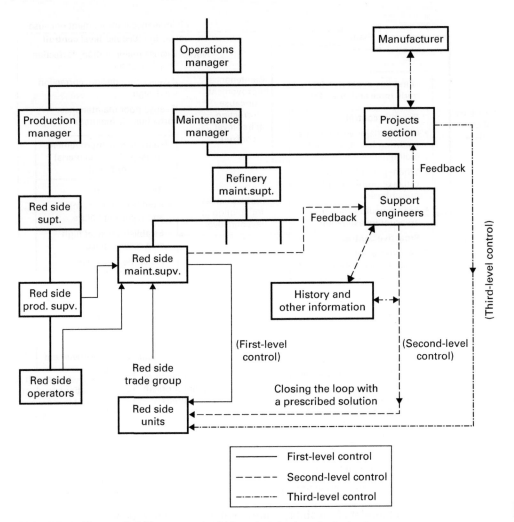

Figure 10.4 Plant reliability control within a batch chemical plant

the organization (satisfying point (a) of the control requirements). The major effort, however, will lie in the diagnosis of failure causes (point (b)), by interrogating the plant history, and in the prescription of corrective action (point (c)), an effort which will need to come from the investigative engineers.

In general, it is the root cause of any problem which will be sought, and because investigate effort is necessarily limited only a small number of problem items can be looked into at any one time. The criterion for selecting these is usually based on some kind of equipment ranking, by downtime, direct cost or failure frequency (see, e.g. Figures 10.6(a) and (b) which show such rankings, Pareto analyses, for a mining vehicle fleet) [1].

A possible third level of control lies in the contact between the various users of a given type of equipment and its manufacturer. This offers the opportunity for maintenance information to be collected from a much larger pool of experience. However,

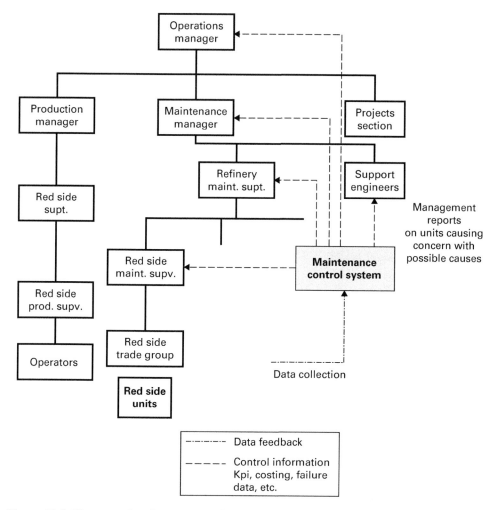

Figure 10.5 The use of maintenance information systems for reliability control

because more than one user company will, in practice, be involved it is the least effective level of control. The onus for ensuring the success of such an activity rests with the equipment manufacturer.

Review Questions

R10.2   Explain the importance of 'human factors' in the successful operation of the control of plant reliability. Discuss total productive maintenance (TPM) in terms of proactive control. (You may need firstly to carry out a brief search on TPM.)

R10.3   Draw a simple model to explain how plant reliability control might operate in a traditional functional organization, i.e. where production, maintenance, etc. have their own departments reporting to the plant manager.

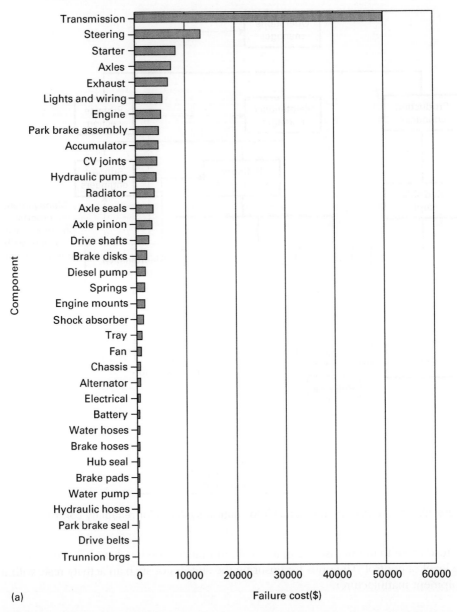

(a)

Figure 10.6 Pareto chart (a) failure cost (b) failure frequency for four wheel vehicles used in an underground mine

Exercise

E10.2   For your own company draw a model to explain how 'plant reliability control' operates within the organization. Use Figures 10.3 and 10.4 as a guideline. How effective is this system in controlling reliability? How could it be improved?

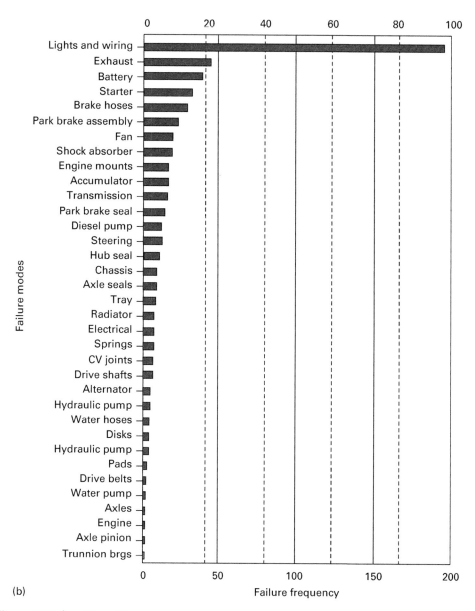

(b)

Figure 10.6 (*continued*)

Reference

1. Healy, A., *Effect of road roughness on the maintenance costs of four-wheel drives* PhD thesis, Queensland University of Technology, Brisbane, Australia, 1996.

Review Question Guidelines

R10.1   Reactive control of plant unit reliability is concerned with collecting and ana-
        lyzing the history of previous events (failures, etc.) to establish the root cause
        of failure and to prescribe corrective action.
            Proactive control of plant unit reliability is concerned with a process of con-
        tinuous improvement of plant reliability via a thorough understanding of the
        operation, maintenance and quality needs of a unit. The idea is to identify and
        eradicate potential reliability problems before they occur.

R10.2   Good human factors at trade force/operator level is essential for proactive
        control of reliability. Identifying and designing out potential reliability prob-
        lems requires considerable effort (and training) at the trade force level, it is
        beyond the duties that these people are normally expected to carry out. The
        function of continuous improvement at trade force/operator level (kaisan) is
        part of the organizational philosophy of TPM.

R10.3   See Figure 10.4.

PART 5

Exercises

11 Exercises on maintenance strategy

'If at first you don't succeed, try, try again.'

Edward Hickson *et al*

Chapter aims and outcomes

This chapter allows the reader the opportunity to attempt two exercises, each of which is aimed at testing his/her understanding of some of the ideas that have been presented in this book (before answering these exercises the reader should study the case studies of Chapter 12, in particular Case studies 1 and 2). Solutions to the exercises are given at the end of this chapter.

Chapter route map

Book divisions	This chapter in the division	Chapter topics
Introductory chapters		11.1 An alumina refinery
Maintenance objectives and task selection		
The top-down bottom-up approach		
Controlling plant reliability		11.2 A gold mine milling process
Exercises	Chapter 11 Exercises on maintenance strategy	
Case studies		

Exercise 11.1 An alumina refinery

The operating characteristics of the refinery can be derived from Figures 11.1 and 11.2. Figure 11.1 shows the relationships between the mine, power station, refinery and the

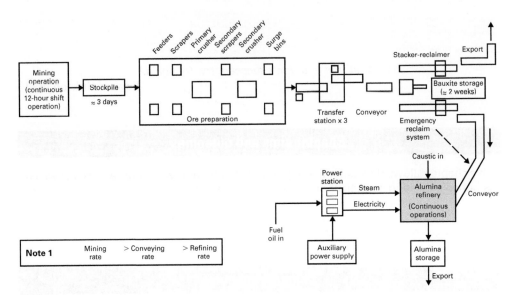

Figure 11.1 Outline process flow, mine and refinery

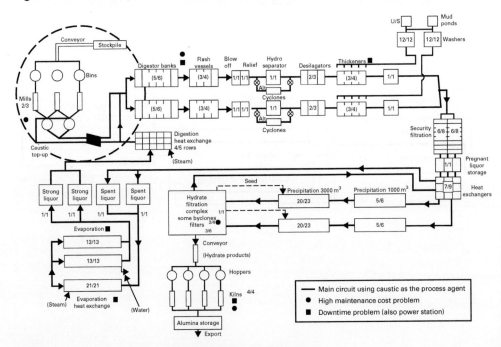

Figure 11.2 Process flow: diagram of alumina refinery

various transportation systems, and indicates that, as regards alumina production, the refinery is the rate-determining process. The refinery and the power station are integrated from a production point of view and both are, therefore, production-critical.

Figure 11.2 models the refinery process flows at plant unit level (e.g. a bauxite mill is represented as a single unit). Units incurring high maintenance cost or exhibiting low reliability are indicated.

The refinery can be thought of as a series of process functions operating on a circulating working fluid. Bauxite and caustic are added at its front end, and impurities and product are extracted at various stages downstream. Caustic is the main constituent of the working fluid. There are two identical circuits, each with spare (standby) capacity incorporated either in parallel (as in the mills) or in series (as in the digester banks), or in both series and parallel. In some processes (e.g. the evaporator heat exchangers) there is no standby capacity. There is also some inter-stage storage in the main circuit – because of the involvement of precipitators – but its exploitation incurs a production-loss penalty. Although not part of the primary circuit, a number of subsystems (e.g. the hydrate conveyor and kilns) spur off it. In each case these can be considered to be in series with the main circuit.

The refinery is operated continuously, it never comes offline at plant level. The offline maintenance work has to be scheduled by taking advantage of the extensive redundancy at unit level. The other important characteristic is that most of the maintenance is caused by time-dependent failure mechanisms such as wear, corrosion and fouling. A typical maintenance shutdown of a unit is estimated to involve a crew of 9 artisans for about 4 days. The main exception to this is a kiln shutdown, which could involve up to 20 artisans for 3 weeks.

The existing unit life plans (e.g. for the bauxite mill) are based on fixed-time maintenance. A typical life plan would be as follows:

- Minor preventive work: Lubrication schedule; online inspection schedule (extremely limited); service schedule (basic and not carried out well).
- Major preventive work: Major repair or overhaul at frequencies estimated from experience and plant history.
- Corrective guidelines for critical items.

Note that the major offline work has been scheduled at fixed-operating periods. The maintenance schedule has been arranged to spread the workload evenly across the year. The availability level is 92% and management considers that the direct cost of maintenance (men, spares, materials) is too high.

Problem
Senior management wants to improve the availability level of the plant to 95% and at the same time to reduce maintenance costs by 10%. They believe that one way to help the achievement of this aim is to introduce a condition-based strategy.

Question A
List the main factors that should be included in the maintenance objective. If the aim is to raise availability at the same time as reducing maintenance costs, what are the factors that might inadvertently be neglected? How would you guard against this happening?

Question B

Do you consider that the adoption of a condition maintenance policy for determining when units come offline and the work to be carried out would be a better maintenance strategy? How would such a policy affect the maintenance workload and organization?

Question C

It has been suggested that a maintenance life plan for a plant (e.g. for an alumina refinery such as this) should be made up of a mix of maintenance tasks based on the following policies:

- fixed-time maintenance,
- condition-based maintenance,
- operate-to-failure,
- design-out maintenance.

If you were asked to formulate a strategy for a large complex plant, how would you go about deciding what mix of maintenance tasks to employ?

Question D

In general, a maintenance strategy for a power station as based on fixed operating periods (of 3 years or so) between major shutdowns. Why do you think this is so? How does this approach affect the workload and the organization? What is the fundamental difference between the refinery strategy and a power station strategy?

Exercise 11.2 A gold mine milling process

Figure 11.3 shows the process flow of the milling plant of a gold mine. The mine is decoupled from the milling plant by the inter-stage ore storage. The milling process is the mine's rate-determining process. For the foreseeable future (the next 5 years) management want to operate the milling process continuously. This will result in no plant-level windows of maintenance opportunity. Downstream from the cyclone towers the offline maintenance can be scheduled at unit level by exploiting redundancies (e.g. at any one time only three of the available five thickeners are required).

Scheduled offline maintenance, or failure of the crusher circuit, can stop the whole plant, although the plant can then be kept going for 3 days via the 'alternative' crushing process, but at four times the cost of normal crushing. Scheduled offline maintenance or failure of one of the Ball Mills (or its ancillary equipment) causes a 50% loss of milling production.

Most of the maintenance results from time-dependent failure mechanisms (e.g. wear, corrosion or fouling).

The crushing circuit has a mean running time to failure of 6 months. Failure predictability is poor because of the large number of failure modes many of which are induced by randomly occurring production events. The Ball Mills also have a mean running time to failure of about 6 months but with good failure predictability. The main items needing replacement are the rubber lifters and liners.

The location of the mine is such that contract labor is extremely expensive. The resident labor force is manned up to the peak offline maintenance workload and hence is

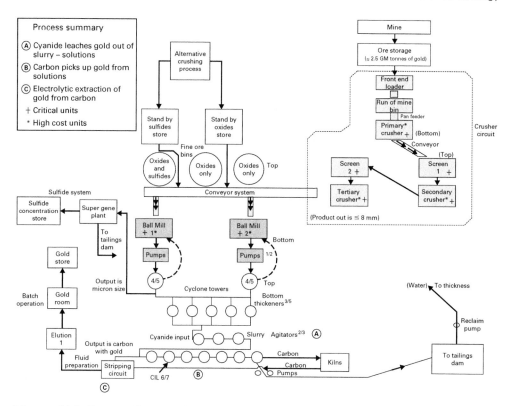

Figure 11.3 Process flow: gold mine milling plant

not very productive for most of the time. The quality of the labor is good, with an excellent knowledge of the plant, and in particular of the corrective maintenance methods. Because of the high cost of production downtime the maintenance objective appears to be to maximize milling plant availability.

The existing maintenance strategy is based on the following actions:

- The crusher circuit is operated-to-failure (or near-failure as indicated by the operators' informal monitoring). Since failure is expected there is a considerable level of pre-planning (e.g. preparation of spares, job methods, decision guidelines). When the plant is offline because of failure, *opportunity maintenance* (including inspection) is carried out on the other units of the crusher circuit. Plant operation is sustained via the alternative crushing process.
- The Ball Mills are on a schedule of 4-monthly overhaul. The main job is the repair or replacement of the lifters and liners, but other work is carried out on the mill to ensure its reliable operation over the following 4 months. In addition, preventive maintenance is carried out on other units in the stream (e.g. the conveyors). This causes a workload peak and contract labor has then to be employed. Some of the work is time-based, some deferred corrective maintenance, but most is repair-on-inspection.
- A minimum level of maintenance (mainly lubrication) is carried out on all other units.

Note: Apart from informal monitoring by operators and by the maintenance supervisor, little online inspection work is undertaken.

Question A
What would be the difficulty in using a fixed-time maintenance approach for the crusher circuit?

Question B
Do you consider that there is a better way of maintaining the crusher circuit? Outline your approach?

Question C
While the existing fixed-time approach (4-monthly shutdowns) for the Ball Mills may not be the *best* policy it is regarded as an *effective* one. Explain why this is so? How do you think this approach could be improved?

Exercise Guideline Solutions

Solutions to problems of this kind cannot be the exact ones. The proposals below must be regarded not as *optimal* solutions but as guidelines to *good* solutions. Various number of points raised are open to debate.

Exercise 11.1

Question A
The factors that could be neglected are standards of safety and plant condition (longevity). Corporate management *must* be made aware of the link between maintenance effort (and resources) and safety. The budget must take into account the longer-term major maintenance work that influences equipment longevity.

Question B
The adoption of a condition-based approach could extend running time of units without reducing equipment reliability. This, however, assumes that a monitorable meaningful parameter can be found. If this is the case, condition-based policies would improve unit availabilities and also reduce maintenance costs. The downside of this could be that the workload might fluctuate erratically (perhaps with very large peaks). It would not be easy to co-ordinate maintenance work with production requirements or to use the 'common centralized maintenance resources' efficiently. If the workload varied erratically across such a large plant, the organization would need to be designed to match, i.e. resources would have to be *plant-flexible* or greater use would have to be made of contract labor.

Based on the limited information given it would seem likely that if condition-based maintenance were introduced as the 'strategic driver' it would be a more cost-effective strategy. Because of the nature of the process equipment (failure mechanisms such as wear, corrosion, etc.) it should be easy to find condition-monitoring techniques that would be effective in 'predicting the onset of failure'. The 'lumpiness of the maintenance workload' that might result from such a policy should be able to be overcome by improved production-maintenance planning coupled with condition-based lead times and resource flexibility.

If the fixed-time policy were largely retained, condition-based procedures might still be adopted, for two reasons, *viz.*:

- To help predict the corrective work needed during shutdowns, this improves planning.
- To avoid unexpected failures.

Question C
Use the *top-down bottom-up* approach (see Figure 9.3).

Question D
A base-load power station shutdown might well take 12 weeks and employ as many as a thousand artisans. The date must, therefore, be fixed some considerable time ahead, to facilitate the necessary extensive planning and resourcing. The maintenance workload might have a peak/trough ratio (shutdown/normal) of up to 10:1, which would necessitate the employment of contract labor. The fundamental difference between the power station and refinery strategies is caused by the difference in the way the plant is designed and operated. This in turn governs the shape of the workload. For the refinery, the major work can be smoothed over the year and carried out by an internal labor force; for the power station, extensive use of contract labor – for resourcing the shutdown peak – will be necessary.

Exercise 11.2

Question A
The crusher circuit fails randomly so a fixed-time policy for the circuit is not effective in controlling its reliability.

Question B
The alternative policies are:

(i) design-out,
(ii) condition-based,
(iii) operate-to-failure.

Option (iii) is already in use and is proving too expensive. If option (i) is considered (as it must be) the causes of failure need to be identified and options considered for their elimination. This, however, is a long-term approach and the most cost-effective attack is likely to be the adoption of a condition-based policy. The information given is that the main causes of failure are wear, corrosion or fouling. Therefore, for most items, monitoring techniques for predicting failure can probably be found and effort would need to be directed at the historically unreliable items. This might allow maintenance of the crusher circuit to move from operate-to-failure to a policy based on condition-based shutdown (albeit with short notice) plus opportunity maintenance. Even with such short notice the monitored information (and history) should facilitate improved preparation and planning.

Question C
The main reason for Ball Mill shutdown maintenance is the replacement of the lifters and liners. Their deterioration is time related and is statistically predictable so fixed-time replacement is an effective policy for controlling their reliability. It is not unlikely, however, that some form of condition monitoring might facilitate running the Ball Mills for longer periods before the lifters and liners need replacing. In many cases this would take the running time past 6 months and in some cases it might be as little as 4 months. However, if the inspection techniques gave an adequate planning lead time, the advantage is that the shutdown could still be scheduled.

PART 6

Case studies

PART 3

Case studies

12 Case studies of maintenance strategy

'What we see depends mainly on what we look for.'

John Lubbock

Chapter aims and outcomes

The main aim of this chapter is to provide the reader with case studies that will reinforce his/her knowledge of the maintenance strategy of process plant. In addition, case studies will be used to illustrate the similarities and differences between the maintenance of process plant and that of other physical asset systems, *viz.* of coal mines, of transport fleets and of power utilities – the main differences arising from the different ways in which these various physical asset systems are structured and operated to generate the product or service, and which in turn requires a revised approach to scheduling the preventive maintenance.

The case studies presented are as follows:

- An audit of the maintenance strategy at an agricultural chemical plant.
- Maintenance strategy review at an aluminum smelter.
- Maintenance strategy review for a petroleum refinery.
- Maintenance strategy in the coal mining industry.
- Maintaining an open-cut coal mine
- Maintenance strategy for a passenger transport fleet.
- Maintenance strategy review for a gas-fired power station.
- Maintenance strategy review for an oil-fired power station.
- Mapping the maintenance strategy for an electricity transmission grid.
- The maintenance of an electrical distribution system.

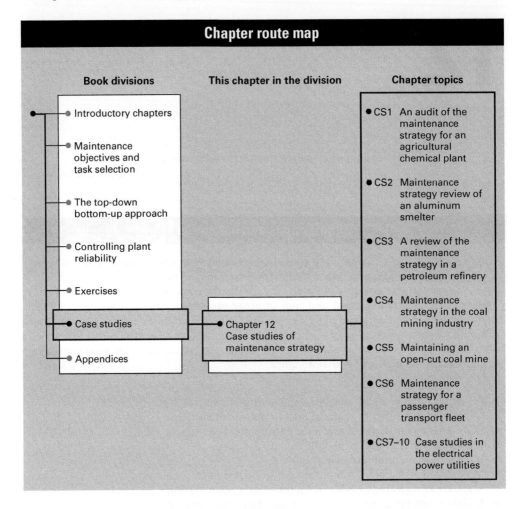

Chapter route map

Book divisions	This chapter in the division	Chapter topics

- Introductory chapters
- Maintenance objectives and task selection
- The top-down bottom-up approach
- Controlling plant reliability
- Exercises
- Case studies
- Appendices

Chapter 12
Case studies of maintenance strategy

- CS1 An audit of the maintenance strategy for an agricultural chemical plant
- CS2 Maintenance strategy review of an aluminum smelter
- CS3 A review of the maintenance strategy in a petroleum refinery
- CS4 Maintenance strategy in the coal mining industry
- CS5 Maintaining an open-cut coal mine
- CS6 Maintenance strategy for a passenger transport fleet
- CS7–10 Case studies in the electrical power utilities

CASE STUDY 1: AN AUDIT OF THE MAINTENANCE STRATEGY FOR AN AGRICULTURAL CHEMICAL PLANT

1 Introduction

This case study concerns a full audit (strategy, organization and systems) of Fertec Ltd – a company manufacturing fertilizers for the agricultural industry. Fertec Ltd is made up of two plants: Plant A and Plant B located in different cities. This audit was carried out on the maintenance department of Plant A. Fertec is owned by a parent company Cario Ltd.

The purpose of this case study is limited to giving the reader an understanding of how the audit procedure was used to map and model the *maintenance strategy* in order to identify the associated problems and to prescribe possible solutions.

2 An overview of Fertec

The plant layout of Fertec A is shown in Figure 1 indicating the location of the main process areas and the maintenance resources (labor and parts store). The labor resources are identified by a letter code that carried through to the organizational models (not shown).

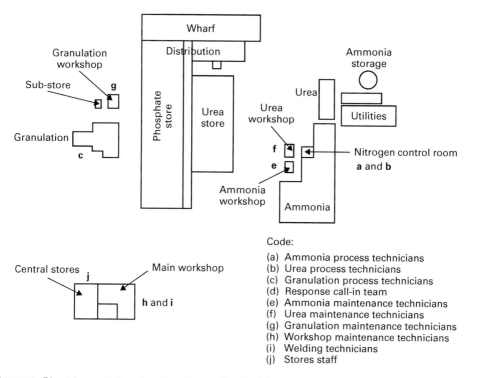

Code:
(a) Ammonia process technicians
(b) Urea process technicians
(c) Granulation process technicians
(d) Response call-in team
(e) Ammonia maintenance technicians
(f) Urea maintenance technicians
(g) Granulation maintenance technicians
(h) Workshop maintenance technicians
(i) Welding technicians
(j) Stores staff

Figure 1 Plant layout showing locations of technician resource

An outline process flow diagram is shown in Figure 2. The ammonia plant is production critical since it supplies the other plants with ammonia and CO_2. There is some inter-stage ammonia storage. The plant can also be supplied with imported ammonia, which is much more expensive than that produced internally.

The complex is some 30 years old but has been up-rated especially in the areas of instrumentation and control systems. The urea plant is currently being up-rated. The cost of energy (natural gas) is a very high percentage of the ammonia-plant-operating cost. The energy efficiency of the ammonia plant is low compared to the worlds best because it has 'old technology'. The reliability of the plant has a major influence on energy efficiency and needs to be improved.

Fertec Ltd is one of a number of companies that belong to the parent group Cario Ltd. The senior management structure of Fertec A Ltd and its relationship with Fertec B Ltd, and its parent group is shown in Figure 3. It should be noted that the Reliability Manager has responsibilities that cover both Fertec Plant A and Fertec Plant B.

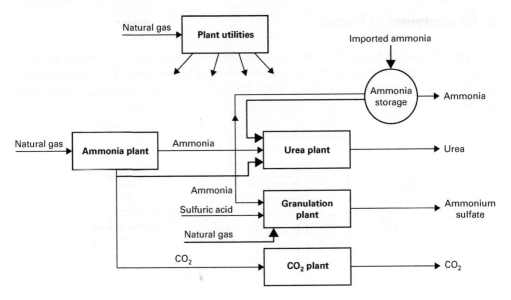

Figure 2 Outline process flow diagram of Fertec Ltd

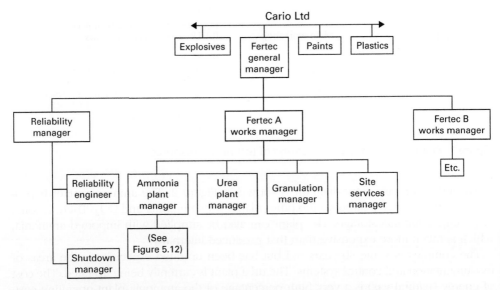

Figure 3 Senior management administrative structure of Fertec Ltd

A number of the senior positions in Fertec A had recently changed and had been filled with a young forward-looking team. The new team commissioned the audit because they felt that in order to remain competitive they needed to improve plant reliability and at the same time reduce maintenance costs.

3 Objectives

An outline of the process of setting objectives and business plans is shown in Figure 4. This is a form of management by objectives (MBO) closely allied to the authors business-centered maintenance approach.

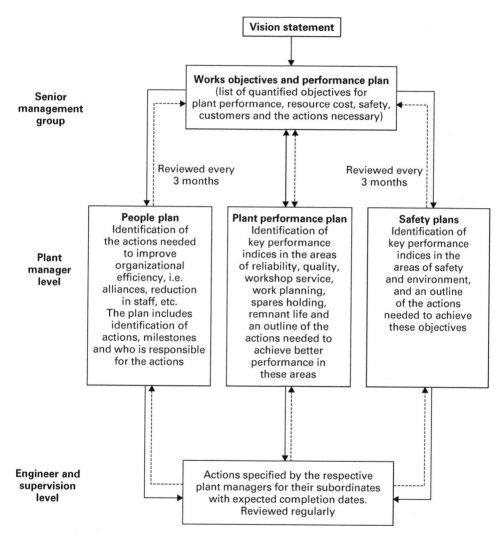

Figure 4 MBO at Fertec Ltd

The Fertec A senior management group (to include the group Reliability Manager) establish a 'works objectives and performance statement'. Objectives at this level are concerned with manufacturing performance. Maintenance objectives are set for those areas that directly affect manufacturing. For example, an objective is set to improve the availability of the ammonia plant from its current level of 88% to match the world best at 96%. Objectives are also set to improve energy efficiency.

4 Maintenance strategy

4.1 Plant-operating characteristics

The outline process flow diagram for the Fertec A complex was shown in Figure 2. The ammonia plant is the rate-determining process, it is production limited. Ammonia plant failures can only be made up via imported ammonia (which is costly). The auditors were given the figure that a 1% loss of annual availability translates into many hundreds of thousands of pounds. The ammonia storage tank gives some protection (days) to the ammonia plant in the case of urea plant downtime. Failure of the ammonia plant also brings out the urea and CO_2 plants. The granulation plant is largely independent of the rest of the complex. In terms of downtime cost the following is the rule of thumb:

| Ammonia plant downtime costs | >> | Urea plant downtime costs | >> | Granulation plant downtime costs |

This case study will only describe the maintenance strategy of the ammonia plant (the audit covered the strategy for the full complex).

An outline process flow diagram for the ammonia plant is shown in Figure 5. At unit level it can be seen that plant is a series process with limited redundancy. There are many units whose failure can affect the output of the ammonia plant and those that present the highest risk of failure are regarded as *critical* (e.g. the syn-gas compressor, SGC).

4.2 Ammonia plant strategy

The current strategy is to operate the ammonia–urea–CO_2 complex for a 4-year period before a 4-week shutdown. This operating period is a function of statutory inspection of the pressure vessels (now self-regulating) and the need to inspect/repair/replace other plant units whose reliability falls off after 4 years. The timing of the shutdown is set to coincide with low annual urea demand.

The 4-year operating period has been determined by the reliability group based mainly on an empirical study of the 'risk of failure factor' vs the period of operation of pressure vessels before inspection (i.e. how long can we operate the plant for without affecting safety integrity?) They have established that the critical 20% of units carry 80% of the 'risk factor'.

Continuous vibration monitoring is used on the large machines mainly for operational safety but also for maintenance prediction. A number of other online monitoring techniques are used both on the large machines and the pressure vessels to aid condition-based maintenance.

The ammonia plant strategy has its center of gravity well toward condition-based maintenance. While the plant is operated for a 4-year period the shutdown workscope is mainly based on the work predicted from:

- online inspections,
- offline inspections from previous shutdowns,
- history from previous shutdowns.

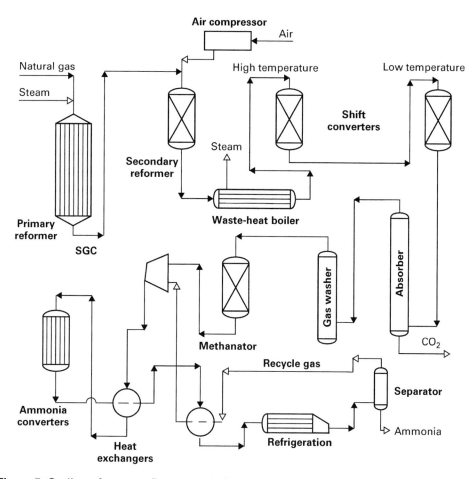

Figure 5 Outline of process flow model of the ammonia plant

The duration of the shutdown is normally 4 weeks which includes a 'dead-week' needed for shutdown and start-up. The critical path during the shutdown is the reformer inspection (pressure vessel) and the SGC (large machine).

In terms of maintenance characteristics the plant can be categorized into large machines, pressure vessels, ancillary equipment (e.g. duplicate pumps and electrical/ instrumentation equipment). The audit selected plant units from each of these categories and mapped their existing 'life plans'.

Life plan for the SGC

A schematic diagram of the SGC is shown in Figure 6 which includes details on spare parts holding. The condition-based maintenance carried out on the machine is shown in Table 1. The machine is expected to operate continuously for 4 years. The shutdown workscope is established from previous shutdown history, deferred corrective maintenance and the online monitoring information. Additional work is identified as a result of the offline inspection during the shutdown (unplanned).

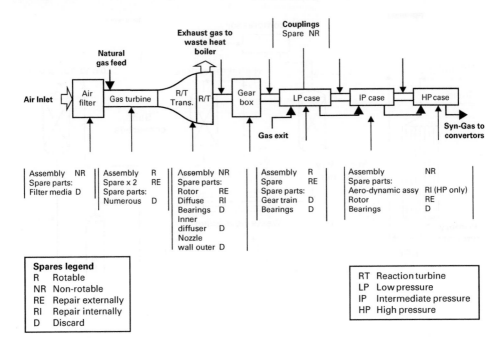

Figure 6 Schematic diagram of a SGC

Table 1 SGC condition-based maintenance

Bently Nevada system
- This sophisticated system records various data and has the ability to combine inputs to produce multidimensional displays.
- It produces data in real time plus long and short trend patterns.
- Items measured include:
  - Radial shaft displacement
  - Axial shaft displacement
  - Bearing temperatures: radial and thrust
  - Accelerometer readings (gearbox and gas turbine only)
  - Shaft orbit readings (multidimensional)
  - Shaft phase angle (multidimensional)
- In addition to the above approximately 200 process variables are monitored.
- All the above have alarm points and key items have shutdown settings.

Oil analysis
- Routine oil analysis.

Seal bypass test (compressor only)
- Routine seal accumulator drop test.

Oil debris analysis (gas turbine only)
- Online continuous monitoring.

Standard job procedures are in use, e.g. inspection overhauls of the high-pressure case. These are comprehensive and detailed. The machine history records have not been formalized, are hard copy and reside in a number of locations looked after by a number of different people. The life plan has not been formally documented.

Although not shown in Figure 6 there is an automatic lubrication system for the SGC. There are simple documented service routines associated with this system which have been computerized.

Life plan for pressure vessels

The generic life plan for pressure vessels is based on condition-based maintenance. The maintenance carried out during the shutdown is based on condition prediction from previous shutdown history and on any online non-destructive testing (NDT) monitoring performed between the shutdowns. Additional work is identified from inspections carried out (open and closed) during the shutdown.

There are variations on the life plans to suit specific vessels. Those that are high on the 'risk factor analysis', see Table 2 for the basis of the calculations, are subjected to an in-depth analysis to up-rate the life plan. Every pipe, weld and hot support that might give rise to failure is examined to develop the most appropriate NDT technique and inspection methodology (e.g. see Figure 7).

This inspection-based life plan is backed up with a comprehensive computerized information base – the pressure systems database which includes for each vessel the following information:

- Process and mechanical data sheets.
- Inspection history.
- Inspection procedures and test plans (see Figure 7).
- The vessel life plan (which has involved risk assessment and remnant life analysis).
- Hard copy reports of previous shutdown case studies.

This computerized database is independent of the recently purchased company-wide computerized enterprise system.

Ancillary equipment*

The life plans of such equipment is based on 'service routines' which are embedded in the main computerized maintenance system (linked to other company systems). A typical routine would be as follows:

Pump preventive routine: 3-monthly frequency

- Oil change
- General inspection
  - Check coupling
  - Lift-bearing cap, etc.

These routines were established some 20 years ago and are in need of review. Many of the routines have been put into the new computer system without review. Vibration monitoring is also used for the rotating equipment in this category (mainly portable instruments but some periodic permanently wired systems).

---

*For example, pumps, pressure relief valves, control valves, etc. – equipment that can be maintained outside of the main shutdowns.

Table 2 Assessment of criticality ranking for a pressure vessel

Pressure vessel CF601 sulfur drum

Likelihood of failure		
Is there a known active metallurgic damage mechanism?	No known damage mechanism	0
Is there a known active mechanical damage mechanism?	Vibration fatigue	2
Have the inspections been effective?	Ineffective – no confidence	5
What is the frequency of inspections?	More than 30 years	4
How reliable are the control systems + operating parameters?	Poor	1
Are the vessel limits exceeded in plant upsets?	Yes	1
Are the vessel's limits exceeded in normal operation?	No	0
Have process conditions changed (but still within design)?	Yes	1
Are the vessel limits exceeded in plant start-ups or shutdowns?	Yes	1
Are the vessel's protective systems effective?	No	1
As detection of damage previously warranted further investigation?	Yes	1
Have repairs been required in the past?	Yes	1
How old is the vessel?	Over 30 years	3
Is the vessel original design to current standards?	No	1
Is the vessel material specification to currently acceptable?	No	1
Total		**23**

Consequence of failure		
Is the vessel contents . . .?	A lethal gas?	7
What is the temperature of the vessel contents?	Above 500°C	3
Are the contents flammable if they leak?	Auto ignites	3
Would a failure promote consequential damage elsewhere in plant?	Yes	5
Would emergency services help be required to contain a situation?	Yes	3
What is the vessel pressure?	Above 10 MPa	3
What is the volume of worst rating contents in the vessel?	Over 1000 m^3	8
Will a leak cause secondary damage to other equipment?	Yes	1
What is the distance to internal personnel?	Less than 10 m	2
What is the distance to the general public?	Less than 10 m	4
What is the business impact of a vessel failure?	Over £10,000,000	11
Total		**50**

Criticality risk ranking number $= 23 \times 50 = 1150$

EQUIPMENT NUMBER: T503   PRESENT CLOSED FREQUENCY: 4 years   PRESENT OPEN FREQUENCY: Yearly   INSTALLATION DATE: 01-01-1968

DESCRIPTION: Ion Exchanger   VOLUME:

OPEN INSPECTIONS

Equipment item	Visual	Ultrasonic	Radiography	Mag/part	Dye/pen	Thermovision	Vibration	AE	Attenuation	Metallographic	Other
2RK65 to Tray Ring Weld	Yes				x						
Alignment	Yes										
Associated piping	Yes		O/head line only								
Davit/Lifting devices	Yes	Prior to S/D		Prior to S/D							
Earth connection	Yes										
Heads	Yes	Bottom									
Instrumentation	Yes	Evidence of bulging									
Insulation	Yes										
Internal liner	Yes	4 per petal			To Bot Tray						
Manway and bolting	Yes	Manway plant									
Nozzles	Yes	Manway liners		Internal							
Platforms/handrails	Yes										
Pressure relief devices	Yes										
Protective coating	Yes										
Shell	Yes	Lower 1.5/m			Liner welds						
Supports and bolting	Yes										
Thermowells and sockets	Yes				x						
Vessel bolting	Yes										
Vibration	Yes										
Welded joints	Yes										

Figure 7 Open inspection test plans for exchanger

In general the monitoring procedures have not been tied into the routines.

In addition to the routines a 'contract lubrication system' has been introduced operated by one of the large oil companies.

The auditors noted that the operating procedure for units with duplicated drives was as follows:

- Electric motors: change over weekly.
- Electric motors and steam turbine: use the electric motor and proof test the turbine weekly.

Electrical/instrumentation equipment

The life plans are based on clean, inspect and calibrate where necessary. These preventive routines were set up many years ago and need review. It was noted that much of the more recent equipment, e.g. PLCs were not included on the routines and had not been reviewed. The large electrical machines had no documented life plan. More importantly the whole of the electrical/instrumentation equipment had not been reviewed in terms of 'spares criticality'. The information base data (job specification, modification and plant history, etc.) was either on hard copy (in a number of different locations) or held in peoples' memory.

4.3 Comments and recommendations on strategy

(i) When auditing maintenance strategy the auditors ask the interviewees their opinion of preventive maintenance in use in their plant. The following are some of the comments:

The main shutdowns are carried out well – this is where most of our preventive work is carried out.

We must tie up the preventive routines with vibration monitoring.

Routines are used as fill in work – they are not regarded as important.

The electrical routines are in peoples' heads – they must be documented.

The refrigeration units in the plant services are in poor condition and are operation critical – we must sort out our spares.

We should rethink our operating period – the USA plants do it differently and at lower cost.

Our condition monitoring is heading toward international benchmark levels.

We should be replacing old gear – monopumps out and granfar pumps in.

Our life plans for large machines are not right yet – we should seek help from the original equipment manufacturer (OEM).

(ii) The auditors observed that the operating period of the plant has been extended from 2 to 4 years and will shortly extend to 4½ years. This is due to the considerable efforts of the reliability group in the area of pressure vessel maintenance (NDT techniques, good computerized information base, criticality and remnant life analysis, and metallurgic knowledge).

However, it appears from ammonia plant failure data that the main production losses occur as a result of problems with the large machines. The data shows that the large machines fail more often and more randomly than the pressure vessels with a mean-time-to-failure (m.t.t.f.) <4 years. This is not surprising since they are up to 30 years old and are a complex arrangement of many rapidly moving parts. Over the years as a result of numerous overhauls, often carried out without standard job procedures, their condition appears to have fallen away from the OEM standard specification. This leads to the following comments:

(a) If the company are to get the best out of a 4½-year operating period they will have to bring the condition of the large machines back to an 'as new standard' – perhaps with the assistance of the OEM. Since the machines are old this is almost equivalent to a life extension decision and relates to the probable remaining life of the plant.

(b) It is recommended that the company use the top–down bottom–up approach (TDBUA) [1] to review the life plans of the large machines. This should include a criticality analysis of the spares holding. In addition the large machine 'plant information base' should be brought up to the same standard as the pressure vessel database.

(iii) The auditors are aware from discussions with the company engineers that companies in the USA operate a different maintenance strategy than that outlined above. For example, some companies use an operating time of 2-year and a 2-week duration shutdown.

Many factors affect this decision to include:

- The period for statutory pressure vessel inspection (now self-regulating).
- The shortest expected running time of other critical units before requiring maintenance (e.g. the large machines).
- The remaining life of the plant (remnant life) – in this case 7 years (the existing gas contract is 7 years) and uncertain.
- The market demand (assumes the plant is production limited).
- The shutdown duration needed to complete the workscope. This must take into consideration a 1-week dead period for shutdown and start-up. (Thus, a 2-week shutdown with a 2-year operating period has only 66% of the maintenance time of a 4-week shutdown with a 4-year operating period, see Figure 8.)

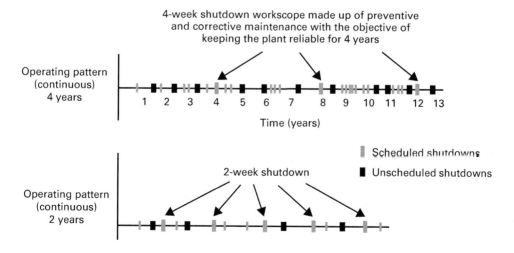

Figure 8 Illustration of strategy based on 4- and 2-year operating periods

The maintenance objective for this situation can be expressed as follows:

Minimize = Planned downtime costs + Unplanned downtime costs

This is a complex problem involving information not available to the auditors, e.g. Why is the dead period apparently shorter in the USA? Can the 4-week shutdown duration be reduced by shortening the reformer critical path? If so, how much would this cost? Do the large machines need realignment/offline inspection at 2 years? In spite of this (and without the use of statistical/cost modeling), it is the auditors opinion that if the company comply with the points listed in (ii)a and (ii)b they are moving toward an optimum maintenance strategy.

(iv) It is recommended that 'opportunity scheduling' should be used to compliment the existing strategy, i.e. when a failure of a plant unit occurs unexpectedly all other outstanding work should be looked at with a view to carrying it out in the 'opportunity window'. The auditors accept that the planning system will also have to improve if opportunity scheduling is to be used.

(v) Both mechanical and electrical/instrumentation routines are in need of review and update. Such a review should use the TDBUA to focus the routines on necessary and worthwhile tasks. In addition to modify as necessary the policy and frequency of routines, e.g. the changing of replace/repair of pumps/motors from fixed time to condition-based.

CASE STUDY 2: MAINTENANCE STRATEGY REVIEW OF AN ALUMINUM SMELTER

1 Introduction

The purpose of this case study is to illustrate some of the principles of preventive maintenance decision-making, i.e. how much, and what type, of preventive maintenance should be used to maintain an industrial plant. In addition, the case study shows the importance of the relationship between maintenance strategy and the workload it generates – there is no point in selecting a maintenance strategy if it cannot be resourced!

2 An overview of Smeltall

Smeltall Ltd is one of the largest aluminum smelters in the world. The plant layout is shown in Figure 1 and the outline process flow is shown in Figure 2. The heart of the process involves the electrolytic reduction of alumina (aluminum oxide) in a series of large cells (a Pot) – the *Potlines*. A schematic diagram of a cell is shown in Figure 3. In order to operate the cells (some 1080 in this case) a continuous supply of carbon anodes is required. These are manufactured in the *carbon plant* and after use each spent anode is returned for renewal. The molten aluminum is collected from the cells for transport to the *casting and finishing area.*

The smelter organization was built around manufacturing units in each of the main plant areas, e.g. the carbon plant (similar to the ammonia administration of Case study 1). Thus, the carbon plant had its own maintenance engineer and staff, and a maintenance

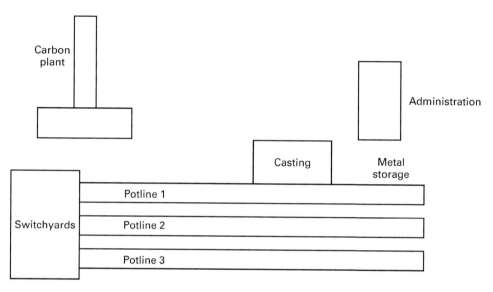

Figure 1 Smeltall: site layout

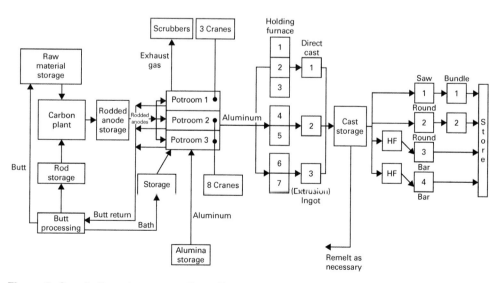

Figure 2 Smeltall: main process flow diagram

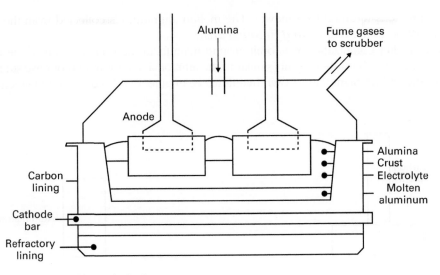

Figure 3 Electrolytic cell (a Pot)

resource group for the first- and second-line maintenance work. For major work the carbon plant used Smeltalls Central Service Group and/or contract labor.

The maintenance strategy had evolved over a considerable period of time without external review. In addition, there was concern that the existing strategy might require modification in order to cope with a recently completed expansion of the Potlines that had increased output by 30%. The Chief Engineer, in particular, wanted advice about the future direction of maintenance strategy within the plant. The author reviewed the strategy for the complete smelter but in this case study only the carbon plant strategy will be covered.

3 Carbon plant process flow: overall operation

Figure 2 shows the process flow diagram of the smelter and Figure 4 shows the process flow diagram of the carbon plant.

The smelting operation is continuous and there are no smelter-level windows of opportunity for maintenance. Figure 3 shows that the carbon plant and Potlines are decoupled by a 24-hour storage of anodes.

Figure 4 shows that the carbon plant can be considered as being made up of three separate, different, but interrelated sections or processes separated by inter-stage storage. The front-end process involves the manufacture of the unbaked or 'green' anode blocks – which are subsequently baked in the ring furnace (the second process) and then rodded (the third process). After this the finished anodes go into the anode store and from there to the Potrooms. The rate of production of anodes from the carbon plant was governed by the rate of production of the ring furnace – the bottleneck process.

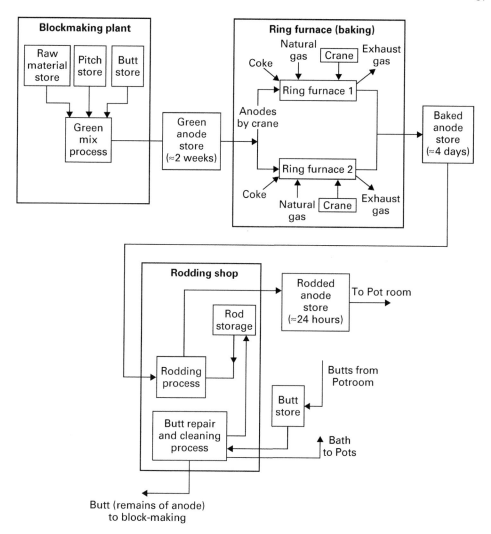

Figure 4 Smeltall: process flow, carbon plant

The average rate of production of green anodes from the green mix process exceeded (by far) the average rate of ring furnace production. The green anode stock was used to decouple these processes and could hold 2 weeks of stock. Similarly, the rate of production of the rodding process exceeded the rate of supply from the ring furnace and in this case the baked anode store served to decouple these processes. It was also important that the rate of butt[1] cleaning and rod repair was able to at least equal the

---

[1]Butt is the remains of a used anode. The rod is repaired for reuse and the remains of the block material returned for reuse in the green mix plant.

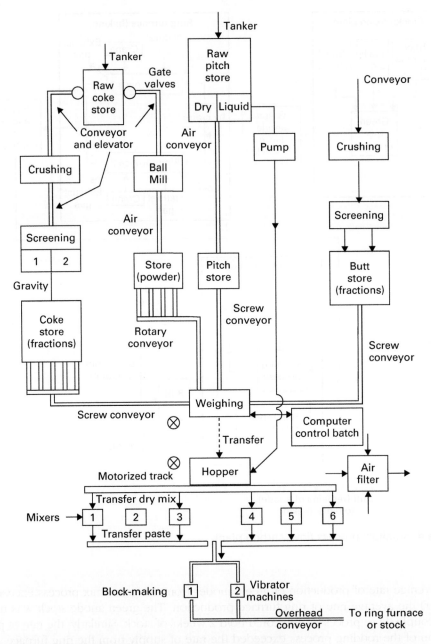

Figure 5 Smeltall: process flow diagram, green mix plant

baked anode production. This, in part, was a function of the number of 'floating butts' in the rodding/smelting/cleaning cycle.

The following review of carbon plant maintenance strategy will concentrate on the green mix plant and the ring furnace.

4 Green-mix plant-operating characteristics and maintenance strategy

4.1 Operating characteristics

A process flow model of the green mix plant is shown in Figure 5 (third-level model). The plant was made up of four raw material process subsystems, each with short-term storage, feeding into a weighing, mixing and blocking process.

Each of the raw material subsystems could be considered as critical to green mix production which could therefore be modeled as a series reliability system. There was some spare capacity in the mixing process and block-making process. The plant operated 13 shifts per week which left 8 shifts free for possible maintenance. Additional windows could be generated by building up the green anode storage level. Windows were also available during normal production through plant redundancy (mixers) and inter-stage storage (Ball Mill). In terms of lost production a green mix unit could only be considered critical if its repair took longer than the time covered by green anode storage (could be weeks). However, production insisted on high reliability over the 13-week operating period because failure had a major effect on the green block quality.

4.2 Maintenance strategy

The equipment life plans were based on simple preventive service routines (inspection, lubrication and minor component replacement) for each unit of equipment. Table 1 shows the life plan for the butt breaker of Figure 5. These services were reinforced for the critical units with extensive condition monitoring. For ease of execution of the preventive jobs the plant was divided into routes (e.g. the butt route), i.e. all the equipment on this route is tied together in some way (e.g. by process and/or isolation), etc. Every week the due services for each route would be carried out as a 'route-service'. The

Table 1 Outline of life plan for butt breaker

Butt breaker: online work				
Weekly	Butt breaker	Online inspection	No. 81 inspection sheet	
Butt breaker: offline work				Specification No.
Fortnightly	Guide	Inspect	Crusher jaw Ram	3901 0101
Monthly	Guide	Check clearance	Crusher jaw Ram	3901 0102
Monthly	Bolt	Check tension	Guides	2800 0101
Monthly	Stripping hand	Inspect and adjust	Stripping head	4000 0001
2 years	Cylinder	Inspect and test	Main Ram and Auxiliary cylinder	3002 0202
2 years	Lubricator	Replace	Stripping head	2301 0101
2 years	Lubricator	Replace	Stripping head	2301 0101

'route-services' for the plant were scheduled over the year into a 'green mix preventive schedule'. The schedule tries to smooth the workload over the year.

The *corrective work* resulting from the preventive inspection, or coming from production requests, was carried out by the local trade-force supplemented as necessary by central services and contract labor.

4.3 Comments and recommendations

The center of gravity of the strategy is based on condition-based maintenance (CBM). In general, the lead time resulting from the inspection procedures allowed the corrective maintenance to be carried out in the weekend window or if necessary by using the inter-stage storage. The carbon plant engineer justified this strategy (compared to fixed-time maintenance (FTM) or operate-to-failure) as follows:

- The low probability of a maintenance job (planned or resulting from a failure) in the carbon plant incurring a loss of anode production.
- The prevention of green mix plant failure (the inspection should identify and prevent failures – failure can cause product-quality problems).
- The avoidance of overmaintenance (which inevitably comes from the use of FTM[2]).
- The relative smoothness of the workload generated from such a plant in conjunction with the ability to cater for unexpected peaks with contract labor (most of the equipment is different, has already been overhauled and has different running times to major maintenance, i.e. the incidence of major jobs has been randomized and therefore the operation of the condition-based strategy should not result in large workload peaks – see Figure 6).

The author was impressed with the above strategy and its justification.

5 Ring furnace maintenance characteristics and strategy

5.1 Operating characteristics

A process flow model of the ring furnace and associated plant is shown in Figure 6. The rate of production from the furnaces was a function of the firing and cooling cycle (a period of 1 month) for a line of pits. Figure 7 shows an illustrated sketch of a pit. The

---

[2]The policy for maintaining the green mix mixers at the sister company is based on FTM. Such a policy comes from knowing that the life of the critical parts of the mixer is 2 years ± 3 months (from history records). An overhaul takes 30 shifts. The mixers are overhauled at a rate of 1 per 4 months. This policy is considered more economic than operation-to-failure or CBM (sigma arm wear, lining wear). The advantages are obvious in terms of planning, spares provisioning and a greater degree of confidence in ensuing 'mixer output' reliability. The disadvantage is overmaintenance. However, the key to this decision is the predictability of the mixer life (overhauling at, or about, 2 years minimizes overmaintenance).

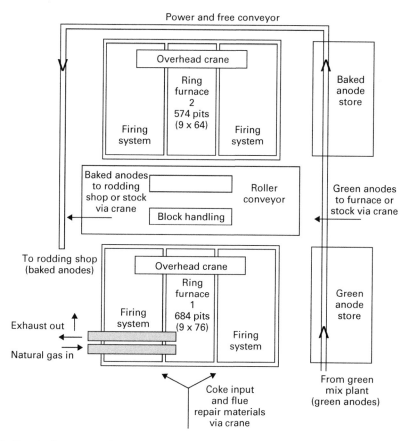

Figure 6 Smeltall: process flow diagram, ring furnace

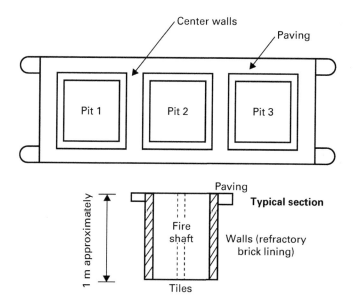

Figure 7 Illustration of a ring furnace pit

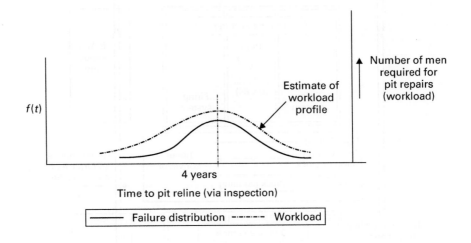

Figure 8 Ring furnace pit failure distribution

main maintenance work associated with the pit was the repair of the brick lining. It appeared that about 5 days were available within the cycle for repairs, i.e. if a repair was completed within this time no pit unavailability was incurred.

The ring furnace was perceived by the author to be that plant which was most critical to the operation of the whole smelter.

At the time of the audit the output of rodded anodes exceeded the Potroom's demand by only a small percentage. Thus, any unit within the ring furnace process would have been critical to the total performance of the smelter, if its failure would have led to a reduction of ring furnace output. Units identified as having that level of criticality were the power and free output conveyor, roller conveyor and cranes. In general, these units could be maintained in the windows arising out of the production-operating pattern and/or unit duplication. The pits themselves could also be considered as critical. A small percentage of pits could be unavailable, without affecting the Potroom production but unavailability above this percentage would have adverse effect.

5.2 Ring furnace maintenance strategy

Before the commissioning of Potrooms 2 and 3, the core of the recent expansion, the ring furnace had excess capacity. The maintenance strategy was based on inspecting pits after unloading and repairing as necessary. Unusable pits would go into a backlog until repaired. There was enough spare capacity to maintain Potroom 1 production. The author did not ask (neither was he told) if sections of the furnace were taken out for fixed-time repair under this regime. Experience from this operation had shown the mean pit life to be about 50 firing cycles (approximately 4 years). The distribution of times to pit repair was analyzed by the author who found that it showed the classic form for units failing by wear-out (see Figure 8 for an illustrated sketch).

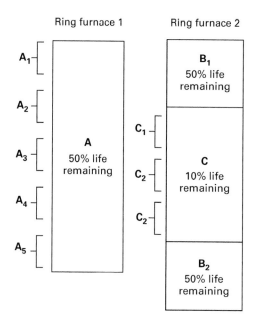

Figure 9 Condition of ring furnace pits

After Potrooms 2 and 3 were commissioned the maintenance strategy appears to have remained unchanged. The author estimated the proportion of pit life remaining at the time of audit and this is shown in Figure 9. Approximately 70% of the pits (A + B1 + B2) had about 50% of their life remaining; the remaining 30% had 10% of their life remaining. Thus, it was likely that the pit repair workload could build up to a major peak in 2 years (see Figure 8) assuming that pits would be left to go to their full life. Such a strategy would maximize pit life but would only be acceptable if the production rate from the furnace continued to be sufficient to meet Potroom needs. This would only be the case if the pit repair rate, during the 5-day maintenance windows, could be set to match the increasing workload. Any estimate of the rate of such repair would need to take into consideration the higher failure rates of the 'center walls' and the consequent likely need to work on adjacent pits. *Given the available internal resources such work appeared not to be possible.*

5.3 Comments and recommendations

The author proposed the following two alternative courses of action to overcome the pit maintenance problems:

1. Retaining the current policy of CBM and employing contract labor (if available) to overcome the imminent, and 2 years hence work peaks. Perhaps carrying out the repair over a three-shift roster. The subsequent work peaks would be lower, would

have a wider spread and would therefore be easier to resource. This policy would maximize pit life.

2. Using fixed-time repair for sections of the furnace; *this would mean pulling the pits out prematurely and forfeiting part of their useful life.* For example, Sections B1 and B2 required immediate attention, perhaps necessitating contract labor; Sections C1 through to C3 would then be dealt with and then Sections A1–A5. The faster the repair rate (a function of the gang size and shift system) the longer the pits could be left before premature repair. Such a policy needed only to be adopted once because thereafter the failure rate of the pits would be randomized. In the latter event the pit failure rate (and therefore the workload) could be constant and the repair gang size could be matched to this to achieve high utilization.

It was recommended that these alternative actions should be investigated (in terms of available contract resources and material) and costed, and a decision taken without delay.

6 Summary

In the case of the green mix plant FTM would have been an alternative maintenance policy to CBM since sufficient data was available showing that most of the equipment failed due to some form of time-dependent mechanism (e.g. wear). Thus, both CBM and FTM could be considered as effective policies for controlling plant reliability. In this case, CBM was the more cost-effective policy because it allowed a longer operating period before maintenance (it avoided overmaintenance). *In addition the maintenance workload generated by this policy could be easily resourced.*

At first glance it would appear that the existing CBM policy was also 'best' for the ring furnace pits. *However, in this case the maintenance workload generated by such a policy (see Figure 8) could not be easily resourced.*

CASE STUDY 3: A REVIEW OF THE MAINTENANCE STRATEGY IN A PETROLEUM REFINERY

1 Introduction

The author has audited the maintenance management systems of several petroleum refineries. The main purpose of this case study is to highlight the maintenance strategy problems that are typical of such plant.

2 Plant-operating characteristics

A simplified process flow diagram for the refinery is shown in Figure 1. The plant had been on the same site for over 40 years and in that time had major extensions and modifications. Each of the plant sections shown could be represented by a process flow diagram analyzed to unit level, as in Figure 2.

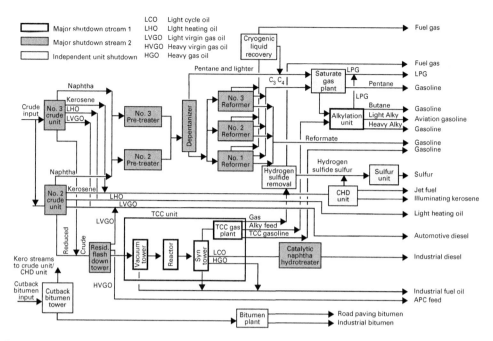

Figure 1 Refinery process flow

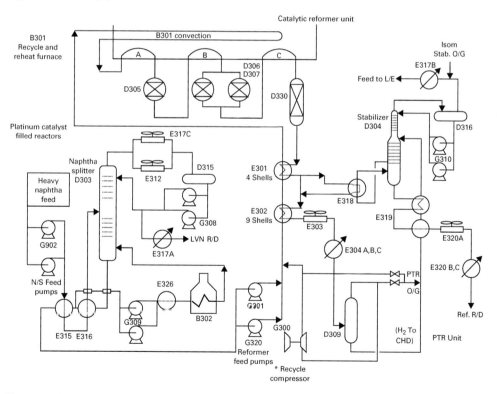

Figure 2 CFU process flow

The plant was production limited. Thus, for the foreseeable future there were no plant-level production windows. The plant consisted of two main process streams: one of which included the crude unit (CU) and the other the thermal catalytic cracker (TCC). Several other plant sections (e.g. the sulfur unit) could be taken offline while the rest of the refinery continued to operate. With the process streams it was not possible to operate (or operate effectively) with one of their major plant units down. However, there was a considerable level of redundancy at item level (e.g. many pumps were paired, one being normally online, the other on standby). There were also several windows at unit level caused by production maintenance (e.g. by catalyst changes).

The 'critical units' could be considered as any unit where failure would affect product output or quality (e.g. the recycle compressor of Figure 2) or would create an immediate or potential safety hazard. Since this was a plant that handled hazardous chemicals there were many safety critical items (e.g. all the safety relief valves and any pump or vessel from which there could be leakage of flammable or toxic fluid).

3 Maintenance strategy

This could be summarized as follows.

3.1 A schedule of outage work for the main process streams

The CU stream was shutdown for a 28-day overhaul – based on the statutory pressure vessel inspections – every 4 years, and the TCC stream for a 28-day overhaul every 2 years (the estimated time for various wear-out effects to become significant). The remaining units came out independently at intervals appropriate to their optimum running times. The work content of these outages comprised the following actions:

- Condition-based maintenance prompted by information from previous shutdowns or from online monitoring.
- Condition-based maintenance prompted by inspections carried out in the current shutdown.
- Fixed-time repairs and overhauls.
- Deferred corrective jobs.
- In practice, more than 30% of the outage work originated from current outage inspections. This was because information from online inspections (which were themselves less than satisfactory) and from previous shutdowns was poor.

3.2 A schedule of maintenance work for the standby equipment (e.g. for pumps)

In general, such a schedule did not exist. The pumps were wither operated-to-failure or replaced via *ad hoc* operator monitoring. The operating times of the pumps were not recorded and there was no set operating policy for pump systems (e.g. 'operate one pump to failure and keep the standby pump as new').

3.3 Online inspection routines

- *Dynamic plant*: Several key units (e.g. various compressors) had a fixed-vibration monitoring system in place. Any other such monitoring was requested on an irregular, *ad hoc*, basis.
- *Stationary plant*: A non-destructive testing key point inspection program was computer scheduled.
- *Simple inspection routines*: Although the operators were the equipment owners most of their inspection was process oriented. Little effort was being devoted to simple maintenance inspections.

4 Observations

The main thrust of maintenance strategy for large process plant lies in the major outage (or turnaround work). The maintenance policies, work content and frequency of this have usually evolved over a long period of time – often leading to the establishment of recognized standards and Codes of Practice – and are usually satisfactory. This plant was no exception and, as a consequence, the availability performance was good by international standards. With better online monitoring, however, and better information from previous shutdowns, it should have been possible to pre-plan 90% of the outage work. This would have resulted in better shutdown planning, improved work quality, more appropriate spares provisioning and therefore shorter shutdown durations.

The non-outage preventive maintenance schedules (mainly of routines for ancillary equipment such as standby pumps) were poor. The main reason was that the life plans for such equipment had not been systematically established and documented. (The author has found this to be the case with many of the refineries and other large process plants that he has audited.)

All of the main ancillary items of plant should have had a properly reasoned operating policy and maintenance life plan. Such a document should include:

(a) For standby items, a policy specifying operational checks, and the recording and monitoring of running time.
(b) A lubrication routine and operator-inspection checks.
(c) A service schedule, specifying – where necessary – vibrational or other condition monitoring techniques.
(d) A reasoned repair/replacement procedure based on recorded running time as specified in (a), or an observed condition as specified in (b) or (c).

CASE STUDY 4: MAINTENANCE STRATEGY IN THE COAL MINING INDUSTRY

1 Introduction

The main purpose of this case study material is to show how the operation and maintenance of equipment in the coal mining industry can be modeled to enable strategy review.

2 An overview of COALCOM

Figure 1 shows that 'COALCOM' comprises three underground collieries – operating three shifts per day, 5 days per week and 50 weeks per year – and a coal preparation plant. The coal is transported to the preparation plant by a small truck fleet. In the short term, the raw coal storage (located at the collieries) isolates the colliery supply from the rail demand.

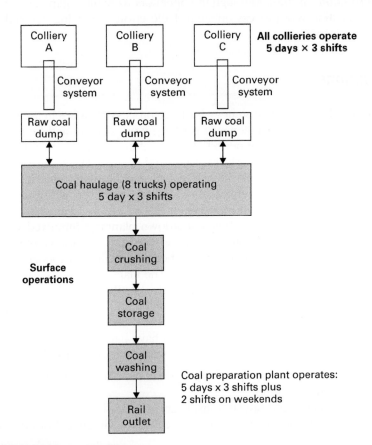

Figure 1 COALCOM process flow

Because all three collieries operate in a similar way, colliery 'A' can be used to illustrate COALCOM's maintenance strategy. The colliery layout is shown in Figure 2. Continuous miners (diesel-driven vehicles with a front-mounted driller-cutter for the development of tunnels through the coal measures) are used to develop the production area and the tunnels for conveyor or worker access. Coal extraction (from the production areas) is achieved by longwall cutting (see Figure 3). Longwall cutting is achieved via a system comprising a shearer, armored-face conveyor (up to 100 m long), main conveyors and services (e.g. electricity supply). The shearer cuts slices of the coal seam (2 m thick) by moving across a 100 m block which has been developed between two tunnels. The

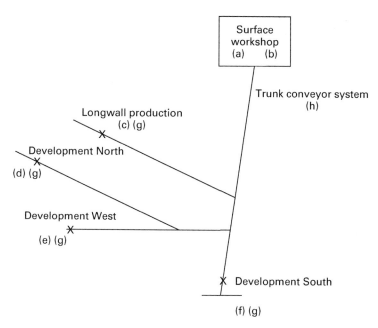

Figure 2 Layout of colliery 'A' showing operating areas

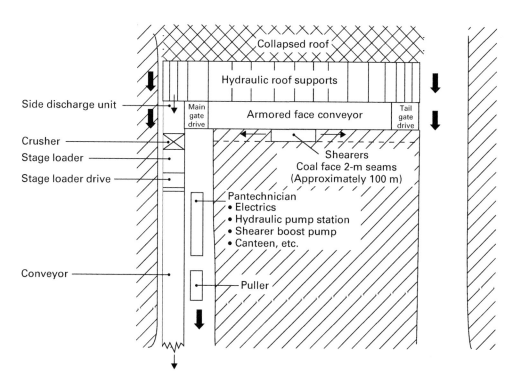

Figure 3 Longwall process

removed coal falls on to the armor-plated conveyor and outwards to the conventional conveyors.

In summary, the underground plant comprises continuous miners, longwall equipment, coal conveyors and diesel-driven vehicles (such as the truck for transporting workers).

The maintenance life plan for a typical unit is outlined in Table 1. It is made up of services and minor work carried out underground (during two scheduled mid-week downshifts) and is the responsibility of the maintenance department. The overhaul of the continuous miner is carried out by contractors off-site. The specification of the major work is the responsibility of the engineering department.

Table 1 Outline life plan for a continuous minor

Minor maintenance program		
Mechanical routines		
MD4M	Change ds rig	(16 weeks)
MOD4M	Change ods rig	(16 weeks)
MOT4W	Oil test	(4 weeks)
MSG2W	Seal gap measure	(2 weeks)
MSR1M	Service	(4 weeks)
MSR1W	Service	(1 week)
MTDS1M	Tension ds nut	(4 weeks)
MTODS1M	Tension ods nut	(4 weeks)
Electrical routines		
ED4Y	Code d	(4 years)
EC6M	Code c	(24 weeks)
EB3M	Code b	(16 weeks)
Note: Each routine is covered by a detailed job specification.		

Major maintenance program
The general condition of each continuous minor is assessed at 3-monthly intervals. The assessments are used to establish the continuous minor overhaul schedule. The minors are overhauled by contractors off-site.

The structure of the physical assets that make up a colliery operation is very different from a process plant and needs to be modeled differently. The process is made up of a coal mining operation, coal transportation (to include a fleet operation) and a process plant. A modified process flow diagram is used to model the overall operation. A schematic is used to model the mining process (development and longwall) and a status diagram can be used to model the fleet (see the next case study). This approach allows the rate controlling process to be identified and the units ranked according to importance. It also allows the maintenance work schedule to be reviewed and modified as necessary. At unit level and below the same approach can be used to establish a life plan as for process plant.

The author believes that this approach can be used to model and review the operation and maintenance characteristics of any mining operation – e.g. see the open cast mining operation which is the subject of the next case study.

CASE STUDY 5: MAINTAINING AN OPEN-CUT COAL MINE

1 Introduction

The purpose of this study is to show how an open-cut mining operation can be modeled as a process flow diagram. In addition, it shows how the operation of a mobile mining fleet can be modeled using 'status diagrams'.

2 Operating characteristics of an open-cut mine

The open-cut mining installation is outlined in Figure 1. The process starts with the stripping and removal of the overburden (the soil and rock above the coal seam) using drilling, explosives and a dragline. The exposed coal seam (meters thick) is then extracted and loaded into trucks for haulage to the coal preparation plant. The coal is crushed in the first operation, and washed and graded in the second one before it was finally conveyed to the railhead for transportation. There are a number of points of inter-stage storage and also final product storage. This gives operational flexibility to each individual process and also to the operation as a whole.

The main feature is that the process depends to a large extent on the performance of small fleets of diesel-powered equipment. For example, five front-end loaders for the

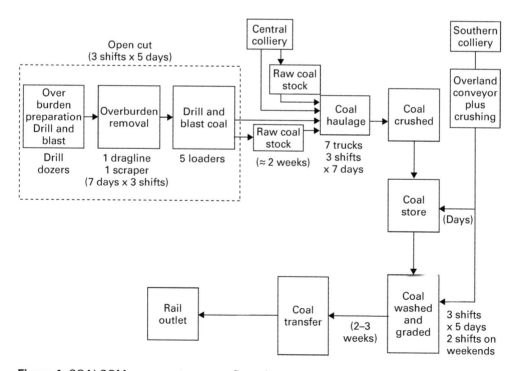

Figure 1 COALCOM open cast process flow chart

mining operations and eight large dump trucks for the haulage operation. (Other mobile equipment includes dozers, scrapers, graders, drills, etc.) It is this equipment – rather than the fixed or semi-fixed units such as coal washing plant, draglines, etc. – that causes the maintenance problems.

3 Modeling fleet operation: status diagrams

Each of the fleet types (e.g. the loaders) can be represented by a status diagram as in Figure 2 (i.e. a loader can be in any one of the states A–E). The availability of a single item can be measured conventionally, i.e.:

$$\text{Availability} = \frac{\text{Time up}}{\text{Time up} + \text{Time down}}$$

$$= \frac{\text{Time in A} + \text{Time in B}}{\text{Time in A} + \text{Time in B} + \text{Time in C, D and E}}$$

Such a measure is useful since it provides an index of effectiveness of the maintenance effort for that unit. It also provides a comparison with the manufacturer's specified availability, which is usually defined in a similar way. For the loaders, the manufacturer had quoted an availability of 85% if the equipment was operated correctly and maintained according to his recommended life plan.

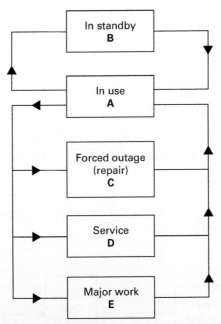

Haulers: 21 shift operation   Operations require minimum of 5 out of 8
Loaders: 21 shift operation   Operations require minimum of 3 out of 5

Figure 2 Status diagram for mobile fleet

However, the important index for the small fleet of loaders was the proportion of the fleet, the fleet demand ratio (FDR) that was required, by production, to be in operation at all times during production shifts. A minimum of three loaders had been specified, and to satisfy this – and to carry out maintenance in states C, D and E – the company carried a fleet of five. Thus, the FDR was three out of five, or 60%.

It appeared, from the manufacturer's availability figure, that the company had played safe. However, the decision to carry five loaders rather than four was based on the following influencing factors:

- The operation was production limited and a high downtime cost would be incurred if the number of loaders operational were to fall to two.
- Production wanted cover when a loader would be undergoing major overhaul (every 2 years) or major repair after failure.

The specification and measurement of availability ratios could have been usefully supplemented by some monitoring of the level of in-service failures. The best way of doing this would have been to keep a simple count as a function of shift, day, unit number, unit type, etc. (It could be argued that unavailability costs did not occur in the same way as with fixed plants; they had been 'bought off' in the capital cost of the extra fleet capacity).

4 Summary

An interesting point is that the maintenance supervisors felt that their objective should be *to ensure production a minimum of three loaders at all times, at minimum maintenance cost.* The maintenance manager, however, felt that it should be *to achieve a loader minimum availability of 85%, at minimum maintenance cost.* His view, which the author sympathized with, was that such an availability would also meet the production requirement. The availability or reliability of mobile mining equipment is normally less than that predicted by its manufacturer, and its maintenance costs often considerably higher. There are several common reasons for this, *viz.*:

(a) The equipment selected may not have been the most appropriate for its duty.
(b) For many reasons (e.g. pooled use) there is little sense of ownership by its operators. This leads to much maloperation, especially when coupled, as it often is, with severe operating conditions and bonus payment arrangements.
(c) For several reasons – including (a), (b) and poor maintenance organization – the preventive program is often neglected, equipment condition deteriorates and more corrective work is needed. This in turn results in even less preventive work being done – and so on until the whole fleet maintenance becomes purely reactive.

All of this was evident in this particular case. Clearly, the long-term solution was to upgrade the fleet with new, wholly appropriate, equipment. Recommendations for the shorter term included:

- Improving the sense of ownership by allotting operators, who would carry out simple pre-shift inspections and other minor maintenance, to equipment. Improving their training in both operation and maintenance, this to include improving their understanding of the links between symptoms and the failures.

- Carrying out a condition audit of the existing equipment and establishing a corrective maintenance program to bring the equipment up to an acceptable condition (a 'catch-up' strategy). In conjunction with this corrective effort, reviewing and modifying, as necessary, the equipment life plans.
- Changing the maintenance organization to set up a preventive and overhaul group and a corrective group. Ensuring that the work planning system and its priorities reflected the importance of the preventive program.

CASE STUDY 6: MAINTENANCE STRATEGY FOR A PASSENGER TRANSPORT FLEET

1 Introduction

The purpose of this case study is to reinforce the principles and concepts, as introduced in the previous study, of fleet maintenance.

2 Fleet-operating characteristics

The transport authority concerned operated from 20 or so garages located in different parts of a large conurbation, each providing transport in its own area and also the necessary parking and maintenance facilities. The garages were divided into three groups and in each one the major maintenance work (overhauls) and reconditioning was carried out at a central works. The system for a single garage and works is outlined in Figure 1.

The buses employed were mostly of the double-decked, front entrance, rear-engine type. The various models are enumerated in Table 1, which also shows the peak demand. The existence of a surplus of vehicles, i.e. above this peak level, provided a small standby pool on which essential maintenance could be carried out. In the analysis of the previous case study it was assumed that the production demand for fleet units was constant, i.e. it was always for a minimum of three. In most fleet operations, however, it fluctuates with time and the bus fleet of this case was no exception (see Figure 2, which indicates numerous 'production windows'). Because of the difficulty and expense of night-time and week-end working the most convenient windows occurred mid-week (from 9 a.m. to 4 p.m.) and facilitated the routine inspections and servicing, and other minor maintenance.

Although time for maintenance was available *outside* these mid-week windows, the number of buses being 16% in excess of the peak demand, it was clearly advantageous to try to make maximize use of the opportunity they provided because this would reduce the need for excess buses and hence the capital cost of the fleet.

3 Outline of the existing maintenance strategy

At the time of the study, the maintenance *life plan* for a bus was based on 'inspection, service and repair as necessary' policy. The basic service frequency was carried out at

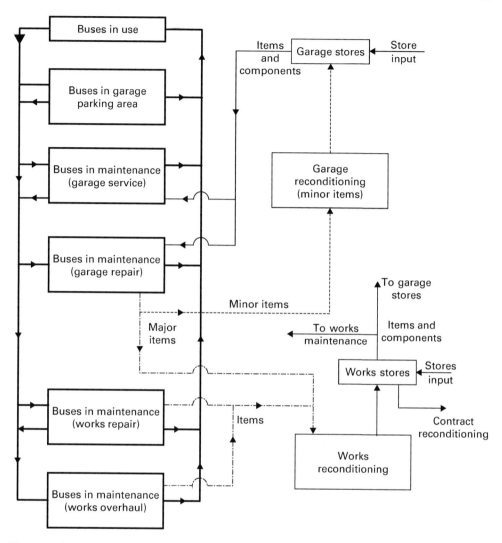

Figure 1 Status diagram for a large passenger fleet and its maintenance system

3-weekly intervals (3000 miles). Additional work was added to this basic service at 6000 miles, 12,000 miles, etc. and at the end of the year the bus was prepared for the annual statutory test. Overhauls were carried out at intervals of approximately 3 years. The services and minor repairs were scheduled to be carried out (the *preventive* schedule) in the mid-week windows (see Figure 2). The scheduling of the major work needed in the excess buses in the fleet. This strategy had evolved over a period of time and was in need of review because it was felt that:

(i) The fleet demand ratio (FDR, see previous case study) was too low.
(ii) The incidence of in-service failures (and unscheduled corrective work) was too high.
(iii) The existing inspection procedures were too subjective and often not carried out.

Table 1 Fleet inventory and maximum demand

Bus type	Bus make	Number in fleet	Maximum demand
Single deck	A	6	4
Double deck	B1	1	
	B2	14	
	B3	16	
	B4	13	
	B5	40	
	C1	23	
	C2	86	
	D	10	
		203	177
	Total all buses	209	181

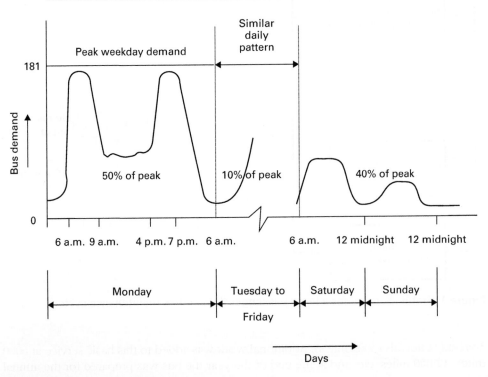

Figure 2 Bus demand pattern

3.1 Maintenance strategy review

The existing life plans for each bus type – which had evolved via custom, practice and manufacturers' recommendations (and were felt, by the supervisors and trade-force, to involve a degree of overmaintenance, especially as regards routine servicing) – were reviewed. The main thrust of this exercise was to extend the basic service period from 3 to 6 weeks (see Tables 2(a) and 2(b)) and to move toward thorough and comprehensive inspection procedures (not shown).

Table 2(a) Revised bus life plan: minor work

Work and frequency	Outline description
Daily checks	Tire pressure, engine oil, cleaning, etc.
Weekly safety checks	Steering gear and lubrication, etc.
6-weekly service	Basic service.
12-weekly service	Basic, plus engine oil change and oil analysis check. Also valve clearances and fuel cylinders.
18-weekly service	Basic, plus gearbox oil change and oil analysis. Gearbox calibration and bearing adjustment on front axle.
24-weekly service (continued to 48 weeks in multiples of 6 weeks, then repeated)	20-weekly service plus checking of fuel system, king pin bushes, gearbox, piston seals.

Table 2(b) Revised bus life plan: major work

Frequency	Inspection and corrective maintenance	Inspection time	Duration (weeks)
3 yearly	Complete bus inspection and repairs at works. Thorough inspection/replacement/repair of all items and/or components. On completion bus to undergo a FFD test.	4–5 hours	10
6, 9 and 12 yearly	Same as 3 yearly.	Same	10
15 yearly (economic life of bus)	Fixed by management on a criterion based on a combination of economic obsolescence, and condition factors.		

Only minor changes were felt to be necessary to the preventive schedule.

The *services and minor repairs* were carried out in the respective garages in the mid-week windows. The basic 6-weekly service was scheduled by dividing the year into 86-weekly periods, leaving 2 weeks for holiday and 2 weeks for statutory work preparation. Because the total number of buses was 209, this required 7 buses to be serviced per day. The estimated time for each service is shown in Table 3(a), and the daily loading – which does not take into consideration the resulting corrective work – in Table 3(b). In the majority of cases the servicing, and any corrective maintenance, could be completed within the window; where this would not be possible, the bus would not be available to meet the peak demand and this would count against the peak demand ratio (PDR). In addition, this planned workload could be augmented by the unscheduled corrective work resulting from in-service failure, which could be minor or could demand several days' effort.

Table 3(a) Maintenance service type

Service period (weeks)	6	12	18	24	30	36	42	48
Estimated time (hours)	½	1½	1½	3	½	1½	½	4
Maintenance class	A	B	B	C	A	B	A	D

Table 3(b) Daily workload for red group

Maintenance period (weeks)	Maintenance class	Red group: 35 buses				
		Day 1	Day 2	Day 3	Day 4	Day 5
6	A	–	–	–	–	–
12	B	–	–	–	–	–
18	B	–	–	–	–	–
24	C	–	–	–	–	–
30	A	–	–	–	–	–
36	B	–	–	–	–	–
42	A	–	–	–	–	–
48	D	–	–	–	–	–
Buses per day		7	7	7	7	7
Hours per day		12.5	11.5	10	11.5	12.5

The *overhauls and major repairs* were scheduled to be carried out in the central maintenance workshops shown in Table 2(b), the timing of major work was governed by the freedom from defects (FFD) test and by the 3-yearly overhaul. Thus, the buses could be scheduled for overhaul and FFD test, at the central workshops, on a 3-yearly basis. Taking into consideration the time (10 weeks) needed to carry out an overhaul, about 15 buses would be in the works for overhaul at any one time. As before, this would count against the PDR.

4 Comments

Would the new strategy reduce the combined costs of unavailability and of resources used? The daily, weekly and 6-weekly scheduled preventive work would be carried out in the windows and would therefore not affect the PDR – and would not involve an increase in the workload. Changes in the major preventive work would be small and they also would have little effect, therefore, on the PDR or on the resources used. The most important point was whether the revised inspection and servicing procedures would lead to fewer in-service failures and less unscheduled corrective work. The level of such work that would result from the new plan was difficult to estimate. The more thorough consideration of the maintenance procedures for each item, the resulting increase in the number of items covered and the greater objectivity of inspection procedures should result in a reduction of corrective work. Even a small reduction would result in fewer buses being in repair, a higher PDR and a smaller workload.

Three additional recommendations were made, *viz.*:

1. The 3-yearly overhaul period should be extended, initially to 4 years and, after experience with this period, to 5.
2. The time required for an overhaul (10 weeks, sometimes more) was excessive. The procedures should reviewed with a view to its progressive reduction.
3. The economic life of the buses should be extended to at least 20 years.

These last were not accepted. At the time, the bus company was publicly owned and controlled. It has since been privatized and these and many other changes (not all positive) have been implemented.

> It will be realized that the 'physical asset structure' of fleets is very different to process plants. There are many identical (or similar) units (buses) and the best way of modeling their operation and maintenance is via status diagrams (see Figure 1). This approach in conjunction with the bus fleet demand pattern allows the scheduling problem to be understood. From unit (bus) level downwards the generic approach to establishing a life plan can be used.

CASE STUDIES 7–10: CASE STUDIES IN THE ELECTRICAL POWER UTILITIES

1 Introduction

The purpose of these case studies is to show how the principles and concepts of business-centered maintenance can be applied to the diverse equipment and processes of electricity generation, transmission and distribution. In many respects the operational and maintenance characteristics of electrical utilities are similar to other utilities (e.g. gas production and distribution; water and sewerage).

2 Operating characteristics of an electricity supply system

Figure 1 is a schematic of a generation and supply system. Typically, demand for electricity varies throughout the year as shown in Figure 2. (The demand will also vary, of course, throughout the week – there will be less demand at the weekends – and throughout each 24 hours – there will be less demand at night.) Several generating units (GUs), of various sizes, will feed the distribution grid. The most efficient of these, usually the larger ones, will supply the base load (the non-varying demand), the less efficient ones being brought on intermittently to meet peaks in the demand. Not uncommonly, gas turbine and/or hydro units will be employed to meet demand peaks of *short* duration (a practice sometimes referred to as *peak lopping*).

It will be appreciated that in most situations, different companies own and operate the major functions of the system shown in Figure 1, *viz.* generation, transmission and distribution. Indeed in many countries the power generators (gas, oil, coal, hydro, thermal) may be owned and operated by a variety of companies.

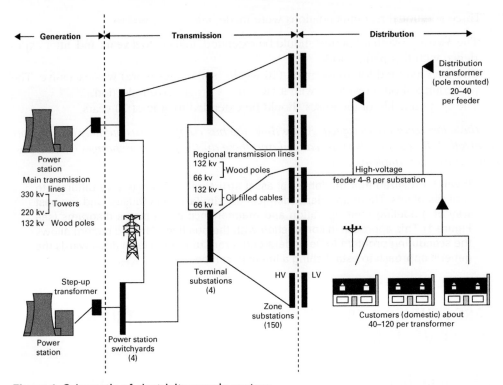

Figure 1 Schematic of electricity supply system

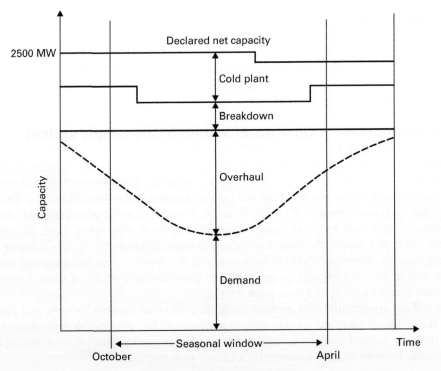

Figure 2 Annual variation in demand (southern hemisphere)

CASE STUDY 7: A GAS-FIRED POWER STATION

Concerns a maintenance strategy review of a gas-fired power plant. The case study also illustrates the importance of the linkage between production policy and maintenance strategy.

1 The station and its operating characteristics

The station concerned had an installed capacity of 600 MW(e), made up of five 120 MW(e) sets, each of which comprised a gas-fired boiler and steam-driven turbine. Until a year before the maintenance review the station had been part of the base-load supply. It had then moved down in the merit table and at the time was being used on a two-shift operating pattern, i.e. it tended to be used each day from 6 a.m. to 8 p.m. but was not required at night, when the demand fell.

Relatively little offline work could be carried out at night because of shortage of time for cooling and isolation, and also because the station was expected to provide a 'spinning reserve'. However, production-related windows for one or more of the generating units (GUs) occurred on a more random basis and could be up to 2 weeks in duration. Such windows occurred – mainly during the annual low demand period – on average, about three times per year per GU. The planning lead time for these randomly occurring windows was relatively short (about 1 week, at most).

2 The maintenance strategy in use when the station provided base load

The major outage life plan for a GU when the station was operating to provide base load is shown in Figure 1. This program was the main thrust of a GU's life plan. Relatively little work other than lubrication and simple inspection was undertaken outside the major shutdowns. The *major shutdown schedule* took account of the pattern of grid demand and also of the availability of internal and contract labor. For the station as a whole there was a 10-year plan, a maximum of two units being overhauled in any 1 year. This generated a workload of the kind illustrated in Figure 2.

3 Maintenance strategy review for two-shift operation

The work content of a major shutdown was examined and, as far as possible, reduced by the following actions:

(i) Jobs were identified which might possibly be scheduled into the randomly occurring windows.
(ii) Jobs which could be carried out in windows provided by the presence of redundant or spare plant, e.g. work on duplicate pumps, were identified and rescheduled.

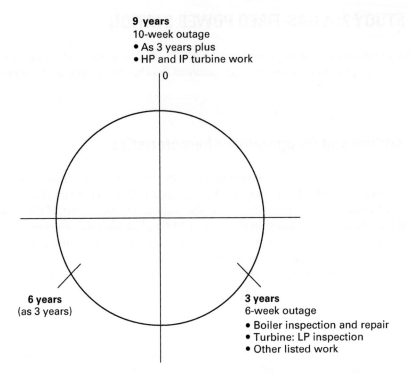

Figure 1 Outline of the major-outage life plan for the GUs

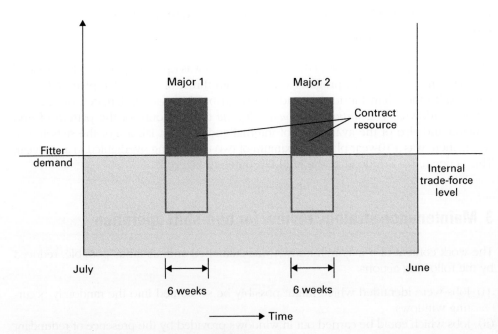

Figure 2 Workload pattern and its resourcing

(iii) On review, many jobs that were previously done at fixed intervals became condition-based ones; in some cases it was decided to do them only after failure.

The review resulted in an improvement of availability, mainly due to the reduction of the duration of scheduled outages (the maintenance transferred into the randomly occurring windows not then having any direct impact on availability) but also because the revised maintenance policy was more effective. *In order to implement this revised strategy and, in particular, to facilitate the necessary opportunity scheduling, improved work planning systems (based, among other things, on better computer software), were needed.*

CASE STUDY 8: AN OIL-FIRED POWER STATION

This study will illustrate the linkage between production objectives and maintenance objectives, and shows how pursuit of the latter can drive changes in the life plan and maintenance organization.

1 The station and its operating characteristics

An installed capacity of 360 MW(e) was achieved via five 60 MW(e) sets, using oil-fired boilers and steam-driven turbines, and a 60 MW(e) gas turbine. The steam-driven units were some 30 years old and the gas turbine 22 years old. By the time of the study the station was privately owned, having been run down – with a view to decommissioning – under its previous state ownership. The existing management had a contract to supply electricity using the steam-driven units until the year 2000 and the gas turbine units until 2010. This would depend on many uncertain factors, among which were whether the local grid would be connected to other grids, the future demand for electricity, environmental legislation, and so on.

The station provided a peak-lopping service to the grid. For this, the gas turbine could provide an immediate response while the steam turbines could respond with as little as 4-hour notice. The contract for the steam turbines was for four units out of the five (i.e. 240 MW(e)) to be available at any time. Thus, these units could be considered separately from the gas turbine as regards most aspects of maintenance strategy. The presence of the extra steam unit provided numerous windows for scheduling offline maintenance work without losing system availability. Taking the gas turbine offline for maintenance always meant, at any time, a total loss of *its* availability.

2 Production and maintenance objectives

Production objectives were determined by factors which had been set under contract. For the steam units, payment was based on availability rather than supply. Full payment resulted from achieving 100% availability of four units (i.e. of 240 MW(e) capacity); various checks and penalties could then modify this. The availability actually achieved at the time of the study was about 98%. For the gas turbine, payment was based partly on availability (e.g. 50% of maximum payment could be obtained by achieving 100% availability) and partly on operational reliability (e.g. 50% of maximum payment could be obtained by achieving 100% successful response to all the demanded starts). At the time of the study the gas turbine availability was over 80%, its operational reliability of the order of 90%.

Environmental and personnel safety standards were not discussed so it was assumed that they were satisfactory. A plant condition audit was not carried out but it was known that the equipment was old and that, during the last 10 years, it had been allowed to deteriorate. An important question was *What was the expected remaining life of each steam unit, given its age and condition?* The answer to this would have a major influence on its maintenance life plan.

The management were aware of the above considerations and their interrelationship. They had identified the maintenance objective as being:

> *to maintain or improve the present output performance of the generators while reducing the resource cost via improvements in maintenance organizational efficiency.*

3 Maintenance strategy before privatization

3.1 Steam units

The life plans could be summarized as follows:

- A major outage of 12-week duration every 6 years, to carry out statutory inspections, boiler, turbine and ancillary equipment overhaul.
- A major outage of 3-week duration every 26 months. The frequency of the shutdown was that of the statutory inspection of the boiler but other necessary work was also carried out.
- An annual outage of 1½-week duration, to undertake boiler and turbine inspection and ancillary plant maintenance.
- Online lubrication and simple inspection routines.

The station maintenance schedule was aimed at spreading the outages as evenly as possible over the 6-year cycle, in order to smooth the station workload. Essentially this meant that, on average, there were 25 weeks of outage work per year. The station's internal maintenance labor was manned up to this shutdown workload. Little use was made of any contract resource.

3.2 Gas turbine

The life plan was built around a major outage, every 4 years, of 6-week duration and an annual outage of 2-week duration. Because of its specialized nature and the high cost of spares holding, this work was contracted out to specialists, except for the first-line work which was covered by internal labor. This policy remained the same after privatization.

4 Maintenance strategy after privatization

After privatization, considerable effort was devoted to changing the life plans and station outage schedule in order to maintain the steam unit availabilities and reliabilities at reduced maintenance cost. This was achieved via the following actions:

(i) Discontinuing, after 1995, the 6-yearly outage because the steam unit lives would come to an end by the year 2000. The remaining two 12-week outages were scheduled for the summers of 1994 and 1995 (the last of these being a precautionary outage).

(ii) Discontinuing the traditional annual outage and incorporating its work into the 26-monthly statutory outage. This extended the duration of that outage to 4 weeks. These outages were scheduled for the summer months at a rate of three in 1 year, two in the next year, and so on.

(iii) Reviewing all the shutdown work to identify the jobs that could be undertaken outside the main shutdowns by taking advantage of plant redundancy. This work was incorporated in an ancillary equipment preventive maintenance program (a 'window' schedule) and was scheduled to smooth the workload between outages.

The changes in workload and resourcing are shown in Figure 1. Peaks were resourced via a combination of contract labor (mostly) and overtime. The main benefit was a reduction

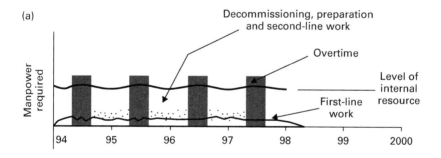

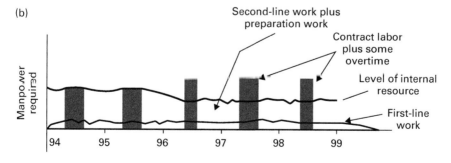

Figure 1 Workload and resourcing (a) before and (b) after strategy change

of 40% in the internal maintenance trade-force and of an overall 30% in labor costs. In other words, *the change of strategy allowed an improvement in organizational efficiency without a loss of maintenance effectiveness.*

The management of the station was also embarking on measures to reduce labor costs by improving flexibility, i.e. by reducing the non-trade workforce, improving inter-trade and operator–maintainer flexibility. *This would lead to the same workload being carried out by less labor and at lower labor cost.*

CASE STUDY 9: A TRANSMISSION SYSTEM

This case study is concerned with mapping the maintenance strategy of the transmission physical assets.

1 Equipment-operating characteristics

The transmission grid was outlined in Figure 1. Its function was to transmit power from the generating stations to the zone substations and then to the local distribution systems. In order to transmit the power efficiently the station transformer stepped up the voltage to 330 kv; the power then going via the main switchyards to the grid.

The grid itself comprised main substations, zone substations, main transmission lines carried on steel towers, and regional transmission lines carried on wooden poles and in oil-filled underground cables (see Figure 1); these were the *primary assets*. In addition there were the following *secondary assets*:

- *Grid control system*, including the host computer at the control center and the transducers, etc. at the power station and substations. This was mostly solid-state electronic equipment.
- *Communication systems*, including the grid protection communication system and the microwave systems which passed information from the transducers to the host computer.
- *Protection systems*, made up mainly of solid-state electronic equipment that protected the power stations, substations, etc.

The *maintenance objective* for the transmission grid could be expressed as for process plant, i.e.:

> **to achieve the agreed system operating requirements, with agreed and defined plant condition and safety requirements, at minimum resource cost.**

The system-operating requirements were set as 'transmission practice standards'. Supply reliability, and safety, were measured via various quantitative indicators, and targets were set based on these indicators. These requirements could then be translated into user requirements at main asset (e.g. substation) level and used to develop maintenance life plans.

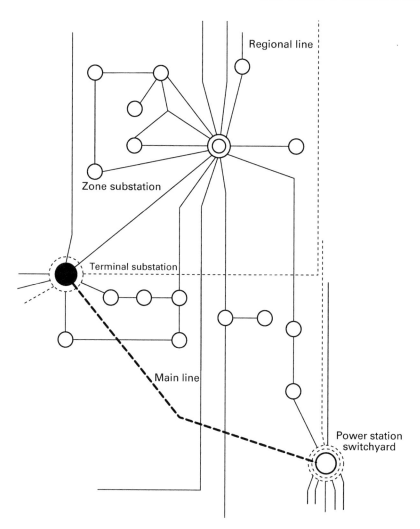

Figure 1 Part of the transmission grid

2 Maintenance strategy mapping

As a part of the strategy review the author developed an equipment criticality ranking (similar to the procedure for process plant, see Section 9.2.2). For example, consider the outline, in Figure 1, of a part of the transmission grid. The thick line indicates a main transmission line that could be regarded as critical, in the sense that if it failed it would restrict the flow of electricity from the power stations. If this line were to be required for offline work it would have to be taken offline when one (or perhaps two) of the generating units (GUs) were on outage maintenance. This particular transmission system was audited and one of the main resulting observations was that more attention would have to be given to identifying and ranking those lines, switchgear and failure modes which were critical to system reliability or safety. Such a *criticality ranking* was probably understood but, as far as could be seen, had not been documented as a part of the transmission system maintenance strategy.

The maintenance life plan for the *primary assets* had been developed in the conventional way. The plan for a typical substation, e.g. was as outlined in Table 9.1.

Table 1 Substation life plan: outline

Inspection and lubrication routines	Monthly
A-grade service (a combination of inspection, proof testing, minor adjustment, replacement of simple items)	3 yearly
B-grade service (broadly similar to A-grade)	6 yearly
Overhaul	Based on the results of the services

In general, the life plans for the *secondary assets* were different because they were largely solid-state electronic equipment. The plans were therefore based on routine cleaning and calibration, some proof testing and some planned corrective maintenance.

The maintenance schedule for the *main lines* was driven by the outage requirements for the GUs. This in turn drove the outage schedule for the switchyards, main terminals and substations and hence influenced the schedule for the secondary assets.

Although this scheduling seems straightforward it should be appreciated that the GUs, main lines, regional lines, switchgear and secondary assets were the various responsibilities of different parts of a large organization. Thus, the effective co-ordination of effort throughout such a large organization required excellent communication systems.

CASE STUDY 10: A DISTRIBUTION SYSTEM

This study will complete discussion of the generation and supply system of Figure 1. It is instructive because it will show that, even if an otherwise satisfactory maintenance strategy is being followed, preventive maintenance can be neglected if objectives and work priorities are not clearly laid down beforehand.

The distribution system boundary was at the zone substation of Figure 1. Even in this example's relatively small grid of 2500 MW, the size of the distribution assets was considerable, *viz.* 150 substations and thousands of wooden poles each one carrying some appropriate equipment.

Although both corporate and maintenance objectives had been specified for the generation and supply systems they had not been interpreted into objectives for the distribution system. Simple life plans – broadly similar to those for the transmission substations (i.e. based on inspection-oriented services) – had been formulated for each of the substations. In general, there were life plans for the pole-mounted equipment, based on simple inspection when the wooden pole structure was being maintained (which, because of the age of the poles – as much as 30 years – and the prevalence of adverse ground conditions, was itself the main source of work). The maintenance policy for the pole structure was as indicated in Figure 1. An additional maintenance task in some areas was tree clearing around the lines.

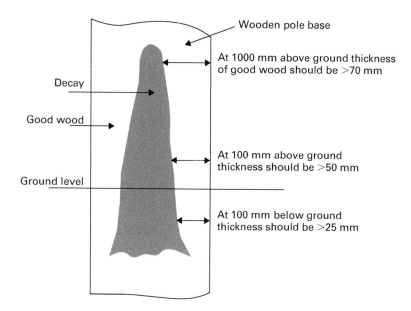

4-yearly inspection, based on the following:

- If below-ground criterion is met then chemically treat base only.
- If below-ground criterion is not met but upper criteria are met then reinforce the base with steel stakes and chemically treat.
- If lower and upper criteria are not met then replace pole.

Figure 1 Pole maintenance policy

Audit of the distribution system maintenance revealed a backlog of work on the poles, and on the equipment mounted on them, which was many years long. The condition of these assets was clearly deteriorating and causing senior management concern, both for safety and for security of supply. The basic cause of this problem can be deduced from Figure 2, which shows the maintenance workload for a typical distribution area. The trade-force had to carry out not only the maintenance of the existing network but also the expansion of the network to new homes and industries, which generated new income and therefore took priority. The absence of asset condition and safety standards led to continued deferral of maintenance. At best it was carried out only when expansion work eased off.

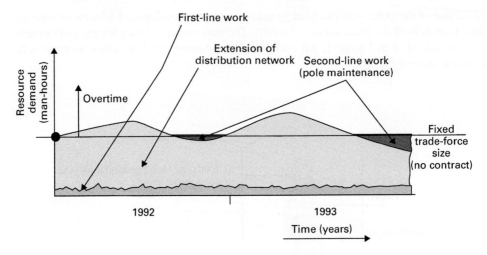

Figure 2 Long-term workload for line trade-force

The following recommendations resulted from the audit:

- Distribution maintenance objectives should be set and translated down to main asset level. Safety and longevity standards should be specified.
- Either a separate 'maintenance group' should be formed or work priorities changed so as to ensure that maintenance is carried out at the required time.

Appendix 1 Maintenance terminology

Definitions are given below for some of the more important terms used in this book. They are broadly in line with those given in the British Standards publication BS 3811:1984, but some have been significantly amended or extended by the author. The list does not include definitions already given clearly in the main text.

Maintenance:	The combination of all technical and associated administrative actions intended to retain an item in, or restore it to, a state in which it can perform its required function.
Preventive maintenance:	The maintenance carried out at pre-determined intervals, or corresponding to prescribed criteria, and intended to reduce the probability of failure or the performance degradation of an item. Preventive maintenance is planned and scheduled (or carried out on opportunity).
Condition-based maintenance:	The preventive maintenance initiated as a result of knowledge of the condition of an item derived from periodic, routine or continuous monitoring.
Condition monitoring:	The periodic, routine, or continuous measurement and interpretation of data to indicate the condition of an item.
Corrective maintenance:	The maintenance carried out after a failure has occurred and intended to restore an item to a state in which it can perform its required function. Corrective maintenance can be planned and scheduled.
Emergency maintenance:	The corrective maintenance which is necessary to put in hand immediately to avoid serious consequences. Thus, emergency maintenance cannot be scheduled. In some cases, however, it can be planned for by ensuring that decision guidelines have been prepared and that necessary resources will be available.
Unit life plan:	The program of preventive maintenance work to be carried out on a unit of plant unit over its entire life.
Preventive maintenance schedule:	A schedule of preventive maintenance work for the whole of a plant (or plant section). The schedule is listing of jobs, with trades, against plant units and dates.
Maintenance window:	The opportunity to carry out offline maintenance on a plant without incurring production loss. Windows can arise at plant, unit or item level.
Online maintenance:	Maintenance which can be carried out while the plant or unit is in use (also called *running maintenance*).
Offline maintenance:	Maintenance which can only be carried out when the plant or unit is not in use.

Appendix 2 *In-situ* repair techniques (from a dissertation by Julia Gauntly, Manchester University, 1986)

Techniques	Principles of operations	Applications
1. Inerting of flammable material storages	Foam generator used to inject inert gas.	Makes safe for welding.
2. Welding up and machining	Building up worn metal parts by welding until oversize and then machined back to size.	Normally carried out in workshop but portable machines and welding equipment are available for on-site work (worn shafts, bearing housing gears, etc.).
3. *In-situ* machining	Full range of machine tools and hand tools available.	Machine tools have emphasis on portability with special emphasis placed on devices to fasten the machine to the job. Limitless applications, e.g. *in-situ* grinding of rollers, machining the back face of a heat exchanger.
4. Flatness checking with monochromatic light and optical flat	An optical flat (flat piece of glass used as a reference) is placed on the surface to be tested. Surface and flat are placed under a monochromatic light source. Interference fringes allow surface to be compared to optical flat.	Used in conjunction with on-site machining operations such as grinding.
5. Alignment checking with lasers	Laser light is collimated (it propagates in narrow beams which have low divergence). A laser beam is emitted from a laser/detector unit mounted on the shaft of a stationary machine. It is aimed at a prism mounted on the shaft of the machine to be aligned. The beam is reflected back to the detector. The two shafts are rotated and the misalignment can be measured by the laser unit and corrected.	Alignment of roller bearings in conveyor belt systems, drive shafts, fan motors, etc.

(*Continued*)

Techniques	Principles of operations	Applications
6. Laser cutting, welding, cleaning	A laser beam can be focused onto a small spot in order to give high-energy densities of the order of those used for electron beam welding	Can be used for high-quality precision welding and cutting. Not yet used extensively for *in-situ* repair.
7. Laser gas absorption	This is a form of leak detection. It can be used to scan every area of a plant in seconds for leaks of a gas which absorbs radiation in the infrared spectrum of a carbon dioxide laser. The system is based on a laser, mirror and detector.	Used to scan a plant for gas leaks after a major overhaul and start up, e.g. ammonia leak.
8. Leak sealing under pressure via sealing compounds	Manual or hydraulic injection of thermosetting compounds into, or around, a leak. The application of heat, either externally or internally, from the contents of the pipe, e.g. steam, causes the compound to cure and seal the leak.	Sealing flange leaks, heat exchanger joints, turbine joints, etc.
9. Leak sealing under pressure (other methods) (a) Welding	Pinhole leaks can be closed by welding an ordinary nut around the leak. A bolt, with a sealing compound is then screwed into the nut.	Pinhole leaks. Larger leaks can be tackled using a specially prepared plate rather than a nut.
(b) Clamping	A range of clamps can be purchased for sealing leaks in pipes.	As above but do not require welding. Used for low-pressure leaks.
10. Pipe lining	A terylene felt tube, impregnated with polyester resin, is inserted into an existing pipe and cured *in situ*.	Used for the renewal of brick sewers, cast iron pipes, concrete culverts, etc.
11. Pipe freezing	A method of isolating sections of pipe or plant (where valves are not available) by freezing the contents of the pipe, using dry ice or nitrogen.	Routine maintenance of service pipes; extension of existing pipework systems.
12. Tube plugging	Used to seal off the leaking tubes in a tube bank by inserting a plug into the ends of the damaged tubes.	Boilers and heat exchangers.

Techniques	Principles of operations	Applications
13. Explosive techniques (a) Expansion	Small explosive charges are detonated within the mouth of a heat exchanger tube to seal the tube–tube plate joint.	All kinds of boiler and heat exchanger tube repair.
(b) Welding	Similar to (a) but the conditions are arranged so that a weld is formed between tube and tube plate.	
(c) Loosening	The loosening of scored threads and other similar seizures.	
14. Hardfacing repair techniques	Covers the techniques listed below which are used to coat components with a surface which is best able to withstand the conditions encountered in service.	
(a) Thermal spraying	Flame spraying with wire – used for thick coatings. Flame spraying with powder – used for small items. Plasma spraying with powder – used for spraying chromium and tungsten carbide.	Pump shafts. Impellors. Fan blades, etc.
(b) Flame plating	Particles of a metallic compound (tungsten carbide) are mixed with oxygen and acetylene in a 'gun' and then detonated. The metal is melted at high speed and 'sprayed on to the surface'.	Fretting surface, gas turbine blades. Worn shafts in gas compressors and steam turbines.
(c) Spray fusing	A two-stage process in which a coating is flame sprayed on to the workpiece, and then fused with an oxy-acetylene torch.	Coating and building up worn pump pistons, sleeves, wear rings, etc.
(d) Depositing	Depositing materials onto surfaces using welding techniques: ● Oxy-acetylene rod and powder. ● Gas tungsten arc or argon. ● Metal arc. ● Plasma.	As for spraying techniques. Worn cutting edges and teeth on excavators, worn shafts and many other applications.

(Continued)

Techniques	Principles of operations	Applications
15. Brush plating	An electrolytic method of metallizing a surface without an electrolyte bath. The surface of the component is 'brushed' with an anode which is wrapped in an absorbent material (cotton which has been dipped into an electrolyte.	For coating worn surfaces or, depositing a corrosion resistant material, e.g. cobalt.
16. Hot tapping	A method of connecting branches to pipes which and are under pressure cannot be isolated. A branch is welded to the line to be hot tapped. A valve is fitted to the branch. A special drill is fitted to the valve. The valve is opened and the line is drilled. The valve is closed and drill removed. A new line is fitted to the branch.	Used for connecting branches to main lines which are expensive to shut down and purge.
17. Cold tapping	Very similar to hot tapping but there is no welding. Instead of a conventional branch a 'tee clamp' is used which is clamped to the line.	Used where welding would be dangerous.
18. Online valve replacement	Used to change valves under pressure (see Figure 7.11).	Valves can be removed without having to drain the system.
19. Thread inserts	Sleeves, usually with internal and external threads, which are used to replace damaged threads.	Repair of damaged threads.
20. Metal stitching	Cold stitching a component which has fractured. Consists of drilling special apertures into both sides of the fracture and then peening matching keys into the apertures.	Can be carried out on any metal over 1/4-inch thick, e.g. machine foundations, gearbox castings, cylinder blocks. Most repairs can be carried out *in situ*.
21. Repair of floating tank roofs	Leaks are often caused by failure of welds and rivets on a roof under the stresses of its movement. Sections of plate are cut to fit over the leak and held in place by specially designed bolts and the edges sealed with a proprietary sealant.	*In-situ* technique for tanks storing all refinery products.

Techniques	Principles of operations	Applications
22. Repair of glass-lined vessels	A number of techniques, e.g. Cement repairs, Tantalum plugs for pinhole leaks.	Can be used for repairing *in-situ* holes of a wide range of sizes.
23. Cold-forming materials	Generally consists of two or more components (liquids or putties) which are mixed together to form a uniform material. After mixing, the material is applied to the surface and is allowed to cure.	
	(i) Metal repairs – mixtures of metals and epoxy resins. (ii) Rubber repairs – rubber-based mixtures.	Holes in pipes, scored shafts, tank seams, etc. Split, embrittled, rubber hoses. Damaged electrical insulation. Rubber flanges, etc.
24. Adhesives	A wide range of natural and synthetic materials which are used to bond together other materials.	Particularly useful for bonding dissimilar materials, dissimilar metals which constitute a corrosion couple, heat-sensitive materials and fragile components.
25. Shrink insulation	An outer insulation sheath can be shrunk on to the existing insulation of a cable. The sheath is heat-shrinkable.	*In-situ* repair of damaged cable insulation where the cables are too difficult, or expensive, to replace.

Appendix 3 Introductory failure statistics

A3.1 The statistical parameters of component lifetimes

Let us assume, as a highly idealized illustration, that we have been able to test 100 identical pumps of a new design by running them continuously until each one has failed, with the results shown in Table A3.1.

Table A3.1 Pump failure data

Time-to-failure (hours)	Number of pumps failing	Fraction failing	Fraction failing per hour
(Class interval)	(Frequency)	(Relative frequency)	(Relative frequency density)
300–399	2	0.02	0.0002
400–499	9	0.09	0.0009
500–599	21	0.21	0.0021
600–699	40	0.40	0.0040
700–799	19	0.19	0.0019
800–899	8	0.08	0.0008
900–1000	1	0.01	0.0001
Totals	100	1.00	

Note: (a) The second row of the table shows the standard statistical terms ('class interval', etc.) for the types of quantity evaluated; (b) the figures in the fourth column are obtained by dividing those in the third by 100 hours, the width of the class interval used.

Using the data in the fourth column a *histogram* can be constructed, as in Figure A3.1.

The assumption might now be made that the pattern of failure of this sample is typical of all such pumps; i.e. the *observed* relative frequencies truly reflect the *expected* probabilities of failure. The probability that any one pump of this kind will last longer than, say, 700 hours is then given by the shaded area in the histogram, i.e.:

$$0.19 + 0.08 + 0.01 = 0.28 \text{ or } 28\%$$

We now require some numbers which will indicate the general *nature* of the variable quantity (or of the *variate* as it is called in statistical terminology) that we have observed.

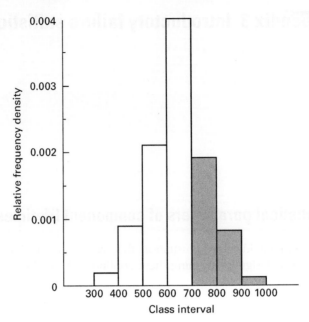

Figure A3.1 Relative frequency density histogram

(i) For its average magnitude, or *central tendency*, we use the *arithmetic mean*:

$$m = (0.02 \times 350) + (0.09 \times 450) + (0.21 \times 550) + \ldots, \text{etc.} = 642 \text{ hours}$$

(ii) For the spread or *dispersion*, we shall calculate the *variance*

$$s^2 = 0.02(350 - 642)^2 + 0.09(450 - 642)^2 + \ldots, \text{etc.} = 13{,}500 \text{ hours}^2$$

where, as before, the first bracket, say, refers to the data for the first quoted class interval and 642 hours is the previously calculated overall mean. A quantity measured in hours-squared is rather mysterious (although it is, in fact, indispensable in most statistical calculations), so for presenting information on the observed spread of the times-to-failure we quote its square-root, the *standard deviation*:

$$s = (13{,}500)^{1/2} = 116 \text{ hours}$$

A3.1.1 Probability density functions

If many thousands of pumps had been tested, instead of just one hundred, the width of the class intervals in Figure A3.1 could have been reduced and a virtually continuous *probability density function* or *pdf* obtained, as in Figure A3.2. Many failure processes generate pdfs of time-to-failure which can be represented fairly accurately by simple mathematical expressions. This can be useful in reliability calculations.

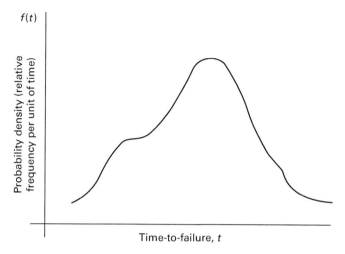

Figure A3.2 Continuous probability density distribution

A3.1.2 The Normal or 'wear-out' pdf

Some engineering items exhibit definite wear-out, i.e. they mostly fail around some mean operating, age, although a few fail sooner and few later. The distribution of times-to-failure often approximates to the symmetric, bell-shaped, *Normal* pdf, a distribution which is of pivotal importance in statistical theory. (It is often called *Gauss's* distribution because he derived it – by formulating a simple model of the way in which errors of measurement are generated.) If the times-to-failure were to be distributed in this way then 50% of them would fall in the range $(m - 0.67s)$ to $(m + 0.67s)$, and 95% in the range $(m - 2s)$

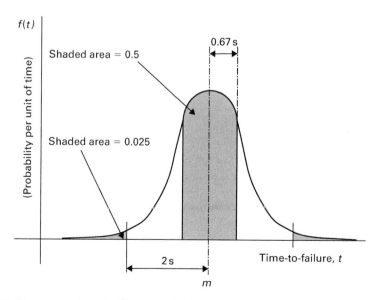

Figure A3.3 The normal probability density function

to $(m + 2s)$, where m is the measured mean of the distribution and s its standard deviation (see Figure A3.3). Statistical tables give other percentage probabilities for other ranges (expressed as multiples of s) about the mean.

A3.1.3 The negative exponential, or 'random failure' pdf

During their 'as-designed' lives many engineering components, if properly operated, do *not* 'wear-out'. On the contrary, they are as likely to fail sooner as later. The probability of failure is constant (and probably small), i.e. the component is always effectively 'as good as new'. This indicates that the cause of any failure is external to the component, e.g. overload. It can be shown that, in this case, the distribution of time-to-failure t is given by the *negative exponential pdf* (see Figure A3.4), i.e.:

$$f(t) = \lambda \exp (-\lambda t)$$

where λ = mean failure rate (failures/unit time/machine) and
$\quad 1/\lambda$ = mean-time-to-failure (m.t.t.f.).
Also for the negative exponential case Reliability $R(t) = \exp (-\lambda t)$

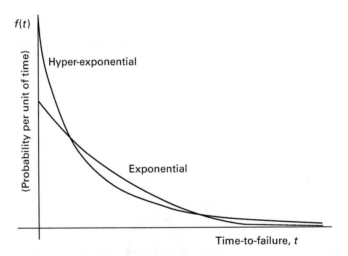

Figure A3.4 Hyper-exponential and exponential pdfs

A3.1.4 The hyper-exponential, or 'running-in' pdf

Sometimes, the probability of failure is found to be higher immediately after installation or overhaul than during subsequent operation. This can be represented by a pdf of time-to-failure which exhibits two phases, an initial rapid fall and a later slower one (see Figure A3.4). This is evidence that some of the components concerned have manufacturing defects, or have been re-assembled incorrectly, faults that show up during the running-in period. Components that survive this period are without such defects and go on to exhibit the sort of time-dependent failure probability previously discussed.

Hazard rate, *Z(t)*

This is defined as:

the fraction, of those components which *have* survived up to the time *t*, expected to fail, per unit time.

Thus, at any time, *t*,

$$Z(t) = \frac{\text{Fraction of original pumps failing per hour at time (t)}}{\text{Fraction of original pumps still running at time (t)}}$$

$$= \frac{f(t)}{R(t)}$$

So, for the negative exponential case,

$$Z(t) = \frac{\lambda e^{-\lambda t}}{e^{-\lambda t}} = \lambda$$

that is, the failure rate is constant, the component is always, 'as good as new' as already explained. For the data of Table A3.1, *Z(t)* is calculated, tabulated and plotted in Table A3.2 and Figure A3.5.

Table A3.2 Variation of hazard rate: pump data of Table A3.1

Time (hours)	t	350	450	550	650	750	850	950
Fraction, of original pumps, failing per hour, at time (t)	f(t)	0.0002	0.0009	0.0021	0.0040	0.0019	0.0008	0.0001
Fraction surviving at time (t)	R(t)	0.99	0.94	0.79	0.48	0.19	0.05	0.005
Hazard rate (conditional failure probability per hour)	Z(t) = f(t)/R(t)	0	0	0	0.01	0.01	0.0160	0.02

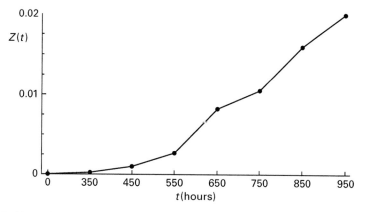

Figure A3.5 Hazard rate plot for pump data

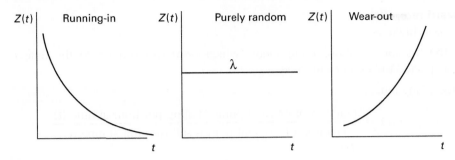

Figure A3.6 Principle modes of failure

In Figure A3.6, $Z(t)$ is shown for the three basic types of failure – running-in, useful-life and wear-out.

A3.1.5 The whole-life item failure profile

By combining the three $Z(t)$ curves of Figure A3.6 a single $Z(t)$ curve as in Figure A3.7 can be obtained which, broadly speaking, gives the whole-life profile of failure probability for the generality of components. This is the much quoted – and much abused – 'bath-tub curve'.

This is only the 'bath-tub curve' when the variable on the y-axis is the hazard rate, $Z(t)$, as we have defined it here. The actual level of $Z(t)$, the time scale involved and the relative lengths of the three phases, will vary by orders of magnitude and from one sort of component, and one application, to another. Furthermore, in any specific case one or two of the phases could be effectively absent (e.g. in the case of high-reliability aircraft control gear where running-in failure is negligible and wear-out non-existent).

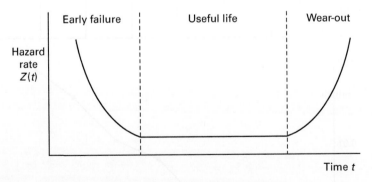

Figure A3.7 Typical $Z(t)$ characteristics for engineering device

Reference

1. Kelly, A., *Maintenance Planning and Control*, Butterworths, Oxford, 1984.

Index

Printed and bound by CPI Group (UK) Ltd, Croydon, CR0 4YY

08/05/2025

01864813-0002